Making the World Safe for Existence

Making the World Safe for Existence
Celebration of the Saints among the Sierra Nahuat of Chignautla, Mexico

Doren L. Slade

Ann Arbor
THE UNIVERSITY OF MICHIGAN PRESS

Copyright © by the University of Michigan 1992
All rights reserved
Published in the United States of America by
The University of Michigan Press
Manufactured in the United States of America

1995   1994   1993   1992   4   3   2   1

Library of Congress Cataloging-in-Publication Data

Slade, Doren L., 1945–
    Making the world safe for existence : celebration of the saints
among the Sierra Nahuat of Chignautla, Mexico / Doren L. Slade.
        p.   cm.
    Includes bibliographical references and index.
    ISBN 0-472-10289-3 (cloth : alk)
    1. Nahuas—Religion and mythology. 2. Indians of Mexico—Mexico—
Chignautla—Religion and mythology. 3. Syncretism (Religion)—
Mexico—Chignautla. 4. Chignautla (Mexico)—Religious life and
customs.   I. Title.
F1221.N3S55   1991
972'.48—dc20   91-43631
                                                                          CIP

For Terry and Joan, and Lisa

Preface

This is a book about celebrations held to honor the saints and the meanings attributed to them by the Sierra Nahuat Indians of Chignautla, Mexico, at a moment in time when their traditional beliefs and practices are becoming part of a history that will soon be lost. My intention is to portray the structure of these people's experience of themselves and their world, that stratum of culture that lies below the surface of consciously held beliefs and is unknowable to participants. The shared meanings in acts of propitiation performed to ensure the continuing favor of the saints have always been centrally positioned within the experience of Chignautecos, and, indeed, these celebrations have been a focal point of public life in this society for roughly three hundred years.

We all take for granted certain aspects of our lives whose import becomes clear only after they have gone. Chignautecos do not take these rituals for granted, but they remain unaware of the vulnerability of this institution to the passage of time, and the vulnerability of their way of life to the encroaching tide of national integration. Transformation of this folk-Catholic complex has accelerated since 1972, the ethnographic present of this study. I am saddened by my certainty of what will surely come to pass by the turn of the twenty-first century. Even so, some twenty years of research have yielded sufficient clarity to enable me to portray the nature of being Chignauteco so that the conceptual system of these people will not be completely lost.

As a graduate student in anthropology, stories of those returning from the field fascinated me. I first journeyed to Chignautla in the summer of 1967 as a member of a field training program, a journey that took me first to Mexico City, then on to the regional capital of Teziutlán in the Sierra Norte of the state of Puebla, and finally to the nearby village of Chignautla. Standing in front of my new home watching the field instructor drive away, I found myself wondering if I could tolerate the isolation. I was comforted by my assumption that sufficient common ground existed with the people I was to study. After all, this was not New Guinea. These peasants spoke a language I recognized and practiced Catholicism, and as a neighboring country, Mexico did not seem at all alien. This, of course, was to prove untrue. I gradually came to appreciate how very different the world view of the Sierra Nahuat Indians was from my own, and from the world view of rural Mestizos and Mexicans of urban centers.

In 1967, material expressions of wealth made it obvious that the roughly five hundred Mestizos in the village were not an economically homogeneous group, and from physical appearances, they did not seem ethnically homogeneous either. My first impressions led to me to categorize the family of comparatively modest means with whom I lived as culturally transitional, somewhere between an elite clinging to Spanish traditions and my image of the Indians. The Indians who inhabited the scattered hamlets surrounding the village were consistently spoken of derogatorily. They made their appearance in the village only for celebrations held for the saints. These ceremonial events were well attended, and participants spilled into the village plaza. The Indians, however, seemed extremely reluctant to speak with me, even more so than did the Mestizos. Indeed, during these *mayordomias,* the Indians remained aloof, quite obviously unwilling to entertain questions from a stranger. I felt invisible and shut out, but this only heightened my curiosity and desire to situate myself in Chignautla for my doctoral research.

My return in 1970 had an equally inauspicious beginning. A banner reading "Yankee Go Home" hung across the main square of Teziutlán and, of course, I knew it meant me. Access to civil archives in Teziutlán remained limited, regardless of formal permissions and the support of the various governing institutions of the state of Puebla, the Instituto Nacional de Antropología, the Museo Nacional de Antropología, Chignautla's municipal authority, and the Archdiocese of Puebla, to all of whom I am grateful. Teziutlán had always been a stronghold of the *Partido Popular Socialista,* the national socialist party, which is extremely anti-American. Such attitudes accentuated my experience of the wall of silence that greeted me during the early months of my two-year residence in Chignautla, corroborating Madsen's (1969) description of Nahua peoples as characteristically closed and disinclined to speak to outsiders about their beliefs and ritual practices. The parish priest of Chignautla created further obstacles. He admonished the Indians, and especially *cargo* holders, persons responsible for ritual events, to avoid me because I was dangerous, an insidious anti-cleric who was undoubtedly a communist. These threatening statements followed his attempt personally to dissuade me from pursuing my study of religion for reasons I did not yet understand. He strongly recommended that I investigate some other aspect of community life. Fortunately, the ecclesiastical authorities of

Teziutlán and Tlatlauqui (Tlatlauqui-tepec) were far more welcoming of my search through their archives. Local parochial archives in rural Mexico are often casually maintained. Information about church history may be lost among records of births, deaths, and baptisms and notations of parish and sodality activities during the colonial and later eras that appear unnamed, in ledgers, folios, sheaves of paper, and large volumes stored randomly in trunks or even on open shelves. Rural archival material is rarely catalogued but may yield unexpected treasures, such as the original chronicle of the history of the church in the Sierra Norte written by six priests that I discovered in the archives of the cathedral of Tlatlauqui.

Two factors facilitated my investigations. Women are less threatening figures than men among these people, and my ambiguous status as a woman and an outsider allowed me to accompany Chignauteco men in many activities that a Chignauteco woman would not. I was also allowed entrance to households and access to gossip that would have been beyond the reach of a male researcher. I developed working relationships with women informants who offered a different view of Chignauteco social life. I was grateful to be able to hire Rufino Galindo Camacho of Chignautla, a young Indian who served as my field assistant and became my constant companion. Acting as translator of both language and cultural content, Rufino buffered my experience of the Indians' refusal to interact with me. Over time, mistrust subsided and I was able to work independently, speaking Spanish as fluently as most Indians did, although I was never able to master Nahuat during the two years of my continuous residence. Together, we were able to tackle a household census that gleaned sensitive data on land ownership and usage, wage earnings, and familial and residential composition. Genealogies from a broad section of the Indian population allowed me to focus more directly on the relationship between kinship and ritual participation.

I was not prepared to encounter a ritual system of such complexity. In order to understand the nature of this institution, I made the municipio my domain of investigation. Certain spatial and cultural divisions emerged as significant for the system's operation. The Indians wanted me to confirm, in how I dressed and acted, their expectations of the status they attributed to me. It became clear that in order for them to feel free to be themselves without discomfort, I had to be myself, and not what I assumed they wanted me to be. This mutual understanding grew as my involvement shifted from the Mestizos to the Indians. Although the lives of the Indians and Mestizos were interdependent, both existed in their own cultural universes. The small enclave of Mestizos inhabiting the municipal head town venerated saints whose images were housed in the parish church alongside the images of saints venerated by the Indians, an overt sign of the ethnic bifurcation in important dimensions of life in this community. Mestizo religious practice was structured by different principles from that of the Indians, whose beliefs about the saints carried the earmark of their indigenous past. Shrouded in intentional secrecy, the rituals of the Indians became my central focus and eventually revealed a clear view of Nahuat ontology. Unless otherwise specified by the term *Mestizo, Chignautla* and *Chignauteco* in this book refer to the Indian population, their culture and institutions.

My description of the relationship between Indians and Mestizos and the nature and function of the mayordomía complex in this society offered previously (Slade 1973) reveals a different analytic focus. My earlier view of Chignauteco ideology represented a more limited grasp of the organizing assumptions that lie deeply buried in the experience of Chignautla's Indians. I believe that my description and analysis of the cosmological underpinnings of the institutions I describe in this work present an understanding in depth, made possible through the sustained gathering of data over the past twenty-four years. This is ample time for nurturing openly trusting and enduring relationships with informants, maintained by my return visits to Chignautla for several weeks or more each year since 1972. The difficult task of conceptually bridging individual and collectively shared experience has been facilitated by the completion of my training as a psychoanalyst. My experience as a practicing psychoanalyst since the early 1980s has gradually deepened my grasp of the subjective lives of Chignautecos by adding conceptual and methodological tools previously unavailable to me.

The process of gathering data by listening, looking, and asking yielded a great deal of information about the Chignauteco way of life. Randomly collected, this data made little sense until configurations emerged that enabled me to articulate the principles ordering events I observed and allowed me to become more focused in my questioning and more able to predict behavior. What had remained unclear for so long in the vast array of ritual events I attended as a participant observer suddenly took on meaning. But observation does not produce the same kind of understanding that is gained from the vantage point of placing oneself in another's shoes. What I learned from being an actor in ceremonies that create bonds of ritual kinship was invaluable, and I never experienced a ritual event quite in the same way again. That is, the evocative nature of sacred acts and the anxiety of the performers in carrying out specific duties heightened my appreciation of what it means to undertake a sacred vow toward a saint or toward an individual with whom a sacred relationship is established.

I am especially indebted to my ritual kinsmen, Guillermo Esteban, Bonifacia Bautista, Bartola Vasquez, Benito Esteban, Marcela Camacho, and Camilo Galindo, for opening their lives and homes to me, interrupting my isolation with deep caring and kind support, which I fully reciprocate. The statements made by Chignautecos that punctuate descriptions in this book are from transcriptions of multiple taped interviews gathered during my residence in Chignautla, which have proven invaluable as a permanent record of a mode of thought whose subtleties remained obscure to me until comparatively recently. These verbal documents are not unlike analytic sessions, and they capture the associative process of individuals and highlight causal assumptions Chignautecos make without conscious awareness. Some informants were more perceptive and helpful than others, and I am particularly indebted to León Ramón and his family, Crescenciana Hipólita, and Asunción Castro and his family.

Aside from these Chignautecos, I am grateful to the many individuals who accompanied me in one way or another during my fieldwork and contributed to the fruition of this task, especially Dr. Fidelia Silva Fuentes, Ysauro Rivera, Desiderio H. Xochitiotzin, Lilia Ortega de Xochitiotzin, Fernando Cámara, Dr. and Mrs. Raul Carrillo, and James and Sharon Taggart.

The involvement of many institutions facilitated the field research upon which this book is based. My training in anthropology at the University of Pittsburgh was made possible by a predoctoral fellowship from the National Institute of Mental Health, which funded my first year of fieldwork. A grant from the National Science Foundation allowed my fieldwork to continue for another year, while a Provost Development Fund Award as well as the Andrew Mellon Postdoctoral Fellowship provided needed time to further collect my thoughts on the data I brought home from the field.

Many people, far too numerous to mention, have contributed essential ingredients to the formulation of my ideas. My emphasis on the manner in which Chignautecos experience their world and the importance I give to this perspective rests on a theory and method devoted to the investigation of subjective life as developed initially by Heinz Kohut, which led to the formalization of Psychoanalytic Self Psychology. The intellectual legacy of this man is far-reaching, and his writings have influenced my thinking over a number of years in ways that are beyond my conscious grasp. More recent contributors such as Robert Stolorow have amplified the usefulness of concepts such as the organization of experience for understanding how individuals design and interpret their experience of the world. I wish to acknowledge my long overdue debt to Keith Brown, an anthropologist who nurtured my intellectual growth and my ideas on kinship and religion.

Most of all, I owe an intellectual debt to Hugo G. Nutini, whose rigorous investigation of Tlaxcalan ideology has inspired my concern with the primacy of ideology for the understanding of social life. I was fortunate to have the opportunity to read a draft of a manuscript by Nutini on the cult of the dead in Tlaxcala, which, during my visits to the field between 1984 and 1987, encouraged me to direct my attention to the collection of further data that would test his notions regarding the relationship of efficacy that obtains between ideology and belief, and the structural system in operation. This stimulated many questions concerning the assumptions people make about the nature of their world, and the role of these epistemological entities in the organization of experience. I have found several concepts developed by Nutini (1984, 1988) such as sacralization, desacralization, and vehicles of sacralization particularly useful in the study of folk Catholicism and in elucidating my data.

There are a number of individuals to whom I am grateful for their substantive contributions to the preparation of the manuscript and insightful suggestions, which helped clarify the presentation of my ideas. I wish to thank Robert Friedrich for his meticulous rendering of the maps and for helping to accommodate this project into my life. I am grateful to Suzanne Daycock for the sacrifices she made in manuscript preparation, to Jennifer López for her organizational suggestions and development of the index, to Susan Milano for her painstaking clarification of my writing style, and to Sarai Batchelder and Gregory Tewksbury for their research assistance. I am indebted to Barbara Simon for comments on the text.

The supportive help offered by Jean F. Nutini and Lisa J. Moskowitz was invaluable in the formulation of my ideas and interpretation of the data. I am particularly grateful to Larry Horowitz and my patients, who gave me a gift by understanding the importance of this project to me, and to Jon Fisher and family, and to George and Gertrude Silvernell, for their patience with my limited availability during the writing of this book.

And finally, I appreciate the courage and guidance of my editor, Joyce Harrison, whose interest in the writings of an anthropologist retooled as a psychoanalyst allowed me to offer this contribution.

Contents

Tables

Maps

Introduction

If you are ever asked to serve God, never say no. For this you came into the
world, to serve God. And when you die and return to God, He will ask you
what you have done. And for this we make our commitments.
  —An old man telling his grandson what to expect from life

Interpretations of the nature of existence follow from assumptions about life
and the context in which it is lived, defining notions of the possible, the
probable, and the expectable. Such assumptions frame experience and structure meanings according to a logical design, imbuing experience, personal
conduct, and collective activities with a coherence that confirms what is held
to be true about the nature of being. This book is devoted to an analysis of
what the Sierra Nahuat Indians of Chignautla believe to be required of them
to make their world safe for existence. The system of causality in Chignauteco thinking centrally concerns the role of the saints in human affairs, giving
celebrations held in their honor primacy in the experience of Chignautecos
and in the interpretations of social life offered in this book.

My focus on the cult of the saints has served well as a vehicle of
interpretation for Chignauteco ideology, highlighting the pre-Hispanic roots
of the cosmological premises it incorporates to reveal the set of unitary
meanings that relate the domains of this society to each other to form a
conceptual whole. In my approach to the analysis of interpersonal interactions, I have taken a stance that assumes a close functional relationship
between the structuring of individual experience and the patterning of social
conduct. This approach rests on the premise that the ideological system of a
people that structures social institutions and the core assumptions that structure the experience of the individual are inseparable epistemologically because they share a content and provide the basis for organizing activity that
emerges in the recognizable contours of both social institutions and individual experience.

Chignautecos share a cultural history with other Nahua peoples of the
Central Highlands of Mexico. What is unique to the fabric of life in Chig-

nautla is the vitality of the ideological configuration that evolved there. Although some scholars today argue that there is little to be gained from producing yet another study of a community that may be isolated by its physical and cultural boundaries, it can also be argued that specific attention to conceptual systems as they exist at the local level provides a firm basis for needed perspectives on the processes of national integration that will change these communities forever. Studies such as those of Gossen (1974, 1986), Hunt (1977), Bricker (1973), Nutini (1984, 1988), Vogt (1976), and Knab (1986), to name a few, have shown by their attention to ideology that notions of order in the universe resting on pre-Hispanic conceptualizations persist, buried deep in the unconscious of the people themselves. These notions retain sufficient potency to structure experience but will be found only by looking below the level of surface phenomena. My focus on ideology, to which I attribute the patterning of attitudes and actions seen in the routine of daily living and in the more constrained context of ritual performance, has allowed me to grasp what is meaningful to Chignautecos and sustains their traditions. In this book I argue that the mayordomía complex reflects, affirms, and maintains the value of reciprocity and the importance of respect, sacrifice, and rank, nuclear tenets of traditional ideology in which notions of balance and harmony predominate. These celebrations embody a particular "cosmovision," a world view structured by cosmological premises, in which humans and the saints are interdependent and reciprocally responsive beings whose interactions maintain the balance necessary to a harmonious existence.[1]

The Scope and Content of Chignautla's Mayordomía Complex

Cargo or mayordomía systems have received much attention in the literature. I agree with Chance and Taylor (1985) that it is imperative to isolate the functional components of these systems so that each may be understood in its historical development. The most important functional components are a civil hierarchy, a religious hierarchy, and a system of fiesta or mayordomía sponsorship, usually associated with individual or household assumption of this ritual burden. Regardless of the wealthy, Mestizo population residing in the municipal center, Chignautla is known in the region as an Indian community. This characterization reflects the elaborate array of mayordomias of a traditional nature held in Chignautla and has been true for as long as people of the region remember. This designation is also a self-referent for the Indian population and affirms the value Chignautecos place on their mayordomias.

The nature of life in rural, autonomous, and relatively culturally isolated communities as originally outlined by Tax (1937), Bunzel (1952), Redfield (1941), and others was described in greater depth by later writers who specifically focused on the civil-religious hierarchy. Individuals who could ascended a ladder of hierarchically ranked offices, alternately serving in civil and religious cargos. In this process, they exchanged their wealth for prestige, passed out of the system, and joined the ranks of community elders. While noting that cargo systems were originally established by the Spanish colonial government for the purpose of civil and religious administration, these writers gave their continuing existence central importance in the study of life in these communities. Descriptions of cargo systems and interpretations of their functions offered by Cámara (1952), Nash (1958), Wolf (1957, 1959), and Carrasco (1961) became conceptual prototypes. However, later writers debated the consequences of the operation of these systems: do they level wealth or stratify the population on the basis of wealth and prestige; are they mechanisms of expropriation or do they facilitate redistribution within the community or sustain patterns of reciprocity and autonomous political and ethnic identity?

I agree with Chance and Taylor (1985) that an analysis of function, in these terms, misses the complexity of this institution, whose study is better served, not by treating the cargo system as a category, but rather by charting structural transformations over time and the consequences of these transformations for community life. In their work, and the work of Wasserstrom (1983), Rus and Wasserstrom (1980), and Chance (1990), it has been demonstrated that it is unlikely that civil-religious hierarchies originated in the colonial era. On the one hand, civil hierarchies were set in place under Spanish rule to govern local indigenous populations by giving these posts to members of the Indian elite and adapting this administrative body to indigenous circumstances. On the other hand, religious sodalities, the *cofradias,* were gradually organized as vehicles of conversion. Each cofradía was corporately organized and dedicated to a specific saint or ritual object such as the Holy Sacrament. Corporate lands and other property generated the means for guaranteeing that ritual obligations taught by the friars would be fulfilled. Cofradias operated independently of a hierarchy of civil offices.

Individual sponsorship of fiestas held in honor of the saints did not occur until the nineteenth century, after the struggle for Mexican independence from Spain. By this time, cofradía organization had been undermined by economic recession and war (Chance 1990). Because the cofradias had been stripped of their material means for carrying out ritual duties toward the saints, the sponsorship of mayordomias fell to individual members. The resulting system of individual sponsorship was ranked and hierarchically arranged to form a body of formally appointed cargo holders who continued to organize and perform the necessary activities of the cult of the saints.

Whether or not these formal offices dedicated to civil and religious duties formed a single administrative body with authority to govern public affairs remains controversial. What is clear is that after the War of Independence, civil and religious duties became further divided with the establishment of formal municipal governments in the second half of the nineteenth century. Each duly constituted civil office had designated duties, authority, and a domain of power, making civil administration on this level a local branch of a national system of governance. This left the religious cargo system to function in relative autonomy. Rather complete summaries of the evolution of these systems exist in the literature and need not be repeated here (see especially Gibson 1952, Carrasco 1961, Cancian 1967, DeWalt 1975, Nutini 1976, Greenberg 1981, Chance and Taylor 1985, Stephen and Dow 1990, and Chance 1990). However, these are not studies of the cult of the saints. The nature of religious beliefs and practices often remains subordinate to a focus on the hierarchy itself.

Over the years two approaches have developed, one looking outward from the local community toward the nation beyond, and the other placing the small-scale community in the responsive position, charting the political and economic forces impinging upon the nature and function of cargo systems. This latter interest moved research further away from a study of cultural processes, specifically the study of indigenous cosmology (Taussig 1980) or syncretic ideology (Assad 1983; Ingham 1986). In my view, and without quite understanding why, there appear to have developed divergent, dichotomous positions at war with each other in Mesoamerican research: those studies guided by political economy and those centering on ideology; those studies dedicated to a structural analysis and those dedicated to an analysis of function; and finally, those studies wedded to diachrony and those wedded to synchrony. I agree with Gossen (1986) when he writes of the "advent of theoretical perspectives, interpretive strategies, and comparative methods that may facilitate some progress in breaking the impasse between the so-called reactionary voyeurs and antiquarians who still do serious local ethnography, on the one hand, and, on the other hand, the prophets of the left, who believe that local social facts, such as hierarchy and ethnicity, are actually class phenomena belonging to a global configuration, and that culture is obfuscation" (1986, 3).

As for cargo systems, they appear to have become an institutionalized topic, but not without falling prey to these conceptual cross currents. What appears in the literature is a study of the cult of the saints as a vehicle of political economy, not a religious complex. Thus the meaning and practice of the cult are reduced to "popular religion," which is then seen as a purely political mechanism for both the state and the local community (Stephen and Dow 1990). On the one hand, popular religion is the new bottle for the old wine of folk religion, making primary the political objectives of opposition to social and economic inequalities that have always existed in one form or another. On the other hand, these writers argue that because religion continues to serve an important function within the local community, religious complexes in whatever form they occur today cannot justifiably be seen as secularized. I believe this to be a contradiction in terms. From my perspective, when sacred meanings are no longer present in the experience of the actors, activities and actions have become desacralized, that is, no longer have the sacred references they once did, regardless of their sociological functions within the societies in which they occur.

Rural communities in Mesoamerica have been in a state of transformation for nearly half a century, and no institution is immune, although the range of transformation varies from region to region. In the last twenty years, this process has intensified and accelerated. Cargo systems are not only structurally altered, but some have disappeared entirely. Chance (1990) notes that the most common form of cargo system today consists of a hierarchically ranked array of public offices whose purpose is to serve the local pantheon of saints, enabling community members to maintain a clear and firm local identity. Whether in the form of mayordomias whose sponsors are granted prestige, or cofradias, or church committees organized to make general collections for fiesta sponsorship (Brandes 1988), these activities reflect local beliefs and ideology. To the degree to which there is continuity in social attitudes, and an expectable form for ritual activity, this complex may be seen as instrumental in the experience of its practitioners. Given that the ideological basis of the cult has endured for three hundred years despite structural transformation resulting from extraneous factors, I feel justified in the use of the term *traditional* for Chignautla's ritual complex.

Religious cargos in Chignautla are held by a constantly changing group of individuals. No one can be forced to serve the saints, and men who request cargos will typically hold them for one or two years. Those individuals selected are usually household heads. Gender is not a basis for exclusion, since women may also be formally appointed to cargos even though this is relatively uncommon given the nature of kinship, marriage, and residence in this society—issues that will be addressed in detail in chapter 4. The complementary roles of men and women in ritual reflect their interdependence in all aspects of life. In fact, men cannot carry out the duties of sponsorship without the contribution of their female kin, for it is members of the sponsor's household who contribute essential ingredients to ceremonial performance, mirroring the value and functional significance of household groupings in this community.[2] Sponsorship invariably includes contributions by ritual kinsmen as well, thereby widening the circle of involvement created by a single formal appointment.

Much has been made of the hierarchical ranking of cargos. The ceremonial ladder, as emphasized in Carrasco's (1961) writing, draws attention to the nature of participation in these systems, which has come to be seen as characteristic. There is a hierarchy of ranked positions through which individuals are expected to pass in a certain order. The concept of hierarchy implies a priori assumptions about the nature of participation, whether or not we understand the meaning behind a preferred or proscribed ritual order that determines which sponsorship enables or prevents an individual from holding one cargo before or after another. Consequently, mode of participation becomes a correlate of progression and a conceptual correlate of the notion of hierarchy epitomized by Cancian's (1965, 1967) concept of the "cargo career." For Zinacantan, Cancian showed that wealth both determined and limited mode of participation and therefore the prestige earned by cargo sponsors. Yet, Zinacantecos were unable to rank the cargos in terms of a prestige scale while easily relating the cargos to each other in terms of costs, forcing Cancian to assume that cost is the basic component in prestige. The more costly the cargo, the greater the prestige accrued by the sponsor. Cancian is not an exception; hierarchy, prestige, and progression appear to be inextricably linked to each other in the way these systems have been conceptualized.

In Chignautla, the cargos are differentially but not necessarily progressively ranked, and cargo holders are respected according to their ritual rank. Yet, an individual does not earn respect by holding a specific series of cargos of increasing importance to ultimately achieve the status of *hueytatoani,* a great and wise leader. Rank validates respect but rank cannot produce respect. Chignautecos hold assumptions about what follows from a life lived in the appropriate manner. They also believe that wisdom grows with age. In combination, wisdom and proper conduct throughout life merit the type of respect that underwrites the influence of an individual recognized as a hueytatoani. However, while cargo sponsorship does indeed affect an individual's reputation, cargo sponsorship, positive reputation, and respect are not causally linked. Chignautecos do not experience sponsorship as a means for earning prestige, for complex reasons that will be addressed as they become relevant. Suffice it to say that attributes of reputation tend to coalesce around poles of "goodness" and "badness" that are associated with a sense of safety or danger.

All ritual sponsorships in Chignautla are dedicated to achieving the same purpose regardless of the specific duties assigned to each cargo as indicated by its formal title. Hence, a *mayordomo* (religious steward), a *fiscal* (fiscal officer), a *sacristán* (sexton), and a ceremonial dancer have different ritual duties to perform, but at some point in their tenure, each will be engaged in an event structurally analogous to a mayordomía celebrating a specific image. The mayordomía, then, emerges as a central, sacralizing vehicle by evoking a meaning and purpose that reflect pivotal tenets of ideology central to the cult of the saints as practiced in this community. A sacralizing vehicle activates a process in which a structural and ideological coalescence occurs to create a pattern of interaction and thought that evokes the sacred yet pragmatic contract between the saints and the human community by intensifying the nature of their interdependence. Such experiences lie below the level of conscious awareness but mark these moments and interactions and the contexts in which they occur as sacred. When I use the term *desacralization* I refer to a loss of one or more critical elements that have sustained the ideological bases upon which this society rests. It is for these reasons that I favor the term mayordomía system over others in common usage in the literature for this religious complex.

The language of the mayordomía represents a sacred lexicon of harmonious and balanced interdependence, confirming and justifying the bases for an ordered social life. Ritual sponsorship is experienced as a burden and a sacrifice by Chignautecos but uplifts those who directly and indirectly participate, since it is a reminder that all is well in the universe. From this perspective, it has been more useful to ascertain the meanings behind sponsorship than to focus on the hierarchical arrangement of cargos as it would be drawn by an observer. I also believe that the concept of hierarchy, and the meanings that have been associated with it, have distracted us from this sacred lexicon and have been emphasized because of their weight as motives in Western thought, wherein time and money, wealth and prestige are linked to issues of cost, power, and self-enhancement. Even though this may be true in the future, no Chignauteco, wealthy or poor, will refuse to participate if asked, because the meanings surrounding money are not yet as compelling as the meanings surrounding sacred acts.

In recent years, certain activities associated with the cult are showing signs of desacralization, making them available for transformation into secularized fiestas. A number of factors are significant in this process. Mestizos and Indians share a church and a civil administration, but the meanings they impart to these institutions are radically different. The Mestizos of Chignautla, eager to enhance their position in the mainstream of national culture, reject that which is rural and therefore Indian, encouraging some Indians to reject elements of their own identity. Mestizos have also usurped certain events that were traditionally Indian, to which they have added meaningful symbols of their own cultural heritage. Indian mayordomias consist of a complex chain of discrete events that occur during the year of a mayordomo's tenure and are typically not held in public view, although those mayordomias held to honor San Mateo during Easter and Christmas draw many people who come to watch or participate in the festivities that occur in the town plaza. Over the past decade, some Indians have retreated from participation in things traditional because of a sense of shame in being Indian while others have built residences near the Mestizos in the municipal head town. Culturally neither Indian nor Mestizo, these individuals straddle both social worlds. The events in which they engage are in their experience largely devoid of tenets that are crucial to the structural expression of Indian cosmology.

The parish church in the municipal center houses fifty-two foci of veneration, including statues and portraits of saints and various manifestations of Jesus Christ and the Virgin Mary, and other ritually significant objects such as the monstrance, crosses, and carved angels. Both Indian and Mestizo images are housed in the church, and on certain occasions the Mestizos will borrow an Indian image, as will the municipal government for particular events. While there may be several likenesses of a particular named saint, Chignautecos regard each image or sacred object as a separate supernatural entity and accord to each a sponsored celebration referred to as a mayordomía. Also, some images are the focus of multiple mayordomias sponsored by different individuals or different groups of individuals. The result is a very complex series of venerative acts that have been sustained for as many as two to three hundred years, depending upon the era in which some form of ritual event was organized in the sacred object's honor.

More than the church, the household of the mayordomo is the focal point for the ritual activities of mayordomía sponsorship. Through sponsorship, the mayordomo becomes the household and community representative in relation to the saint celebrated. As previously stated, the mayordomía itself is a series of ritual acts performed in honor of a particular image venerated as part of the Chignauteco pantheon of supernaturals. The mayordomo relies upon the cooperative efforts of a social network of individuals drawn from his residential extended family and nonresidential kinship group (Nutini 1967, 1968), their ritual kinsmen, and neighbors from the barrio. The mayordomo is also accompanied by formally designated assistants, who enlist their circle of kin and ritual kin. After vespers the previous night, a mayordomía mass is held in the church. A procession with the image follows, and then the mayordomía entourage leaves to attend a ceremonial banquet in the mayordomo's house.

The single most salient attribute of the way humans and supernatural beings are conceptualized as relating to each other is the reciprocal bond that obtains between them, which is viewed as contractual and binding. Reciprocity represents the most fundamental organizing principle structuring ritual activities and interpersonal relations between individuals significant to each other. This central principle is cosmologically thematic and is woven into Chignauteco thought regarding what must and must not be done, and expectations of what should or should not occur as a result of actions taken. In the vernacular of human experience, interpersonal relations hinge on an on-going exchange of favors in which giving generates an expectation of receiving in turn. The propitiatory aims central to celebrations held in honor of the saints are an enactment of this mode of engagement. According to the assumptions Chignautecos make about the universe and the interdependence of all beings existing within it, giving only to expect to receive in turn assures the saints that people are minding the store, in exchange for which participants are assured of a safer and more fulfilling journey through life.

There is no connotation of gift-giving in this conceptualization that would imply a certainty and power to obligate. Such an attitude is antithetical to the Chignauteco way of thinking about their relationship to the saints. Assuming the burden of ritual sponsorship is seen as a sacrifice voluntarily offered in repayment for supernatural beneficence already received without any guarantee that such favor will continue. Reciprocity conceived in this manner differs from the discussion of dyadic contracts conceptualized by Foster (1961b, 1963) and Brandes (1988) for Tzintzuntzan. In their work, interpersonal and personal-supernatural interactions fall within the class of exchange, in which the power resides with the giver, who by the act of giving obligates repayment. The existence of the contractual bond hinges on the substantive nature of the exchange, and whether or not it materializes. Foster (1963, 1283) states that "no contract exists until the request is granted and no contract exists after the supplicant complies." The people of Tzintzuntzan make very specific requests to the saints, which, if met, result in vows. This is not supplication as it exists in Chignautla. The capacity for manipulation inherent in patron-client contracts implies a sense of power over the saints that Chignautecos do not believe human beings have. Vows made are in repayment for health and good fortune already received; it is in this sense that the venerative acts performed to honor the saints represent acts of propitiation.

To the outsider, mayordomias are colorful fiestas with dancing, elaborate meals, and processions. To participants, an essential step is being taken to ensure safety in a world fraught with uncertainties. Chignautecos conceive of the individual as intrinsically vulnerable, unable to determine his or her fate without participation of the saints. Concomitantly, Chignautecos believe that the saints care about mayordomias given in their honor and that mayordomias predispose the saints to return the favor and to share the burden of maintaining harmony and balance in the universe. What is to be gained from an exchange of favors, then, derives from a cosmological premise and subjective truth and is implicit in the structure of these exchanges, creating an endless web of necessary and reliable interchanges in which each partner is bound by the action of the other. In this ongoing exchange of provisions that are both substantive and symbolic, individual and collective, failure to comply makes further engagement uncertain. In principle, reciprocity is at once sacred and pragmatic, serving to sacralize interpersonal interactions in which reciprocity is normative and to intensify the potency of constraints and imperatives inherent in its contractual basis.

For Chignautecos who are only subliminally aware of the breadth of structural implications reciprocal obligations create, this organizing principle governs the mode of interaction between individuals who consciously experience a sense of obligation toward each other. Given verbal expression in mundane events involving exchanges of goods, labor, and other types of material support, reciprocal exchanges are referred to locally in Nahuat by the term glossed as *makwis makepis,* translated as "to lend a hand." This term captures an interpersonal ethic that implies a system of interpersonal obligations. Reciprocal exchanges are crucial between members of the residential extended family and nonresidential kin group and serve as the basis for cooperative efforts, guaranteeing that what is needed will be provided so that no one is without by promoting reliability in mutual dependency, a fact of life in small communities. This echoes expectations of reliability in its structural and functional analogue, the pragmatic yet sacred contract between humans and the saints to create an endless circle of sacred involvement in which interdependency is an ontological tenet. For the observer, ritual sponsorship becomes the structural and ideological point of coalescence for the most significant organizing principles within this cultural universe.

The Conceptual and Methodological Framework

It is axiomatic that a conceptual and methodological scheme arises from a theory that contains underlying assumptions and organizing concepts about the nature of phenomena to be studied and thus influences the manner in which the data are collected, understood, and ultimately analyzed. The complexities of the lives of those we study in the field must be converted into a comprehensive system of descriptive statements intended as representative while reflecting the experience of individual actors whose behavior and communications we actually chart. Similarly, the structure of a domain, either ideational or phenomenal, cannot be directly observed. Models designed to explain structure do not exist on the empirical level and are constructed after the fact and superimposed on the data they are used to explain (Lévi-Strauss 1953, 1960; Nagel 1961). This is very much the case in a study of the ideas held by a specific group of people and the rules by which they are organized into a coherent body of knowledge and propositions about the nature of existence and the physical world. These are categorical patterns of thought embodied in beliefs, meanings, values, and normative ideals that are displayed in action, a study of which allows us to ascertain themes and premises, assumptions and expectations that order the experience of those we observe. In this study, I refer to this very complex construct as ideology, divided into its separable constituents for the purpose of analysis.

Unlike Western society, the substantive domains of Chignauteco society are relatively undifferentiated both ideologically and structurally, which makes it impossible to describe Chignauteco religion as autonomous and freestanding. The cult of the saints has been treated in this book as the most salient expression of Chignauteco ideology. Beliefs and practices of the cult constitute a discernible system of sacred signification, crystalizing the role of the saints in human affairs and thereby expressing, affirming, and sustaining the most important tenets of Chignauteco cosmology. It is the pervasive influence of cosmological and ideological themes regarding human-supernatural relations that permits me to use the term *sacred* in reference to acts and intentions of participants in various contexts of life that realize the aims of the cult in their broadest implications. Because these cosmological and ideological themes persist from their indigenous roots and continue to form a significant content in the assumptions that organize Chignauteco experience, I have used the terms *folk, sacred,* and *traditional* interchangeably when speaking of Chignauteco religion, beliefs, institutions, culture, and society.

The organization and presentation of the data in this book incorporates a distinction between what occurs in the minds of our informants that we cannot see and the behavior we can observe. Failure to make this distinction, I believe, leads to confusion of those phenomena we have set out to understand. However, the activities we observe never stand by themselves and must be related to the beliefs that give them meaning and purpose. And, beliefs verbally communicated are heuristically meaningless unless we ascertain the role they have in the behavior observed. I sought to discover regularities in the relationship between observable forms and their intrinsic meaning, because cultural reality is by nature structured by inner meanings. Of course, the number of observations one makes of a given type depends on the generalizations one wishes to generate. Once the principles involved are grasped, prediction becomes possible and will be verified by further observation and questioning. Such is the basis for a growing understanding during investigation while in the field.

My struggle to comprehend the nature of being Chignauteco began with an initial study of the Mestizos residing in the municipal head town even though the Mestizos and Indians led lives belonging to different centuries. It was obvious that I would not be doing a "village" study since the cult of the saints is a municipal phenomenon and interbarrio and interethnic interactions were significant in the operation of the system as a whole. My comprehension of the ideological underpinnings of the cult of the saints in Chignautla took much longer than my period of sustained residence in the community and has been distilled over more than twenty years. Each return visit has provided a deeper understanding of Chignauteco cosmology.

Important structural and cultural data can be extracted from observing rituals and much of my time was spent in this endeavor. Our informants teach us about their world by how they relate to us, and only occasionally does questioning in depth reveal directly what may be inferred about ideology. Statements made or stories told display their meaning only after some measure of understanding is reached that reveals the ideological contents buried within the subjective experience of the individual. Penetrating insight is often spontaneous, especially after one has done the wrong thing, since these troubling moments clarify expectations held by the people. For a significant period of time I was unable to comprehend why my best informants refused to accept monetary compensation for the time they spent teaching me about their world. On one occasion an informant came to me to borrow a significant amount of money. I refused the request, fearing that the money would not be repaid without understanding the implications of both his request and his refusal to take the money I offered him for his generous counsel. It is clear that he expected me to give him the money, and I, admittedly, had never expected him to make such a request, since we were neither kinsmen nor ritual kinsmen but were involved in a relationship without defined expectations. Only afterward did I understand that harmonious interpersonal interaction had been his operating premise, allowing him to formulate his goal in the manner in which he had. He fully believed that I would give him the money, but he was not aware of the assumptions embodied in his beliefs that led to his expectation of success, assumptions pertaining to long-standing cosmological notions of balance that lie in the background of reciprocal exchanges between individuals who respect each other.

Most of my interpretations of the data presented in this book rest on an analysis of implicit, organizing principles. Clearly, ideology is the major epistemological entity utilized in this study in association with a formulation of the organization of experience, as elucidated in recent psychoanalytic conceptualizations. I have kept in mind that experience bridges the domains of the conscious and the unconscious, and what exists on the level of the collectivity transcends that which exists on the level of the individual. Cultural meanings are invariably articulated within personal experience, and one does not exist independently of the other. Just as cosmological premises are intrinsic to the ordering of the constituent elements of an ideological system, core assumptions create an enduring image of the world that is embedded within the organization of an individual's experience. Core assumptions, held with the certainty of convictions, come to be known by listening to how people talk about themselves, others, and their interpretations of events. A specific pattern emerges that illuminates the system of expectations determinant in the choice of action to be taken.

In other words, it is the ordering of thought, and the logic thought lends to expectations, that reveals the operation of unconsciously held assumptions, which serve as principles organizing the experience of the individual without his or her conscious awareness. Assumptions may be seen as causally linked to expectations. Expectations are interwoven with consciously held beliefs, and function as predispositions to action elicited verbally by inquiries. Expectations, then, are organized by the same principles that order assumptions but deal with causal relationships established through experience about the knowable world.

An ideological system and the organization of experience are complementary and interdependent in content and function. Together, these constructs have deepened my understanding of how Chignautecos navigate their world. My conceptualization of ideology is not unlike Turner's (1974) ideological pole of meaning, which includes normative values, such as reciprocity and respect in Chignautla, and principles of organization, such as patrilineality and rank; but it is also not inconsistent with how Lévi-Strauss (1967) views such phenomena. Many more writers comprise my intellectual genealogy as my mode of analyzing has shifted between anthropological and psychoanalytic formulations in the writing of this book.

I came to know many unspoken truths about the nature of existence in Chignautla by watching and asking, and listening, experiencing, and analyzing. The analysis of experience differs from the raw data of experience, and the collaboration of my Chignauteco informants often expressed their value on hospitality and respect rather than their understanding of my efforts at data collection and analysis, a difficulty El Guindi (1986) attempted to overcome by her methodological approach to ethnoscience. I learned that it was believed dangerous to express angry feelings between cargo holders not from statements made by informants, but rather from listening to comments people made to each other and observing their fears when cargo holders treated each other less respectfully than they should. I learned very early that accuracy and reliability in collecting information was a primary consideration, since direct questions often resulted in distorted answers; but the form distortions took came to have its own meaning and was in itself revealing. I had asked informants directly how they experienced the images of the saints housed in the church, hoping to gain some insight regarding how Chignautecos experience the saints. I was told by one informant that they are just images, like photographs of someone you love! Understanding of such a statement had to be sought on a deeper level of collective meaning. People either hold strongly to their beliefs and can discuss their significance or are unsure of details but can conceive of no other possible way to believe. Similarly, in pursuit of the significance of behavioral and verbal distinctions that Chignautecos make between different cargos, I asked several reliable informants about the relative value of mayordomias and was dismayed by their insistence that all were equal in the eyes of God. This, of course, was a statement of the ideal and does not mean that my informants were unaware of distinctions actually made between one cargo and another. Informants prefer to communicate what they should do and do not necessarily communicate distinctions they make between what ought to be done unconditionally, what the individual should try to do, and how things are actually done given the nature of living. This forced me to pay meticulous attention to the dynamic interplay between ideals, rules, and norms in multiple contexts of daily life and in ritual activities. Observations of verbal and nonverbal action, when combined, constitute the raw data of the belief system. Beliefs can be presented in an "I believe" form, but often they are not, and more is gained from statements of "disbeliefs" (Rokeach 1960). What people believe to be true consists equally in what they believe not to be true or what they believe to be irrelevant. Beliefs are more typically expressed in the form of statements about behavior, especially in gossip or in criticism, and even these statements cannot always be taken at face value. Like gossip (see especially Haviland 1977) and humor (see Bricker 1973), beliefs betray cosmological themes that lie in the background of experience and are never verbalized directly, nor can they be validated by verbal presentation, since in this form, they will typically be unrecognized or even denied.

I had arrived in Chignautla with a number of assumptions about the nature of cargo systems that were based on the literature. In many ways, Cancian's (1965) work in Zinacantan initially served as my bible and field manual. I was determined to discover the "hierarchy" and experience the prestige awarded men who had reached the top. I knew from my study of antecedents of Nahua culture that individuals are valued for their contribution to collective activities designed to preserve cosmic order, and that sacrifice is believed to be necessary in the preservation of that order (Madsen 1969; León-Portilla 1963; Soustelle 1956; Sahagún 1956). I accepted that there is always tension between the personal and common good, and I learned that *communitas* was very much alive in Chignautla. I observed that certain attitudes and characteristics of people were negatively evaluated and elicited negative social sanctions. But once we grant that aims of the collectivity take precedence over the individual, then it becomes clear that self-interest is likely to be considered dangerous. I later came to understand that this personal attribute was indeed experienced as dangerous because it threatened core assumptions that hinge on the balance and harmony necessary for social order. I learned that men who had served collective aims well were considered *importante,* and notable for being steadfast in the performance of their duties. These men were also *recto,* righteous and just, and of good reputation, which earned them respect. In contrast, a demonstration of pride (*orgullo*) in one's accomplishments, especially those stemming from desire for self-enhancement, invited mistrust and was typically associated with prideful ambition. Men who were seen as potentially dangerous would not be granted the cargos that would supposedly earn them a position of prestige among their fellows. What I experienced in interaction with men of high ritual rank was some type of aura that permeated the manner and way of being of these men who in the experience of Chignautecos had been irrevocably altered through their service to the saints.

After initial observations, my own theory began to take form, producing preliminary formulations about central ideological principles operative in diverse domains of experience. Gradually, beliefs became available for systematic charting, but only after multiple taped interviews were collected from individuals who had sponsored cargos and from those who had not, from specialists, agriculturalists, and wage earners, from men and women, and from individuals of different barrios. Interviews were consistently cross-checked with statements by other informants and personal observation. Interviewing was fully open-ended and formal questionnaires were never used because Chignautla's Indians preferred a discursive style, rather like storytelling. Genealogies, censusing, map making, and the use of archives filled in gaps.

Understanding the experience of these people began with a set of intuitive notions about Chignauteco ideology and the structure of their beliefs, developed out of my subjective experience of their subjective experience, because it is within interactions that different world views make themselves available for clear perception. People let down their ideological guard especially under situations of stress when themes of importance are highlighted. If you ask Chignautecos whether they believe that saints are capricious, they might respond by saying they do not, since God is just. But if you observe the inordinate amount of anxiety displayed by men who have been successful and are desperate to secure a cargo, it becomes clear that their desperation derives from a sense of jeopardy that rests on unconscious notions of supernatural debt that must be reciprocated in order to insure the continuing favor of the saints. Thus, validation in this type of study rests largely on an index of coherence. When we are able to predict behavior on the basis of the principles that order the system of meaning of the actors themselves, then we have come to the preliminary stages of discerning their model of the world. Coherence and continuity are characteristic of a cultural system. They are also characteristic of individual experience. Any set of ideological elements that relates various aspects of human experience to each other exists in an orderly arrangement of parts that reveals a recognizable pattern. These interrelationships form a unitary design expressed in the dynamic interplay between these two epistemological entities, reflecting the intrinsic principles that order and sustain social life and human experience.

I have ordered the data in such a manner that Chignauteco ideology can be viewed as a coherent system of unconscious cosmological and ontological assumptions that organize the experience of individual Chignautecos in a form recognizable to others.[3] How Chignautecos experience their world is an expression of the continuing influence of logical rules and imagery crystalized in early life. What individual Chignautecos bring to any life situation is the unconscious organizing activity that reveals their membership in this cultural group. This activity is shaped by structures of meaning encoded in assumptions that underwrite beliefs about the nature of their existence. Once shared, assumptions generate propositions about causal connections between events. Unlike core assumptions, expectations are accessible to consciousness and are comparatively mutable. In this sense, expectations affirm the assumptions generating them when expectations are confirmed repeatedly in experience. At the same time, what a Chignauteco anticipates may not occur. If what occurs is consistently different from what is expected, as is true in a situation of social change, expectations will be challenged without disturbing the core assumptions from which they derive. Yet, such disparities cannot continue indefinitely because of the negative effect this discordance generates in the individual (Rokeach 1960). Given the right conditions, a reorganization of expectations will eventually occur, and disproved expectations will recede because they are no longer tenable. Sustained discrepancies between expectations and assumptions invariably result in an erosion of ideological elements within what was a coherent system experientially, relegating various acts and meanings to the realm of old-fashioned customs that have lost their value. The reorganization of experience in this manner allows us to view expectations as a fluid variable in the functional interdependence of experience and ideology. It is only in the context of massive challenge to expectations that change occurs on the ideological level; that is, when the assumptions organizing experience become irrelevant and are no longer instrumental in the experience of the actors or in the operation of a belief system. If the individual actors in a social system were aware of the dynamic interplay between expectations and assumptions in the patterning and continuity of their experience, then this psychological bedrock of culture would be more available to conscious examination and ideology would lack its elusive, enduring nature.

This leads to the last point I wish to make regarding expectations and assumptions as analyzable elements of culture. My point may be formulated as follows: expectations are to assumptions as beliefs are to ideology. Expectations mediate between specific core assumptions and specific beliefs when they are consistently confirmed in experience, that is, when our beliefs carry us meaningfully through life. If we view ideological principles as organizing individual experience, then ideological tenets are also present in beliefs and underwrite expectations. Individual experience can then be seen to be organized according to what has been called "cultural rules." The performance of ritual activates expectations concerning the aims of sacred acts by bringing them into clearer and collective focus, contributing to the evocative power and durability of religious ideology and belief.

Apart from the approach I have described above, I have been influenced by a complex schema developed by Nutini (1984, 1988) for the analysis of a given structural and ideological domain in which he distinguishes between the ideological order and the structural system in operation to ascertain the relationship of efficacy that obtains between them. For Nutini, explanations must specify those conditions that determine when individuals comply with or depart from what he has labeled ideological injunctions, their derived imperatives, immediate directives to action, and conscious beliefs. Nutini makes a distinction between ideology and belief that is useful for understanding experience, partially because such a distinction underscores the differential function of ideology and belief in the relationship between experience, thought, and action, and also because this distinction accounts for what we can know about ourselves and the actions we take, and what is inexplicable to us about our own behavior. Essentially, I am incorporating a distinction between the realm of unconscious motivation and conscious intention.

On the one hand, the ideological order as described by Nutini (1988) operates unconsciously, and the actors themselves remain unaware of its efficacious properties. That is, they are not aware of the influence ideological injunctions (unconditional oughts), their derived imperatives (shoulds), and immediate directives for action (musts) have on their behavior. On the other hand, individuals are consciously aware of what they believe. Nutini has established the causal relationship between these levels, permitting us to view the structural system in operation as the passive element, and beliefs and ideology as "activating entities." I will present shortly the pivotal ideological tenets and cosmological premises central to the operation of Chignautla's ritual system. These are best understood as contents of core assumptions that organize the experience of individual Chignautecos, serving to explain normative patterns in behavior and what emerge as ideals. In this way, we are able to glimpse the Chignauteco experience and the considerations influencing an individual's actions, as well as the operative assumptions and expected results from actions taken or not taken in a variety of contexts.

Neither experience nor ideology is monolithic. Given the necessary impetus, both will succumb to forces capable of bringing about their transformation. The powerful presence of priests and the influence of Protestant missionaries has only recently been granted the significance it deserves (DeWalt 1975; Sexton 1978; Beidelman 1982; Ingham 1986; Brandes 1988; Earle 1990). The presence of Protestant sects in communities like Chignautla has weakened the vitality of the cult and produced intracommunity tensions, and resident priests have played a major role in the transformation of religious cargo systems. For example, one priest utilized his position to interfere with the traditional mode of selection of cargo holders. His actions politicized the traditional decision-making processes for church affairs so that competition for cargos became a recurrent issue and intensified disputes between interest groups predisposed to conflict over resources perceived to be in scarce supply. This priest's devaluation of the mayordomias increased the people's conflict over their inclination to respect him. His denegration of traditional ritual forms as quaint pagan relics of Indian heritage that needed to be expunged for the sake of their moral well-being led to the Indians' mistrust of his sacred authority. The priest neither understood nor cared about Chignauteco traditions, but he did care about his own income from the services he rendered. He raised the price of mayordomía masses, thereby disturbing the long-standing balance between the burdens of sponsorship and the experience of sacrifice deeply embedded in sacred intentions, making cargo costs take on a significance they had never had before. The Indians' resentment of his power remained contradictory to their compliance to his wishes, and during his residence, mayordomias did not decrease since celebrating the saints was more important than the priest. Potentially stressful situations may enhance the strength of beliefs associated with practices that have generally become residual given the erosion of explanations based solely on supernatural causation. However, the uncertainty lingering in the minds of many individuals continues to produce traditional explanations and responses and Chignautecos will return to supplicatory processions with the image of San Mateo to petition protection when severe storms or lack of rain threaten crops, even though the beliefs generating such supplications coexist with weather forecasting and scientific explanations for natural phenomena made available through radio and television broadcasts.

The Expression of Ritual Meanings

I have designated the mayordomía as prototypical because this ritual form reveals most clearly the operation of principles that embody cosmological premises central to Chignauteco ideology, in turn articulating core values in Chignauteco experience. Six important components are expressed directly in the structure of ritual events and indirectly in other contexts, sacralizing all activities in which they occur. The central cosmological premises are *balance* and *harmony,* which are also existential truths centrally positioned in Chignauteco assumptions about the nature of things. *Reciprocity* and *rank* are the structural principles most clearly articulated in the cult of the saints and in all contexts in which they serve as vehicles of sacralization. Reciprocity and rank are articulated in behavioral and verbal expressions of *respect* and contribute to the intensification and evocative capacity of *sacrifice* as a sacred and symbolic aim. Sacrifice in this system is an organizing metaphor (Knab 1986) relating broad areas of experience to each other in a concrete manner on the basis of a coherent set of meanings.

In my discussion of the mayordomía as a composite of ritual events, I analyze its major symbolic elements. My sole purpose is to enhance analysis of the various forms in which the role of the saints in human life are articulated. Symbols condense many referents and unite them in a single cognitive and affective field (Turner 1974). Symbolic expression, structurally or metaphorically encoded, reinforces what is already conceptualized in belief, but less directly. This reinforcement occurs through the affective resonance that accompanies beliefs and actions. In experience, a ritual event like the mayordomía is a moment of coalescence in which the experience of the ritual actors acquires reliable contours, meaning, and emotional coloration, which gives the event its affective potency. Symbolically expressed, sacred meanings articulate shared experiences that become associated with emotion-laden concerns. These, in turn, trigger the meanings already crystalized in them. Conversely, participation in ritual evokes and affirms associated sacred meanings. Affective resonance, then, may be seen as a reinforcing attribute of a system of coherently organized meanings, acts, and reliable expectations; it provides the subjective basis for the recognition and instrumentality of symbolic forms. It is in this sense that symbolic condensations are incorporated into significant sacralizing vehicles. They have a high degree of subjective potency, and give ritual performances their compelling, uplifting quality.

It would not be incorrect to say that sponsoring mayordomias involves a variety of acts of routine occurrence, which, when dedicated to sponsorship, create sacralizing contexts. Sacralization does not change an act. It changes the subjective experience of it, thereby transforming its meaning and instrumentality. Why, for example, is there an experiential distinction between food prepared and eaten in the daily round of events and food prepared and eaten during ritual meals? Part of the specific design of ritual meals enhances the experience of and the meaning behind the food eaten and its preparation. Cooking on a day-to-day basis is not generally uplifting, but when cooking occurs for a mayordomía meal, it becomes a sustaining and enhancing experience. Women cooking become ritual actors and the tortillas eaten become sacred food. I shall not be analyzing symbolic forms without placing them alongside that which I am able to explain reasonably well within the framework discussed above. That certain elements of belief and structural properties of the mayordomía complex present themselves as evocative signs tells us something about their sociocultural significance, and not about their value as symbols. Symbols, as stated above, have the ability to express a great deal of content in a condensed form, the "why," the "how," and the "what for" of religion. Symbols serve to highlight what is important without necessarily being at the center of attention and portray the latent content of social life.

The Ideological Bases for Belief and Ritual Practice

A number of characteristics of Mesoamerican folk society and Nahua folk religion in particular noted by writers over the years apply equally to the Sierra Nahuat of Chignautla (Tax 1952; Redfield 1953; Wolf 1957; León-Portilla 1963; Reina 1967; Carrasco 1969, 1976; and Madsen 1969). In very general terms, the annual ceremonial cycle is regulated by a calendrical system in which venerative activities represent acts of propitiation to a pantheon of supernatural beings upon whom the human community is dependent, and who are attributed with the power to reward and punish individuals who fail to live up to the dictates of belief. The ritual process in this type of system is highly pragmatic. Basic tenets directly guide and constrain behavior, tenets whose instrumentality is immediately tied to practical consequences. Religious institutions, therefore, function to regulate interpersonal and personal-supernatural relations that mirror each other. In such systems, expectations people hold about the nature of the universe are readily adjusted to changing circumstances. A distinction usually exists between private and public rituals that corresponds to a distinction between the formal doctrines of the church and the beliefs and practices of the cult of the saints as it evolved in local communities while retaining elements of indigenous cosmology.

Locally evolving forms of religious practice represent variations on a theme. What ties these systems together also accounts for their particular adaptations to concrete structural and environmental conditions. In time, both ideology and belief acquire an independence from the conditions that gave rise to them and establish a basis for their own continuity. In Chignautla, the ideology discussed throughout this book developed from a series of historical antecedents, combining what existed in pre-Hispanic communities with elements added by the intrusion of the Spaniards to form a new system of beliefs and ideological tenets that evolved into the cult of the saints as its exists at the present time. For example, the pre-Hispanic belief in sacrifice as a means for maintaining favorable ministration from the gods was transformed by the defeat of the pre-Hispanic gods by what the Aztecs experienced as the gods of the Spaniards. The result was a syncretic complex in which the reciprocal interchange between human beings and the saints became central and still persists.

What follows is a series of representative contents of both ideology and core assumptions, presented in statement form to serve as a backdrop for my analysis of Chignauteco thought and my description of the ritual complex. As will be seen, the beliefs also presented below embody the most significant of these contents, which incorporate nuclear cosmological themes. I have divided the elements of the ideological system in order of their causal entailment and according to their function in the organization of experience. The highest level represents elements that are generally pervasive in their influence and operate from the deepest layer of experience. These are prototypical, and describe the role attributed to the saints in existence.

The following statements lie at the heart of Chignauteco experience and represent the most fundamental injunctions of this cultural system. In this sense, they represent what I believe to be core assumptions that organize experience in much the same manner as cosmological premises order ideology. They are never challenged, nor can they become conscious since they represent the basic structure of experience.

1. Balance is necessary in relationships of interdependence, in which each participant receives his due, thereby maintaining harmony in the universe.
2. The sacred nature of existence must be revered and safeguarded.
3. All that is good and all that is bad is supernaturally predetermined.
4. Performance of duty is necessary to maintain the balance and harmony of the universe.

The next six statements represent what is imperative for proper veneration of the saints in Chignautla. These are explanatory assumptions organizing experience around ideological tenets.

1. All rituals addressing the saints are essential in maintaining a balanced and harmonious existence and are traditionally proscribed.
2. Failure to show appropriate attitudes and display appropriate behavior will result in illness, environmental disaster, or thwarted economic endeavors, especially in the context of relationships that give meaning and order to existence.
3. Venerative attitudes toward the saints and all activities dedicated to them in all contexts, public and private, personal and collective, in the church and household, barrio and community, hold the same sacred value and demand adherence to traditionally proscribed attitudes and actions.
4. All ritual contexts and ceremonial acts indirectly or directly engage the supernatural and cannot be taken lightly.
5. Venerating the saints, whether by entreaty or propitiation, is individually and communally necessary, creating the possibility for an otherwise unobtainable safe journey through life.
6. Ritual sponsorship creates the opportunity for reciprocation for favors received, thereby sacralizing all persons and activities involved.

The next ten statements are assumptions close to consciousness about causal relationships that can be viewed as normative ideals for the practice of the cult.

1. The power of the saints is critical to the well-being of the individual, of kinsmen, of the barrio, and of the community because saints act directly on behalf of their supplicants and can be approached through proper ritual means in personal vows, propitiatory ceremonies, and especially mayordomias.
2. Commitments made to serve the saints, either directly or by helping another who is serving, must be done willingly, humbly, and with respect, holding back nothing in goods and services, for the saints will know.
3. The proper attitude of humble respect predisposes the saints to listen, but favors cannot be demanded or coerced from them.

4. Serving the saints, if performed correctly and with the right attitude, helps insure the continuation of successful endeavors.
5. Sacrifices made in service to the saints must balance the good turns received so that joy, not suffering, results.
6. The saints are benefactors and provision of their favors and good turns must be reciprocated in order to maintain harmonious relations among all concerned.
7. Personal calamities and natural disasters signal that the harmonious balance between the community and the saints is disturbed.
8. Each saint is unique and necessary and will respond in specific ways according to his or her personal inclinations.
9. San Mateo is especially powerful and responsive to Chignautecos and requires elaborate mayordomias with dancing, music, rockets, and regalia offered explicitly in his honor.
10. All mayordomos deserve and require respect and obedience befitting their role in serving the saints for all of us.

The mayordomía is organized reciprocally and reflects the balance intrinsic to reciprocity. Reciprocity subsumes the principle of rank, which is articulated in expressions of respect shown to individuals who have sacrificed to serve the saints. Dedication to collective aims is achieved largely through ritual sponsorship, which implies a willingness to sacrifice on behalf of the common good since the sacrifice of sponsorship enacts deference toward the saints upon whom humans are dependent. Deferential attitudes and gestures are obligatory in ritual contexts, especially toward cargo holders, their wives, and their support personnel. There are many obligatory forms of behavior expressing respect for rank and distinctions of rank are typically enacted in terms of address and in the degree of deference shown individuals based on the value of the sacrifice undertaken by the ritual sponsor. Ritual ranking is determinant and overrides all other bases for distinctions made between times of the day and months of the year, between different natural elements, and between living things, including saints, human beings, animals, and plants. For example, certain saints demand more respect than others, corn is more respectfully treated than any other plant, turkeys have greater significance than any other animal, and the months in which ceremonial dancers perform are more sacred than other months of the year. Interpersonally, youth is subordinate to age, men are primary to women, children owe deference to adults, and younger siblings must obey older siblings. Young children are often compared in their characteristics to animals, whereas adults never are.

Such attitudes display an implicit system of valuation embedded in more generalized notions of the sacred. Interpersonal ranking metaphorically addresses notions of value that are poorly articulated but rest on equally unspecified notions of accretion of what is good and necessary for a safe passage through life. For this reason, older men are expected to be capable of leadership since they have become the repository of wisdom and are valued for this achievement. Similarly, the important mayordomos and the fiscales embody the ideal and are at times called "the fathers of us all." It is clear that in Chignautla, "more" is ranked higher than "less," whether this refers to age, to a position within the family, or to ritual rank, property, land, corn production, children, and animals. But positive valuation is intrinsically tied to the way in which resources are used and not simply to their quantity. An individual of higher rank is *mayor* (senior), *grande* (big, great, or older), or *importante,* just as a father, ideally a household head, would be to members of his family. Time and effort are needed to achieve wisdom and accomplish good deeds, through which an individual can come to embody attributes of the ideal citizen.

Formal teaching of orthodox theology has been haphazard in Chignautla. What the people have been taught by priests has been reformulated by the logic and meanings belonging to Chignauteco thought to become part of an oral tradition. Mass is rarely attended except for mayordomias of importance. The peculiar Chignauteco amalgamation of concepts about God, the Holy Sacraments, the relation of the saints to God, the meaning and substance of the mass, feast days, heaven, hell, the fate of souls, etc., is perpetuated from generation to generation. There is little corrective interference that would cause the Chignauteco reformulation of these beliefs to be directly challenged. Young children come to learn about the Catholic rites of baptism, confirmation, first communion, and marriage, all of which remain embedded in indigenous practices and are maintained as conceptually distinct by the Indians themselves. These differences are neither contradictory nor antagonistic in their experience. What is Catholic in the experience of Chignautecos is, for the observer, syncretic. This becomes clear in the following event. A young man was to marry a woman whose parents were members of a group of Evangelists. The man's only relatives were his mother and sister, who were grateful to be able to establish a relationship with a large family from whom they would receive dependable assistance. However, the marriage ceremony was altered to fit this novel situation. The *xochitis,* a complex ritual of indigenous origin (described in chap. 4), is a central marriage rite that encompasses nothing Catholic and requires a ritual dance and exchange involving the couple, both sets of parents, and the godparents of the wedding. The xochitis for this wedding was held, but without participation by the bride's parents. The explanation offered by the groom's family was that the relatives of the bride were not Catholic!

Chignautecos do not relate to the supernatural as a whole, but rather to individual saints to whom they are cosmologically related. Otherwise invisible in their power, the saints are made palpable through their images, which fits well the pragmatic nature of this religion. It is important to note that there is little difference between the manifestations of Jesus or the Virgin Mary and other saints in the experience of Chignautecos. The patron saint (San Mateo) is conceived of as the most important being in Chignautla's pantheon of supernatural entities, while God remains a remote abstraction, often conceptually merged with any saint and having the same properties as a saint, yet unlikely to intervene as a saint would in immediate ways in an individual's life. God is never directly celebrated in mayordomias. Chignautecos are unconcerned with distinctions between God the Father and God the Holy Spirit, since such distinctions are little understood and are therefore irrelevant. Jesus Christ occupies a position structurally analogous to that of a saint. The saints as benefactors are to be respected, ministered to, and venerated in order to render them favorably inclined to help. Clearly, the folk Catholicism practiced in Chignautla displays its origins in pre-Hispanic polytheism, sixteenth-century Spanish Catholicism, and the complex theological admixture that evolved after the Conquest.

Ideology is available for translation into consciously held beliefs about the saints and about how one must act in relation to them. These beliefs encapsulate how Chignautecos experience the saints, depend upon their protection, and know what is required for the saints to remain positively predisposed to their needs. Verbalized beliefs are readily converted into rules by which the behavior of others is measured. In this sense, beliefs represent immediate ideals for behavior, since the behavior of others is judged according to what is held to be the right and correct way to conduct oneself. Beliefs themselves are mediating entities between unconscious assumptions and preconscious predictive activity; that is, expectations individuals hold. Expectations underscore the validity of beliefs by linking thought and action, allowing beliefs to be confirmed or contradicted by experience. According to Rokeach, a "belief system is conceived to represent all the beliefs, sets, expectancies, or hypotheses, conscious and unconscious that a person at a given time accepts as true of the world he lives in" (1960, 33). Disbeliefs do not mirror beliefs. Beliefs and disbeliefs are distinct conceptual entities.[4] For example, the priest cannot prove to Chignautecos that their mayordomias are pagan rituals because Chignautecos experience his words as neither true nor relevant, since he does not hold the legitimate authority granted to the fiscales or the saints, even though the priest is believed to be necessary for the performance of the mass.

An individual's beliefs or disbeliefs are never totally engaged, and in a given moment and context, only certain beliefs will be activated. Chignautecos believe that it is the voluntary will of an individual that motivates cargo sponsorship. They also believe that cargo sponsorship is obligatory if personal calamity is to be avoided. In the context of public life, beliefs regarding the voluntary nature of sponsorship are activated, whereas in terms of personal motivations, a desire to sponsor a cargo is motivated directly by a belief in supernatural punishment. These beliefs are directly linked, but they are not experienced as interrelated or contradictory. Rokeach attributes this to a psychological process of isolation. In such cases, what is seen as untrue is as important as what is believed to be true, a fact especially relevant in a situation of change in which people retain traditional beliefs and act in ways that contradict them, as is seen in the following case. A woman believed that her pent-up anger toward her husband resulted in her becoming ill. Too much emotion is believed to be dangerous since it implies a loss of balance. This is especially true of anger, a state antagonistic to essential harmony. Chignautecos believe that persistent anger is a manifestation of *muina,* anger sickness, a corruption of the Spanish term *mohina,* or animosity (Madsen 1969). Muina is believed to result from an overflow of bile into the blood and stomach that causes contamination and leads to the development of a disease state called *bilis,* literally bile. The woman mentioned had developed symptoms resembling gall bladder disease, for which she sought medical help from a doctor in a nearby clinic. In fact, she did suffer from this condition, and she received medication and a dietary program from the doctor that improved her condition. But she knew full well that she could not be cured of muina by the doctor. For her persisting muina she continued to seek the help of a curer. In her experience, both her illnesses were valid, as were the remedies she procured.

The beliefs presented below are a condensation of actual, verbalized beliefs or beliefs that have been inferred from behavior observed in a variety of contexts. They are most significant for understanding the mayordomía complex.

1. Paying one's debt to the saints is best achieved through ritual sponsorship.
2. Cargo sponsorship is voluntary.
3. Individual vows to the saints are sacred and binding once made.
4. The cargos belong to the community and individual acts affect the collectivity.
5. The saints must be served with a pure heart.
6. If one is appointed to a cargo, bad luck will occur if the cargo is refused.
7. The saints, if venerated in the appropriate manner with the correct attitude, will not fail to respond to one's wishes.
8. The saints cannot be coerced to grant favors no matter how elaborate a ritual gesture might be.
9. The saints will become angry if what can be offered is withheld.
10. Mayordomos deserve and command respect.
11. Supernatural beneficence must be acknowledged with humility.
12. Pride in good fortune is both dangerous and destructive to the individual and the community.
13. One should not reduce one's material resources through sponsorship.
14. Sponsorship is a sacred commitment and sacrifice.
15. If one does not live a moral life, the saints will not value one's sacrifice.
16. Any cargo is available to any individual in good standing.
17. Only household heads can serve as mayordomos.
18. The images of the saints must be kept in good condition to sustain their favor.
19. All the events of a mayordomía are necessary to proper veneration of the saints.
20. Disrespect shown to a cargo holder is disrespect for the saints and will lead to misfortune.
21. The household altar is a necessary receptacle for the implements and objects belonging to a saint and must be preserved for the offering of candles, incense, and flowers.
22. The celebrations held for San Mateo are the most important for generating his good will.

The values and proscriptions articulated in these beliefs operate in a variety of structural contexts since their instrumentality extends beyond the practices of the cult to the domain of kinship and ritual kinship in which significant economic activities and life crisis events are carried out. These beliefs are relevant in all contexts with a sacred content, such as events occurring in sacred places, apparitions, the cult of the dead, ritual dancing, and mask making, to name a few. All of these contexts incorporate significant sacralizing vehicles that intensify the sacred purposes and intentions of participants and extend and reinforce the sacred truths of Chignauteco cosmology. Some beliefs are more strongly held than others because they are acquired early in life and concern the nature of the physical world, the nature of the self and others. These are core beliefs (Rokeach 1960) and evolve into primary contents and structures of an individual's ontology. Core beliefs, like core assumptions, tend to be convictional and are not easily shaken. All other beliefs derive from such convictions as experience accumulates and affirms, expands, amends, or disproves the attitudes, values, expectations, and assumptions intrinsic to the organization of experience.

A meaningful story was told to me by an informant who seemed to me close to the ideal of what a man of respect should be in Chignautla. Indeed, he had just completed serving three years as first fiscal. A perceptive observer of his culture, he was capable of deep reflection. In the many hours we spent together, he instructed me in the ways of his people, as if I were a child about to enter adulthood with the barest of preparations. He relayed a story about his grandfather, who was a musician and played at many mayordomias. On one occasion, his grandfather was hired to play in the church atrium for a mayordomía mass. Following the mass, there was no ceremonial banquet. His grandfather commented to the mayordomo that this was not the right way to celebrate a saint because it did not reveal his good will toward the saint. Several days later, the mayordomo had a dream, which he recounted in the following way to the musician. "I dreamed I met San Isidro, who said: 'You were mayordomo yesterday. What did you have in your house? It was a fiesta wasn't it?' I responded: 'I didn't have a *compromiso* [literally a commitment not easily left unfulfilled].' Then San Isidro told me to hold the mayordomía again but correctly this time, with *mole* [a dark chile sauce served with chicken, turkey, or pork]. I did, and the people thanked me. Afterward, San Isidro came to me again and said, 'You had your fiesta and spent money, but this will not reach where I am, because what you did, you did without a pure heart. Instead of the gratification you should have, you will be punished because your fiesta did not count with God.'"

Since 1985, I have witnessed rapid changes in the manner of life in Chignautla. It is clear that the traditional practices of the cult of the saints exist on borrowed time. What held the delicate fabric of Chignauteco beliefs and practices together was the integrity of meanings and ritual forms expressed through them. The walls of the eastern Sierra Madre mountains no longer isolate these people from the engulfing processes of monetization and commercialization, from the growing pace of national integration, or from Reform Catholicism, aggressive Protestant missionization, and political movements that are presented in the seductive guise of equality and solidarity. These processes will precipitate a loss that will be experienced by generations to come. Forced to be an unwilling witness to these changes, I have chosen to present the cult of the saints in this community as I came to know it over the past twenty years.

Chapter 1

The Contextual Framework of the Mayordomía Complex

Well within the broken terrain of high ridges and serpentine valleys of the Sierra Madre Oriental mountain range, the community of Chignautla lies near the eastern border of the state of Puebla in the Sierra Norte. This comparatively remote region is situated on the rim of the Central Mexican Plateau just before it drops off into the lowlands of the state of Veracruz. The Sierra Norte is home to a large concentration of Nahuat-speaking peoples descended from Nahuatlan groups that came under the domination of the sixteenth-century Aztec empire (Carrasco 1969). The relative refuge of the Sierra offered a context for the development of beliefs, which are perpetuated in a variety of mutually intelligible dialects called *Mexicano* in local idiom.

The community of Chignautla appears guarded by a high mountain ridge that shares its name. In this uneven terrain, the lay of the land and the abundance of springs, streams, and rivers determines agricultural production. Some sections of the municipio reach an altitude of 10,000 feet while others descend to below 6,500 feet above sea level, allowing for a single corn harvest. During the wet season from June through December, moisture rising from the Gulf of Mexico becomes impaled on the mountain and results in either heavy rains or a constant drizzle that enshrouds the community in mist and produces Chignautla's cool and moist climate. Neither rain nor mist occur after February and the landscape turns brown and dusty so that when the rains return again in June they are welcome. Rain represents security to Chignautecos, since the *milpa,* plots of land devoted to the cultivation of corn and beans, will not yield without it. Chignautecos are characteristically proud of their milpa, but occasional snow and hail dampens the sense of certainty Chignautecos have in what is normally an adequate harvest of these food staples.

The Sierra Norte is a beautiful but not necessarily a benign environment, and the custom of bathing newborn babies in cold water seems an apt meta-

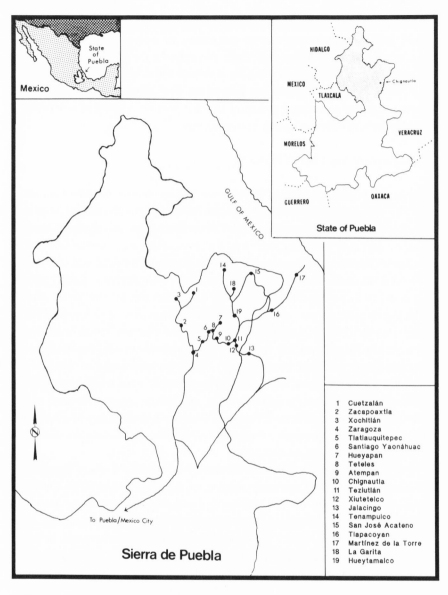

Map 1. Chignautla within the Sierra de Puebla

State
of
Puebla

Mexico

HIDALGO

MEXICO

TLAXCALA

← Chignautla

MORELOS

VERACRUZ

GUERRERO

OAXACA

State of Puebla

GULF OF MEXICO

N

To Puebla/Mexico City

Sierra de Puebla

1 Cuetzalán
2 Zacapoaxtla
3 Xochitlán
4 Zaragoza
5 Tlatlauquitepec
6 Santiago Yaonáhuac
7 Hueyapan
8 Teteles
9 Atempan
10 Chignautla
11 Teziutlán
12 Xiutetelco
13 Jalacingo
14 Tenampulco
15 San José Acateno
16 Tlapacoyan
17 Martínez de la Torre
18 La Garita
19 Hueytamalco

phor. According to belief, a cold bath prepares infants for the difficult lives they will lead. Damaging storms and winds, as well as occasional frosts, encroach upon agricultural endeavors and enhance the validity of explanations in which supernatural causality is central and determinant. The annual round of agricultural chores are interwoven with celebrations held for the saints to create an ordered pattern of life that provides a sense of continuity in the cyclical nature of meaningful moments.

The Parish of San Mateo Chignautla

Spaniards migrated to the Sierra Norte by the seventeenth century in pursuit of the rich mineral deposits of the mountains and rapidly opened several mines relatively close to Chignautla. Franciscan friars accompanied these early colonizers. Under the direction of their superiors in the well-established bases of Puebla and Tlaxcala, the Franciscans were entrusted with the task of converting the Indians of the Sierra Norte.[1] The Indians quickly succumbed to Spanish political, economic, and ecclesiastical domination. The mining of gold, copper, and silver, and the introduction of European fruits and animals (mainly sheep), created the basis for a new social order that altered pre-Hispanic society forever. The initial fervor to colonize the Sierra lessened over the next hundred years, after the institutions of sixteenth-century Spanish Catholicism and town government were set in place. The mines were exhausted, and Indian labor and tribute payment became less crucial than they had been. The Sierra Nahuat slipped further and further from the center of attention, which enabled the Sierra to become the cultural refuge it has remained until recently.

The Sierra Norte was spared the fate of the abutting Pueblan-Tlaxcalan valley, where the land was more suitable for the development of the haciendas whose ruins still dot the landscape. District capitals that were quickly established in the Sierra became thriving commercial centers, attracting an influx of Spanish settlers. The intensity of changes that occurred in the patterns of indigenous life were directly tied to the economic growth of these provincial head towns and the settlement of Indian populations in communities that became dependent satellites. With the passage of time, a class of Mestizos developed to form the upper stratum of regional society. What began in conquest had come full circle to unite Mestizos and Indians in an antagonistic partnership based on their interdependence.

The municipio of Chignautla lies adjacent to the municipio of Teziutlán, whose head town or *cabecera* bears the same name. The national census of

1970 lists a population of 40,742 for the city of Teziutlán. Twenty years later, the official figures have more than doubled even though local officials believe such figures to be far too low. Teziutlán retains its position as the largest commercial city of the Sierra Norte, a position that evolved from its original status as the seat of an administrative and parochial district. As a standard market (Skinner 1964), Teziutlán facilitates the inward and outward flow of goods to regions beyond the Sierra and functions as a source of modernizing influence for its satellite communities.[2] Teziutlán is just five kilometers from Chignautla's cabecera and lies along the same highway that connects the eastern Sierra with the gulf coast, points south, the state capital, and Mexico City. The ethnically diverse and wealthy upper class of Teziutlán consists of Mestizos who consider themselves to be of pure Spanish blood, many of whom are descendants of hacienda families from the Pueblan Valley; families descended from the French; and a large community of Lebanese from Spain. Economically and culturally, Teziutlán offers multiple resources for Chignautla's Indians. In this part of the Sierra, where relatively small land holdings are the rule, the factories and businesses of Teziutlán provide a far greater source of opportunities for wage labor than exists in Chignautla.

The history of Teziutlán set the stage for the events that directly influenced the lives of Chignautla's Indians.[3] As in other large towns of the region, civil and ecclesiastical authorities were set in place to govern the communities of Indians within their districts. By 1620, Teziutlán had become a parish (Church Archives, Teziutlán), and cofradias were organized, modeled after those in Spain during this era (Foster 1953). Formal positions of leadership and authority were also established within Indian communities and included councilmen (*regidores*), a fiscal, an *alcalde mayor* (head of the municipal council), an *alguacil* (constable), a *teniente* (deputy), and perhaps one or more *topiles* (minor officers for policing), all of whom served under the jurisdiction of district officers. These positions were ranked and held on a rotating basis by members of the community to create a system of authority over which the Indians had little control.

The Franciscan friars assigned each Indian community a patron saint, who became the focus of a cofradía. Indian labor was used to construct chapels and shrines to replace indigenous sites and symbols of religious belief and practice. The ecclesiastical affairs of dependent communities like Chignautla are described in some detail in the church archives of the district capitals of Teziutlán and Tlatlauqui. Local appointed officials assisted the friars in their indoctrination efforts by insuring payment of tribute and attendance at religious celebrations. The structure of cofradias in this region of the Sierra appears relatively uniform. Spaniards, Mestizos, and Indians participated in distinct cofradias. Each cofradía owned land either assigned by the church or bequeathed by individuals. Yearly contributions from members helped support ritual activities under the direction of an individual elected as mayordomo. The mayordomo was also in charge of cofradía finances, corporately owned herds of sheep, and the cultivation of cofradía lands. Sheep provided a source of food, and the wool was sold for profit. If funds and profits were insufficient, the mayordomo personally contributed the remainder of what was needed. Records indicate that by the beginning of the eighteenth century, the mayordomo not only managed the corporate property and finances of the cofradía, but individually assumed the burden of financing important ritual expenses, such as the mass and candles. Other members made only small contributions. Mayordomos were elected from the membership for one-year terms and kept account of all payments, expenses, profits, and losses. There is also mention of assistants or *diputados,* but the documents are not clear as to their obligations. Cofradias provided Indian converts with a means for participating in their new faith, and offered them a religious identity that was affirmed through collective efforts. Cofradía membership also insured an inexpensive form of burial and a way to supplement food supplies.

The secular clergy that gradually replaced the friars by the latter part of the seventeenth century continued to use local civil officials to control the conversion process. Once churches and chapels were built, ecclesiastical duties were added to these early civil cargos. For example, the executive and judicial duties of the alcalde were distinguished from those of the fiscal, who became solely responsible for church finances. Religious functions were added to the duties of the alguacil and teniente. The important point is that cargos that were initially civil came to encompass religious duties. This created the possibility for an evolution toward fully differentiated systems of authority in the administration of public life, one concerning the cult of the saints and the other concerning municipal government. The highest civil officials carried staffs of office; the same staffs are carried in Chignautla today by the fiscal, teniente, and alguacil, which are now purely religious cargos grouped together as the three fiscales.

Construction of a church in Chignautla did not begin until after the turn of the eighteenth century. Completed in 1720, the church remained an *iglesia de visita* for nearly two hundred years, dependent upon periodic visits by priests from Teziutlán to perform the mass and other sacraments. Visits did not become routinized until later in the century. During this time, the cumulative effects of a gradual decline in the activity of the cofradias was transforming their organization, a result, perhaps, of the loss of vitality in the colonial economy during the latter part of the eighteenth century (Chance and Taylor 1985).

By 1775, Mestizos of lesser means than those who remained in the haciendas and urban centers of the Pueblan-Tlaxcalan valley began settling in Chignautla, locating themselves in the cabecera. The cabecera had been built to resemble a Spanish town, with the church and municipal buildings surrounding a central plaza. Houses lined the streets, which were arranged on a grid pattern from this central point. The entire community was divided into wards or barrios, superimposed upon the earlier *calpulli* organization, to control the population and facilitate political domination and conversion.[4] Archival material indicates that by 1785, mayordomos, who were invariably accompanied by diputados, were elected by secret ballot to care for the numerous chapels that were built in Indian communities. Mayordomos made an oral promise to fulfill the obligations of their cargos and were given any materials or money that remained from the previous mayordomo's term. Masses were sponsored by general collection from cofradía members, or individually by the mayordomo. A list of expenses incurred by the mayordomo included cost of the fiesta mass, musicians, sky rockets, and candles and payment to a sacristán for ringing the bells and assisting the priest.

A cofradía dedicated to San Mateo had existed since its establishment by the Franciscans. The image of this saint was originally housed in a small chapel in the barrio of Tequimila, the initial nucleus of the community. A crown worn by the image of the Virgen del Rosario bearing an inscription with the date of 1726 indicates the existence of a cofradía for this image as well. Archival records in Chignautla point to an early existence of cofradias for the celebration of Corpus Christi, whose mayordomos were accompanied by diputados. The obligations of the mayordomos of Corpus Christi were largely ceremonial before the existence of a church. Once the church was built, further administrative officers were needed to facilitate the expansion of ceremonial activities. Administrative duties were added to the cargos of the mayordomos of Corpus Christi, who came to assist the fiscales in their tasks, thus accruing the title of *mayordomos mensajeros,* or messenger mayordomos. Their ceremonial obligations became associated with the Holy Sacrament once a monstrance was placed in the church, and their title had to encompass this new referent as well. Hence, these mayordomos came to be known as the mayordomos of the *Santísimo Sacramento,* while their diputados became known as the *diputados mensajeros.*

By this time, the term cofradía was used interchangeably with the term mayordomía in association with San Lázaro, Señor de la Resurrección, and the Sagrado Cuerpo de Jesús, typical early choices by the clergy as objects of devotion. Several sacristanes were required for the upkeep of the church and for assisting the priest when he came to perform the mass. Thus, within two hundred years of the conquest, the core of a system of religious cargos was well established and provided the symbolic and physical means for a syncretic and autonomously functioning ritual complex enhanced by the absence of a resident priest. Not until 1908 did Chignautla formally become the parish of San Mateo, long after the structure and organization of the cult of the saints had become fully institutionalized in the community.

The era following the completion of the church was a time of growth and transition for Chignautla. In the celebration of mayordomias before Chignautla became a parish, the Indians performed a ritual that substituted for the mass in which the three top cargo holders, the fiscal, teniente, and alguacil, officiated. Specialists chanted prayers in Nahuat that had been learned from the priests. But these prayers were already transformed by indigenous meanings. Such "masses" were typically followed by ceremonial banquets, just as they always had been among Nahua peoples in celebration of their gods. It is also clear that the three fiscales, the four mayordomos of San Mateo, and the four mayordomos of the Santísimo Sacramento, along with their diputados, have retained their importance and continue to work closely as a group in the administration of religious affairs. When I asked an informant why there were four mayordomos of the Santísimo Sacramento, he responded by saying that there are four mayordomos of San Mateo, a statement whose meaning was not clear to me until I came to understand the primacy of notions of balance in Chignauteco thinking and cosmology.[5] Many more images were gradually added to Chignautla's pantheon of supernaturals, each requiring celebration in a mayordomía. Interestingly, the cargos mentioned above, those dedicated to veneration of the Virgen del Rosario, and those dedicated to celebrating images of particular manifestations of Jesus, are the earliest in the system, giving them a highly valued place within the total array of ritual sponsorships today.

A permanent market had developed in Chignautla through which goods passed en route to Teziutlán. At the same time, Chignautla was becoming known for its leather industry, which made the community even more attractive to Mestizos, who could locate themselves among the Mestizos already living there. Images of saints favored by Mestizos were taking their places alongside images already housed in the parish church and venerated by the

Indians. The battle for independence from Spain was successfully concluded in 1821 and heralded the establishment of Chignautla's first formal municipal government. The municipalities of the state of Puebla were administratively subdivided into *secciones* (sections), superimposed upon the barrio system, and the business of living in a modern state became a concrete reality for the Indian. Reports from informants, corroborated by municipal records, indicate that the alcalde mayor and secretary were often Mestizos, whereas the regidores were invariably Indians. In actuality, few Indians had the language and sophistication to involve themselves in district affairs. From the perspective of the Indians, public life and service to the collectivity was never differentiated on the basis of the duties performed even as they changed over time, since civil and religious offices were experienced as complementary aspects of the governance of social life. Indians who held top cargos in the administration of religious affairs also held top cargos in the administration of civil affairs simply because they were suited for public office. They were honest and capable leaders, men worthy of respect who would be heard when advice was needed. Often the alcalde and fiscal would make decisions together regarding communal projects and celebrations. Young men serving as topiles could easily serve as sacristanes, and most men who had held the cargo of fiscal readily assumed the responsibility of alcalde. Men who retained a reputation of respectability became *hueytatoanime* (singular hueytatoani) and were sought for their advice, which was universally valued.[6]

The presence of Mestizos and the development of their partisan interests was to change the nature of public life in the community, accentuating a distinction between civil and religious authority and governance that coincided with the growing importance of ethnic difference. Between the second half of the nineteenth century and the Mexican Revolution of 1910, the economic cleavage between Indians and Mestizos widened. A railroad from Mexico City through the Sierra to Veracruz had been completed in 1873. Its construction introduced cash wages and facilitated types of involvement never before possible between the Indians of Chignautla and the Mestizos of Teziutlán. Commercial coffee growing was introduced in municipios close to Chignautla, and the Indians began petitioning the Archdiocese of Puebla for parish status. These simultaneous processes of exclusion and inclusion, differentiation and accommodation, eventuated in the development of fully distinct systems of authority in the hands of adversarial ethnic groups. Further political changes in Mexico had set the stage for the evolution of these distinctions, especially the separation of church and state, which virtually underwrote ethnic differences in rural communities like Chignautla.

Even before church lands and corporate properties were legally stripped from the cofradias by the Reform Laws of Juárez following independence and put into practice late in the nineteenth century, cofradias had ceased to function corporately. Individual sponsorship had long since emerged as the predominant form of celebration of the saints. In fact, the residual meaning of the term cofradía persists in Chignautla in the term *cofraría*[*sic*], which refers to the body of important cargo holders who accompany the mayordomo in the celebration of his mayordomía. In the experience of the Indians, individual sacrifices for the common good were always expected to be a necessary part of public and private life. Cargo sponsorship was not simply a costly burden imposed by outside authorities, as is implied in much of the writing on cargo systems (Tax 1937; Beals 1946; Cámara 1952; Guiteras-Holmes 1961; Carrasco 1961; Cancian 1967). After Chignautla became a parish, the barrio of Coahuixco, located furthest from *El Centro* (the term most commonly used for the cabecera), completed construction of a chapel in 1912 dedicated to the Virgen de Guadalupe, who became Coahuixco's patron saint. The mayordomía for the Virgen de Guadalupe required a mass, and a priest was now available to officiate. Other images placed in this chapel would also require mayordomias, whose sponsorship became the exclusive concern of residents of Coahuixco. The construction of Coahuixco's chapel was the first step in a process of involution of the cult of the saints in response to population growth and a concomitant concretization of localized interests. A chapel in the barrio of Tepepan on Mt. Chignautla was completed in 1945 and dedicated to the Virgen de Guadalupe.

The arrival of the resident priest brought unexpected results, and the collective isolation of this society suddenly ended, making Chignautla's Indians more susceptible to national influences. Traditional ritual practices and the good results expected from them were challenged immediately, shaking core assumptions about the nature of life and the world in which it must be lived. This clash of interests and intentions occurred in the context of the larger conflict brewing between the "haves" and "have nots" in Mexico that eventually intensified and exploded into revolution. Between 1876 and the Revolution under the tutelage of Porfirio Diaz, local forms of *caciquismo,* political bossism, emerged. Illegal purchases by local caciques diminished the communal forests and lands, reducing Chignautla's *tierra comunal* by some 30 percent, and a segment of the tierra comunal was gradually lost to a hacienda lying adjacent to the municipio's southern border. However, a portion remains, which is often the case in remote Indian communities in which communal lands were not very valuable (Beals 1945).

That hostilities instigated elsewhere would come to affect life in this community was accepted as the natural order of things by Chignautla's Indians, since imposition from the world beyond Chignautla was already experienced as inevitable. The strife accompanying the battle between Federalist and revolutionary forces arrived in Chignautla in 1913. For three years, the Indians fled to the surrounding mountains for safety. Life simply stopped. Most of Chignautla's Mestizos fled to Teziutlán, a Federalist stronghold under siege by revolutionary forces who made Chignautla their encampment. The forces at work in postrevolutionary Mexico brought more changes in the form of redistribution of lands and a new basis for municipal government. The corporate properties of both Indian communities and the cofradias had been largely absorbed into private ownership before the Revolution, with a sizeable portion bought by Mestizos, whose ability to make such purchases far exceeded that of the Indian. The ethnic division between Indians and Mestizos that had been accentuated by the establishment of a municipal government and the building of municipal buildings completed in 1884 was further intensified after the Revolution with the creation of the "free" municipio, which granted relative autonomy to municipal governments and established a new basis for their authority and power. Mestizos had largely consolidated their position at the top of a stratified society by furthering their commercial enterprises and making credit available to the Indians.

With the development of a formal civil government in Chignautla, the fiscales became less and less important in public life, reflecting an absolute differentiation between the sacred world of the Indian and the organization of religious affairs and civil governance. The power base the Mestizos had established through their wealth made formal positions of authority less important, their intentions being actualized informally through control of the Indians who actually held office in the municipal government. This was not to change until the 1960s, when heightened efforts by the federal government to bring diverse rural populations into the mainstream of national society made it essential for Mestizos actually to hold the offices they controlled, so that they might serve national party interests and thereby further their own. Neither desiring the ritual cargos of the Indians nor granting them authority in public life, the Mestizos never challenged the Indians' control over church affairs.

The fiscales are essential to the administration of church projects and the activities of the cult of the saints. These offices are differentially ranked and are awarded authority and respect commensurate with the sacred responsibility of the duties performed by each. The teniente and alguacil, the second and third fiscal respectively, are ritual assistants to the fiscal or *fiscal primero*. During mayordomias, the fiscales are seated in the first pew of the church on the left, carrying their staffs of office. As we have seen, the fiscales are assisted by the four mayordomos of the Santísimo Sacramento and their diputados mensajeros and by the four mayordomos of San Mateo. The mensajeros and the fiscales are responsible for the maintenance of the church and its property and for overseeing the organization of individual ritual performances that form the collective activities of the cult. When accompanied by the mayordomos of San Mateo, these eleven cargo holders form the nucleus of the *Autoridad Eclesiástica,* or church authority, a publicly recognized body of officers responsible for the administration of religious affairs. Throughout the evolution of those cargos granted the authority for carrying out the necessary tasks of public life, the basis for the influence of the men of the Autoridad Eclesiástica has remained tied to sacred meanings and normative values, and their actions and influence are delimited by the duties of ritual office. In contrast, the *Ayuntamiento Municipal,* or municipal government, represents a hierarchy of offices with authority based in the legal code of the state.

A small group of Indians who had participated in lowland migratory labor purchased land suitable for coffee production in nearby Hueytamalco as Mestizos and some wealthier Indians entered the market of commercially grown fruits, a market that accelerated with the completion of the federal highway in 1946. Involvement in commercial enterprises and the search for wage income forced many Indians to accept bilingualism and give up their customary dress. The building of schools in Chignautla's largest barrios did not free the Indians from their disadvantaged position in Mexican society, but it did bring this position into clearer focus, making their identification as Indians shameful. The formation of contending national political parties, PRI, the *Partido Revolucionario Institucional,* and PPS, the *Partido Popular Socialista,* marked the arrival of conflicting ideologies at the municipal level.

The Catholic church in Mexico had weathered the anticlericalism of the postrevolutionary period, clearly demonstrating to the clergy where the true sentiments of the people lay. The church in Mexico had always been a political force, and in spite of occasional conflicts over rights and power, most clerics were able to use their authority in political affairs. For the Indians in communities like Chignautla, the Catholic church, the cult of the saints, and PRI were synonymous with the correct and necessary order. It is not surprising, then, that when competing religions and political ideologies arrived in Chignautla in the 1930s, they were met with hostility. In the experience of Chignautecos, individuals who opposed PRI and Catholicism presented easy scapegoats on whom frustrated men could vent their anger in a fully socially and morally sanctioned manner. It is within this context that Protestant sects, agrarian reform, political dissension, and separatist movements are understood.

In Chignautla, individuals who refused to participate in the mayordomía system were and still are linked to Protestantism and communism, since the priest defines both to the people as being antichurch. Individuals who joined PPS were believed to be Protestants because they were anti-PRI. The Indians still believe that political party membership ipso facto determines religious belief: individuals who have turned to Protestantism cannot possibly be for PRI because PRI is simply the civil dimension of the authority of the church. In this manner, religious and political processes continue to be intertwined experientially.

In the region, evangelical sects such as Jehovah's Witnesses have had the most success. These Protestant sects presented the opportunity to deny the divinity of the saints, the authority of the fiscales, and therefore the ritual value of cargos, and thus appealed to individuals who had been consistently denied access to cargos because they could not gain the favor of the fiscales, or to individuals who experienced themselves as disenfranchised from the favor of the saints. These frustrated individuals were equally receptive to the charisma of important PPS spokesmen such as Vicente Lombardo Toledano, who was a native of Teziutlán and whose party promised a more just social order.

Perhaps Protestantism would not have become an essentially political movement in Chignautla nor would PPS have become an essentially religious movement if these forces had not coincided with the rise of non-Catholic sects and the agrarian movement in Coahuixco. My assertion that Chignautecos are in actuality making a political statement through conversion to Protestantism is supported by the work of Sexton (1978) in his study of Panajachel, Guatemala. I believe, however, that a desire for economic enhancement and a flight from alcoholism are also critical factors. Reina and Schwartz (1974) relate the rise of Protestantism in Guatemalan communities to modernization and secularization as experienced by individuals, since conversions occur in the context of an individual life rather than as a phenomenon requiring group action. This may be true, but I believe that conversion when it occurs in the form of a social movement must be explained by social forces within a given social context as well. Conversion to Protestantism in Chignautla is threatening because successful dissenters are obviously able to survive without the favor of the saints; thus they challenge expectations tied to beliefs and the assumptions upon which both beliefs and expectations rest. For those who abandon their faith, personal experience proves that what was expected to be true was, in fact, not true (rather than false). A new interpretation of experience offered by conversion provides these individuals with a means for redefining themselves positively while confirming the value in rejecting what they could cite as the cause of their suffering.

Unlike many in the municipio, Coahuixcaños were unable to increase their wealth through coffee production or the commercial growing of fruits, and they were forced to increase their land base by soliciting *ejido* from the communal lands of the municipio.[7] Much resentment grew around their efforts, and by the 1950s, Coahuixcaños were virtually disenfranchised. The Ayuntamiento refused to appoint Coahuixcaños as topiles or as important regidores, and the Autoridad Eclesiástica opposed their recruitment to cargos. This was rationalized by pointing to the growing number of images in Coahuixco's chapel, when, in fact, the cult developing in Coahuixco was a response to rather than a cause of this discrimination. Thus, the same motives for joining agrarian reform and PPS also provided the incentive for conversion to Protestant sects. The fiscales were targeted more than the Mestizos as a reason for rejection of traditional beliefs, since Coahuixcaños experienced the authority of the fiscales as bringing them suffering. However, the vast majority of Coahuixcaños neither converted to Protestantism nor joined PPS and, in the end, it was the strong belief in the value of mayordomias that led Coahuixcaños to build their own chapel and fill it with images so that their venerative activities would not be obstructed.

The Land, the People, and the Saints

The region's distinctive history, customs, and Nahuat dialect provide inhabitants with a strong sense of identity as people of the Sierra. Today, only a small percentage of Indians do not speak sufficient Spanish to trade in the markets, but Mexicano remains the language of the home. Largely endogamous, each municipality is considered a distinctive sociocultural entity with unique customs, production specializations, and characteristics attributed to the people, virtually forcing municipal inhabitants to develop a strong sense of belonging. The topography of the Sierra has generated both community self-sufficiency and regional interdependence. In this context, a network of specialized markets and festivals for regionally significant saints continues an unchallenged cultural history in which residents feel a sense of "backward difference," forcing them to cling more strongly to timeless ritual truths that form the bedrock of a traditional worldview. Today, Mestizos control all important political and administrative institutions of public life, significant commercial enterprises, sources of wage labor, transportation facilities, and what is offered educationally and medically. Once striking, overt ethnic differences between Indians and Mestizos are disappearing even though the Mestizo style of living in municipal head towns contrasts with how Indians live in more remote settlements.

The municipio of Chignautla contains within its borders some 105 square kilometers. Sweeping down the steep side of Mt. Chignautla to a river and rising again toward a plateau where El Centro is situated, the lands of the municipio continue to climb toward the communal lands and beyond, reaching an area with little vegetation and sparsely scattered houses at an altitude nearly level with that of the mountain. In 1970, less than one-third of the land base of the municipio was occupied by 8,342 inhabitants, only 10 percent of whom were Mestizos clustered in the cabecera. The remaining lands of the municipio are devoted to the tierra communal and the ejido. As of 1990, the number of inhabitants has tripled with a concomitant rise in number of households, which now occupy a far greater portion of the municipal land base.

Chignautecos experience themselves as tied to the land in ways both socially and symbolically important. Private ownership of plots used to cultivate corn and beans is basic to sustaining life among the Indians. Corn and beans are staples of the diet and corn production underwrites ritual sponsorship. Membership in a barrio is established by residence, creating a relationship between a particular barrio, a particular group of agnatic kinsmen, and particular saints, and defines an individual's position in the social structure. Such associations are completely absent among the Mestizos. All land in the settled portion of the municipio is privately owned, except for municipal sites such as streets, roads, rivers, springs, etc., and the sites used for the municipal palace, schools, the church, and the central plaza. Stores, cantinas, and a park make the plaza an ideal site for fiestas like those of San Mateo, which belong to the community as a whole. These community-wide fiestas fill the plaza to capacity with ritual performers and those who come to watch the festivities or sell miscellaneous items and food, making such fiestas the celebratory events that they are. The Centro is the focal point for public life. In the experience of the Mestizos, the Centro is a place of residence, business, and political happenings, and Indians who obtain house lots on its outskirts are expressing their transitional aspirations.

Indians and Mestizos

Chignautecos refer to Mestizos in Mexicano as *coyome,* roughly translated as gentry, and in Spanish as *gente de razón,* knowledgeable people, *gente rica,* rich people, or *gente del centro,* those of the Centro, terms that point to distinctions based on implicit notions of class indicating comparative sophistication, wealth, and residence. Indians believe the Mestizos to be descendants of Spaniards who came to conquer Mexico, while the Mestizos see themselves as racially and culturally mixed with the exception of Indian racial heritage! Mestizos refer to the Indians as *gente indígena,* native people, or *Inditos,* while the Indians refer to themselves as *macehualme* (singular *macehual*), common people who work the land, *gente humilde,* simple folk, *gente del barrio,* people of the barrios, *gente pobre,* poor people, or *naturales,* native folk. There is no confusion in the minds of Chignautecos as to who is Indian or Mestizo. Along with wealth, language, appearance, and residence, a consideration of descent allows Mestizos to trace their ancestry to places other than Chignautla. Beyond these differences, Indians may be recognized by their surnames. Aside from three Nahuat family names that remain in Chignautla, most Indians bear Spanish Christian names originally given to them by the friars.

Intermarriage between Indians and Mestizos does not occur, but ties of ritual kinship are established between more sophisticated Indians who live closer to the Centro and more peripheral Mestizos who live on the outskirts of the village. The Mestizo enclave is tightly knit by ties of consanguinity, affinity, and ritual kinship. Indians of Chignautla cannot simply become Mestizos even if they are monolingual in Spanish, have a Spanish surname, and dress, live, and work in the same fashion as rural Mestizos. Chignautecos believe that the distinction between Indians and Mestizos is a matter of blood. A most important distinction between these two segments of the population, however, is in their manner of participation in the cult of the saints. This creates an insurmountable cultural boundary between them that is reaffirmed in multiple public expressions.

Subtle forms of pressure are exerted on Indians to abandon their traditional customs, but the continuity in their beliefs remains. This is especially true of the mayordomía complex, which has remained resistant to desacralization until the last decade. It is for this reason that the major demarcation between Indians and Mestizos rests on the manner in which the saints are venerated. Indians who attempt to enter the world of the Mestizo do so by acting as religious brokers between Indian and Mestizo ceremonial life. By

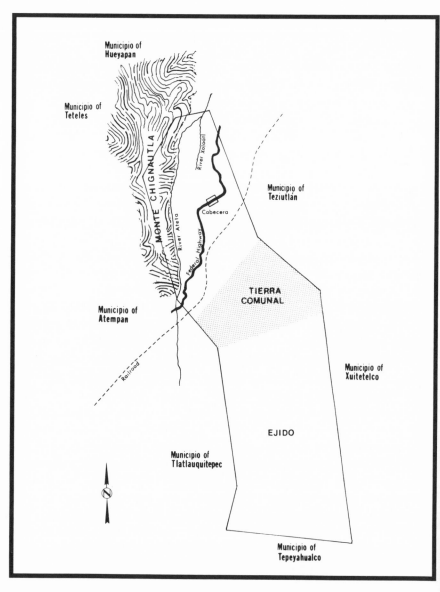

Map. 2.   The municipio of Chignautla

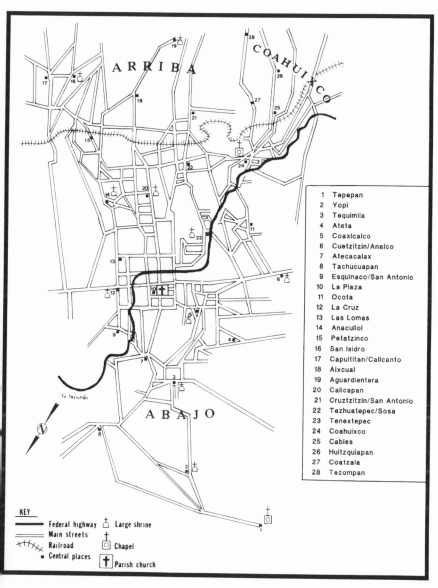

1	Tepepan
2	Yopi
3	Tequimila
4	Ateta
5	Coaxicalco
6	Cuetzitzin/Analco
7	Atecacalax
8	Tachucuapan
9	Esquinaco/San Antonio
10	La Plaza
11	Ocota
12	La Cruz
13	Las Lomas
14	Anacullol
15	Petatzinco
16	San Isidro
17	Capultitan/Calicanto
18	Aixcual
19	Aguardientera
20	Calicapan
21	Cruztzitzin/San Antonio
22	Tezhuatepec/Sosa
23	Tenextepec
24	Coahuixco
25	Cables
26	Huitzquiapan
27	Coatzala
28	Tezompan

KEY

— Federal highway   Large shrine
═ Main streets   †
+++ Railroad   Chapel
▪ Central places   Parish church

Map 3. Chignautla's settlements

virtue of their residence relatively close to the Centro, they have access to certain cargos of the Mestizos, and their mode of sponsorship becomes a function of these intentions. Obtaining a sponsorship of a Mestizo mayordomía will guarantee a certain degree of acceptance among the Mestizos, which, in turn, opens the way for the possibility of exchanging favors otherwise beyond reach.

Spatial and Territorial Organization

Descent, along with residence, is ideologically significant in the organization of Indian society. The principles governing the spatial distribution of groups within this community intersect with those of kinship to create a socioterritorial organization that sustains the structural and ideological integrity of the mayordomía complex. The principle of patrilineality operative in descent, inheritance, and residence merges with the principle of reciprocity in the design of territorial divisions and kinship groupings, each of which has significant implications for the performance of ritual activities. Relationships reckoned in this manner establish the basis for carrying out the tasks of daily living and the means through which ritual activities are assigned and accomplished. Together, their operation creates fundamental contexts for the sacralization of interpersonal relations and determines rights to social, ritual, and productive resources.

Two intersecting modes of spatial organization exist in Chignautla, operating simultaneously and, at times, overlapping. Barrio organization establishes the domain of individuals whose cooperative efforts figure critically in ritual sponsorship. The more recent division into sections organizes the lands of the municipio into discrete localities used for taxation; censusing; elections; birth, death, and marriage registration; school districts; and rights in water and electricity. Mandatory donations in labor and cash, called *faena,* are required for municipal projects and general upkeep and are organized by section under the responsibility of the *regidores de gasto* from each section, who, in turn, report to the municipal regidores representing each section on the municipal council.

Aside from the village, the barrios are either relatively tightly nucleated or widely dispersed settlements. The older barrios may have as many as two hundred households, while more recently established settlements may consist of as few as four households. These smaller settlements are called *lugares* (literally places). Barrios are invariably named and have a recognizable central place such as a fountain, a *capilla abierta* (open chapel), a shrine with an image or cross, or a major crossroads, often with a store and perhaps a cantina. While most barrios are associated with certain families in the minds of Chignautecos, especially by surname, barrio affiliation can change. A change in residence is a response to population increase and the availability of land that may be used in milpa cultivation or for house lots or both. The larger barrios are the oldest settlements of the Indians. Technically any landscape in the municipio with sacred, symbolic, or social meaning—an enchanted cave, a site of an apparition, or a natural spring—is called a lugar. But once a cluster of households establishes itself at this site, a lugar assumes social significance and residents may act corporately to establish a collective identity, making the lugar the functional and structural analog of the barrio. Lugares develop from habitation of uninhabited sites or they emerge from within a large barrio whose population has grown to considerable size so that localized interest groups evolve. In this sense, lugares represent units interposed between the extended family household and the barrio. A lugar may grow to resemble a small barrio by attracting individuals belonging to distinct descent groups, enabling the lugar to develop some form of collective activity and sentiment. However, the larger membership of barrios enables the barrio to successfully support cargo holders in their sponsorship of cargos of the main church.

When an entire municipio is the object of study, it is often not simple to comprehend the manner in which the territorial and social groupings within it are typically experienced or the manner in which place referents are used. The referents used will differ according to individual inclination, the context of the communication, the function of the referent, and the impression the speaker wishes to convey by his or her usage. All barrios in Chignautla are named; the names refer alternately to a specific group of related individuals and to the territorial domain in which at least a majority of these related individuals reside. The sections are formally numbered from one to seven but they are just as often referred to by the name of the main barrio within their limits. Section numbers are typically used in the context of issues of national culture and civil administration whereas the Mexicano name of the largest barrio or some feature of the landscape will be used in ritual contexts. Hence, section names, barrio names, bus stops, capilla locations, etc., are all involved in determining exactly what is meant by a given spatial referent used by the speaker.

In the minds of Chignautecos, each barrio is associated with a specific number of descent groups recognized by their paternal surnames, whose core membership is localized within the barrio; thus, particular surnames call to mind particular barrios. For example, all individuals with the paternal surname of Julian are expected to come from or reside in the barrio of Tequimila, even though various members of this kin group may have moved to other barrios. The barrio of Ateta is associated with a descent line named Bautista, a descent group known to be witches. Despite the fact that not all individuals named Bautista are witches, and that the members of the Bautista family are not the only descent group residing in Ateta, if an individual claims to be from Ateta, people will automatically assume that the individual is a witch. However, the descent group, as described here, is shallow, so that beyond the third or fourth ascending generation, connections between individuals with the same surname will become vague. Yet, there will always be latent assumptions regarding common ancestry, and sharing a surname is a significant constraint in choice of marital partners.

While barrios invariably are associated with ritual activities of the cult of the saints, sections are rarely instrumental ritually. Chignautecos will never refer to a section when discussing issues of descent or mayordomias, since only barrio affiliation has relevance for these issues and individuals living in a barrio act cooperatively to meet the requirements of elaborate events, making affiliation with a specific barrio crucial. The strongest ties are to the barrio of one's birth, especially if this barrio remains the barrio in which the patriline originated and in which core members continue to reside. Men usually inherit land from their fathers, so that an aggregate of patrilineally related men and their families are usually localized within a barrio. These individuals form the core of the nonresidential extended family, a kinship grouping whose households are clustered in the same section of a barrio and whose members are further related through ties of marriage and ritual kinship. It is from within the residential extended family and the nonresidential kin group that the social and material provisions required to carry out ritual activities derive, coalescing with barrio affiliation to define the most significant socioterritorial limits within which participation in ritual sponsorship actually occurs. Affiliation with a barrio other than one's natal barrio may be acquired by de facto residence. Land may be bought by the head of a nuclear family or a generationally extended family on which a house is built and occupied. True barrio affiliation leading to full recognition as a participating member will not occur until the household head has participated in that barrio's faenas and collectively sponsored ritual events and has helped support barrio residents who are mayordomía sponsors. Affiliation gained in this fashion, however, does not yield for the individual the same rights and influence assumed by individuals born and raised there.

Women do not become members of their husbands' descent group in marriage, even though neopatrilocal residence is the norm. Mother's barrio affiliation is insignificant, as are ties to maternal collateral relatives. Cross-barrio ties, when they occur between members of the nonresidential extended family, are sustained through obligatory reciprocal exchanges. Lack of involvement with mother's kin does not present a problem, since spouses are often chosen from within one's natal barrio. A woman, upon marriage, does not change her surname or relinquish ties to her natal barrio, but she joins her husband's barrio affiliation if he should live in another barrio. Today, because of growing population and a rising scarcity of land, it is not unusual to buy land in another barrio. Local antagonism, fear of witchcraft, sanctions related to interests in saints typically sponsored by barrio residents, and strong sentiments involving patrimonial land have prevented this from becoming more generalized. A person may become marginally affiliated with a barrio by owning land, used, rented, or vacant, or by owning a commercial concern such as a corn mill, but contributions must be made to faenas and local ritual events. However, rights will be weaker unless the individual has also established a residence in the barrio.

Barrio names are typically toponymic in Nahuat. Some of the original names have been changed to names of saints and newly established lugares are, more often than not, named after saints as well. At any given moment in time, barrios have clearly defined boundaries delineated by some feature of the natural landscape such as a hill or gully. Emerging from group sentiment and patterns of interaction that have social and religious significance, the barrios can be grouped into two opposing "sets" as they occasionally are in Mesoamerica. In this type of organization, the complementary and converging principles of patrilineal descent and patrilocal residence that create rights in a barrio and produce the residential and nonresidential extended families also produce an affiliation to an aggregate of barrios that forms one of two opposing sets in Chignautla.[8]

The aggregate barrios forming the sets are spatially divided by an artificial boundary that runs through the center of the settled portion of the municipio. The component barrios on the upward slope south of the federal highway become the area known as *Arriba,* literally up or above. The opposing set, *Abajo,* literally down or below, follows the gradually descending slope toward the municipal border. The division into Arriba and Abajo appears in casual conversation as a spatial referent. While barrio endogamy is preferred, set endogamy is achieved by the strength of constraints against marriage between individuals residing in opposing sets. The perceived scarcity of marriage partners within each set readily becomes a source of competitive antagonism, and interset liaisons that otherwise would lead to marriage have instead led to violence. The barrio of Coahuixco lies adjacent to the barrios of Arriba yet it is not a component barrio of this set. Coahuixco's exclusion derives from the settlement of Coahuixco long after the community division evolved. More important but less articulated implications of this division emerge in the operation of the mayordomía complex. The line drawn between Arriba and Abajo is a line of demarcation for ritual sponsorships, creating a system of ritual alliances through a bifurcation between those cargos often held by individuals living in Arriba and those cargos held by individuals living in Abajo, even though all cargos are ideally open to all reputable men of the municipio. When the sets compete, as they do most often over recruitment for cargo sponsorships, barrio rivalries are subordinated to the interest of the set. In effect, Arriba and Abajo become the widest contexts for reciprocal obligations, whose normal limits are the barrio or the households of members of the nonresidential kin group.

Within these socioterritorial groupings, an individual has a large network from whom all forms of assistance may be reasonably expected and reliably received. Traditional antipathy and rivalry between Arriba and Abajo is also expressed in economic terms. Different production specialties exist in each set, creating variations in wealth that crystalize in and are expressed through the distribution of cargos between the sets.

Socioreligious Aspects of the Barrio

Barrio affiliation and therefore set affiliation are primary identity referents and need only the addition of a paternal surname to complete a history of an individual in time and space as well as a history of service to the saints. The articulation of the individual within successively more inclusive social groupings makes possible an ever widening network of people with whom interactions are ideologically regulated and reciprocally sustained. These affiliations imply specific rights and obligations that evoke core assumptions that define ideals for conduct and generate expectations about what will occur in social discourse between specific categories of individuals. Beyond the more intense, face-to-face interaction of members of the household and residential extended family, collective activities of a sacred nature provide the opportunity for the actualization of reciprocal exchanges between members of the nonresidential kin group and between members of the barrio, whose cooperation is reinforced by ties of marriage and ritual kinship.

Chignautecos state that saints watch over the land and the barrios watch over saints. Barrios hold local ritual events structurally analogous to a mayordomía held for the barrio patron saint, for the Holy Cross in May, or for an image whose shrine is centrally located within the barrio's territory. These events are sponsored by a *mayordomo de pila* (literally mayordomo of the fountain), a cargo held on a rotating basis by adult men of the barrio. Such ritual activities mobilize reciprocal, contractual interactions that directly reflect the nature of what interpersonal interactions should be and embody the Chignauteco conceptualization of human-supernatural relations. The cooperative efforts needed for carrying out venerative activities structurally articulate the same meanings clearly displayed in the mayordomía and create an ever-widening circle of actors who individually or collectively participate in a sacralizing context on the basis of a type of interaction that is equally sacralizing; that is, by the implications latent in reciprocal obligations between these individuals.

Descent and residence are critical factors in recruitment decisions and genealogical connections generate rights entitling individuals to request specific cargos. These rights are also used to manipulate recruitment decisions. While no individual owns a saint whose image is housed in the church, and no individual can directly control sponsorship of the events held in a saint's honor, the actions of past and currently serving mayordomos either consanguineally related to a man requesting a cargo or affiliated with his barrio influence who is chosen as cargo sponsor. Barrio residents may discuss and decide upon a mayordomo's successor or may offer to collectively assume a portion of the burdens of sponsorship to assist the mayordomo with cargo expenses so that a sponsorship may continue to circulate among members of that barrio.

Along with a great capacity for solidarity, barrios also inherently have a potential for fission. Legal marriage is becoming more common, giving women rights in property and fostering equal bilateral inheritance to legitimate offspring, thereby undermining the traditional relationship between kinship and locality. Furthermore, the importance of wage work and a dependence on cash has fostered individual disposition in inheritance and in sale or rental of land without regard to corporate interests of the barrio. The availability of land in the midst of population expansion may lead to the creation of separate lugares from within the barrio. Lugares that have achieved some measure of independence through exclusive activities have lost a sense of obligation toward people within the barrio, with whom continuous and intimate knowledge no longer exists. The most common overt expression of this loss occurs in the celebration of exclusive ritual events. When a dependent enclave has sufficient economic and social resources, a shrine will be built for an image bought with collective funds. This process may culminate in the appointment of an individual to a publicly recognized mayordomía who then comes to represent to the saints and the community as a whole an emergent barrio. This type of fissiparous process is captured in the words of an informant commenting about a lugar situated further Arriba from where he lived:

> With some few households they wanted to break away from Calicapan, wanting their own chapel and school. They made their fountain so that they could have a private image. Aguardienterra wants San Angel and put his name on the fountain. They will soon ask for a mayordomía. They are far away, but they will eventually get one.

Cargo sponsorships are limited. Their distribution tends to be relatively fixed within the barrios that form the sets so that obtaining a sponsorship implies its removal from the barrio where the current sponsor resides. Competition is at times fierce, since motives for obtaining a sponsorship are very compelling.

Chapter 2

The Institutional Vehicle
for the Cult of the Saints

Sahagún (1956) recorded the cosmological origins of the peoples of Te-
nochtitlan as told to him by informants. Four warring offspring of Ometéotl,
god of the duality, created the earth, the sun, and ultimately human beings.
Identified with natural elements, spatial directions, and time periods, the
gods Quetzalcoatl, the red and the black Tezcatlipocha, and Huitzilopochtli
struggled for position to dictate the fate of the world once the forces of the
universe were set in motion. The cosmological forces unleashed then combined to explain the destruction and rebirth of the world and the occurrence
of cosmic, natural, and human events. But once human beings were drawn
into the unfolding cosmic drama as collaborators with the gods in maintaining
the balance of forces in the universe, the sacrifices undertaken in ceremonies
dedicated to the gods offered human beings a means to participate in their
own fate.

The pivotal tenets in the cosmology of the Nahua peoples the Spaniards
encountered remain central organizing themes in Chignauteco culture and
become apparent once the structure of ritual activities of the cult of the saints
is analyzed. Not unlike their pre-Hispanic ancestors, the Sierra Nahuat of
Chignautla struggle to make their world safe for existence by balancing the
forces central to existence. The ingredients that sustain life are interdependent elements cosmically related to each other in the experience of these
people and are incorporated into a design for living that serves as the ideal;
with the blessings of the saints, the land of one's father and grandfather
produces corn sufficient to feed the members of the household and sponsor
rituals to venerate the saints. Those who work together in service to the saints
perform sacred tasks that constitute a sacrifice that both requires and creates
harmony among them. Assumptions about the nature of existence are power-
fully evoked in the activities of the cult and lie below a familiarity with
concepts of God, grace, heaven, and hell that represents a synthesis of the
teachings of the friars and indigenous beliefs. Through the performance of

sacred duties expectations are confirmed regarding the beneficial results of ritual practices, which makes the beliefs that guide these practices subjectively potent. In the experience of Chignautecos, life is lived in the present and preoccupations with punishment and reward after death are largely irrelevant. Ethical injunctions are clearly specified in expectations that have coalesced around what could be gained and what could be lost by ignoring the saints and the celebrations dedicated to them.

Ritual sponsorship is a focal sacralizing vehicle in this cultural system. The implications of this institution for interactions between individuals dependent upon each other makes clear the centrality of cargo sponsorship in the thoughts of these people. Strongly held beliefs surrounding cargo sponsorship articulate core assumptions that structure the experience of the individual. Chignautecos expect their chosen ritual sponsors to convey collectively held intentions to the saints and thereby validate the assumption that proper attitudes and conduct sustain the order of the universe. Those who sponsor cargos and fulfill their duties with a pure heart command respect and are vested with the authority to represent the community to the saints. The role the saints have in human affairs is brought into play in the experience of the actors by their participation in cargo rituals. In this sense, cargo sponsorship is directly sacralizing. The prominence of reciprocal transactions, the obligatory respect between ritual actors, the authority of rank and the deference rank demands, and the value placed on the sacrifice of the sponsor mark these contexts as sacred. Reciprocity, respect, rank, and sacrifice emerge as organizing principles intrinsic to the structure of ritual performances. It is for this reason that I have designated these organizing principles as sacralizing vehicles. However, they are not limited to formal ritual contexts but are part of the fabric of daily life. Hence, a sacralizing context is any occasion, event, interpersonal relationship or interaction, or activity in which a sacralizing vehicle is structurally embedded and the sacred aims of the cult are realized.

In this ritual system, respect implements rank just as reciprocity implements sacrifice. Chignautecos believe that successful ritual sponsors avoid vanity, arrogance, deviousness, and greed, for at no time is anyone exempt from these injunctions. Obeying the men of the church becomes obeying the will of the saints, even though all individuals do not equally comply with such dictates. The experience of those who gain and those who lose validates beliefs Chignautecos hold about the power of the saints to determine personal fate and the fate of immediate family members. More than individual prayer or private devotion, cargo sponsorship is an issue of personal responsibility. Collective support legitimizes personal intentions to serve the saints and the support the sponsor will ask for and receive from individuals reciprocally bound to each other. The cult of the saints constitutes a pragmatic system that tests the validity of assumptions Chignautecos make about their world by their results in experience.[1]

The Conceptual Groupings of Ritual Sponsorship

My study of Chignautla's mayordomía system revealed a process of recruitment and selection of cargo holders that was indeed complex, forcing me to question what had been written about the nature of these systems. My initial research was dedicated to how Chignautecos conceptualized the cargos and how they experienced differences between them. I was repeatedly told by informants that all cargos are equally important to the pantheon of saints housed in the parish church and to the community as a whole, and any individual of good reputation can serve the saints as his or her heart dictates. The portrait drawn by informants of participation in Chignautla's system was not upheld when the actual selection of ritual personnel was charted. What required more methodical explanation was the cultural and personal design guiding choice of sponsorship and how individuals actually were able to sponsor the cargos they did during their lifetime, a question Chick (1981, 1984) pursued in his study of a Tlaxcalan cargo system.

Prestige is not a motivating factor in sponsoring cargos in Chignautla, since improving one's standing in the community is not dependent upon sponsorship. The cargos are differentially vested with authority and their sponsors are respected accordingly, indicating the operation of a system of ritual ranking. And although the cargos are differentiated in terms of their importance based on the instrumental value of the duties assigned to each and the ritual significance of the associated image, such distinctions do not produce ranked levels, which allow the array of cargos to be arranged hierarchically and pyramidally. The cargos themselves are not ranked, nor do Chignautecos conceptualize the sponsorship of consecutive sponsorships as a progression or career. Decisions to obtain a sponsorship are far more immediately responsive to the pattern of events within an individual's life.

Chignautecos do not think of the cargos as representing a totality, nor are they interested in the relation of cargos to each other. In effect, Chignautecos do not see their ritual sponsorships as forming a system. Rather, they are concerned with individual cargos, the particular responsibilities of these cargos, and the implications each has for the saints and for the community. Their concerns led me to focus on how individual actors saw themselves and the particular cargos they hoped for, actively sought, or avoided sponsoring. Such personalized strategies invariably enact the sense of indebtedness to the saints that individuals experience and the manner in which they believe these debts must be repaid. Individuals serve the saints for their own reasons, which reflect the personality attributes of individuals and idiosyncratic life experiences that have brought them to a decision to sponsor a given cargo at some time during adult life.

There are also a number of implicit and explicit factors that constrain individual choice directly tied to descent and residence in a manner that is reminiscent of the importance of kinship and locality and the productive use of land characteristic of calpulli organization. Through the collection of genealogies, it became apparent that individuals remember cargo holders of three and four ascending generations in their patriline, all of whom showed a consistency in the type of sponsorships held. For example, an individual born to a family whose members have held important cargos in the past reaches adulthood with expectations that will focus on sponsorship of cargos that bear the burden of administrative decisions. Conversely, a man born to a family with little history of such sponsorship will not anticipate sponsoring cargos requiring this responsibility. Invariably, however, individuals attempt to obtain the most highly valued cargos they perceive as open to them. What emerges is a tendency to pursue a type and quality of involvement with the saints that is perpetuated generationally.

The most encompassing distinction between cargo holders that Chignautecos make separates "the men of the church" from the mayordomos and those who dance in honor of San Mateo. This separation reflects a distinction Chignautecos experience between cargos with administrative responsibilities and cargos vested primarily with ceremonial responsibilities. The phrase *men of the church* refers to the body of cargo holders who work together as the Autoridad Eclesiástica, a group of cargos designated with formal responsibility for the overall practice of the cult and the care of the church and the ritual objects housed there. While every ritual actor in the system must make decisions that affect others, the members of the Autoridad have the duty to select and appoint all other ritual personnel. They are continually under the scrutiny of the resident priest and of the people. It is not surprising, then, that only certain individuals are able to tolerate the constraints of such a position. The fiscales are the central figures in the Autoridad and hold cargos vested with the authority to demand obedience from all other cargo holders, and they are obligated to assume responsibility for the conduct of all other ritual actors in the system. The fiscales are the repository for Chignauteco values as well as a receptacle for blame when ritual performances fail to live up to acceptable standards. Consequently, the fiscales and those who serve directly under them as members of the Autoridad are more ritually and socially restricted in how they act, even though their comportment displays respectful obedience to rather than passive compliance with traditional dictates. The fiscales have a major role in recruitment decisions and must approve those who wish to serve the saints and those selected by others to assist them. They are held responsible for church property and the property of the saints loaned to the mayordomos for their mayordomias. All transactions are recorded in the book of the fiscales. An *escribano* or scribe will accompany them if all three are illiterate. The involvement of the fiscales is essential to the performance of mayordomias, but their duties require participation throughout the annual ceremonial cycle. Men who serve as fiscales are highly respected, especially the fiscal primero, whose cargo is acknowledged as the heaviest burden of all.

Several cargos have overlapping duties, which gives them a combined role in the system's operation. The most important are the four mayordomos of San Mateo and the four mayordomos mensajeros (the mayordomos of the Santísimo Sacramento). Aside from the important mayordomias these cargo holders sponsor, they are members of the Autoridad. The mensajeros are obligated to stand by the fiscales in recruitment decisions and facilitate the flow of information between ritual personnel. While it is optional for all other mayordomos to have a diputado mayor, the mayordomos mensajeros must be accompanied by diputados mensajeros who also serve as members of the Autoridad. One diputado mensajero resides in the church with the sacristanes at all times, his food contributed by his mayordomo and prepared and brought to him by the mayordomo's wife, the *mayordoma*. Each diputado mensajero resides for one month in the church, rests for three, and then serves again. Rotation of the diputados mensajeros is the occasion for an event similar to a minor mayordomía sponsored by their mayordomos in celebration of the Santísimo Sacramento and in reciprocation for the assistance these diputados offer their mayordomos. The diputados mensajeros assist the fiscales in place of or along with their mayordomos in the process of recruitment, in processions, and in the protection of church property. Along with their diputados mensajeros, the mayordomos mensajeros assist in the care of the sacred wax stored in wheels or disks belonging to each image but held in trust by the fiscales to be used in the fabrication of candles consumed during mayordomias. In ceremonial contexts in which the mayordomos mensajeros are the central ritual actors, the diputados mensajeros act as ritual assistants directly responsible to their mayordomos. In the context of the Autoridad, the mayordomos mensajeros are responsible for the diputados mensajeros over whom they have authority.

In an analogous manner, the fiscales have the right to assume direct authority over the sacristanes and are obliged to assume responsibility for their conduct. The fourteen sacristanes are members of the Autoridad and participate in the process of recruitment by providing information regarding potential cargo holders. They are responsible for routine maintenance of the church and also assist the priest in masses and processions, ring the bells, change the holy water and flowers of the main altar, and provide assistance to any cargo holder sponsoring a ritual event held in the church or utilizing the atrium. Because the sacristanes must always be available in the church, they rotate in their duties by residing in the church for ten days every four months. Twelve minor sacristanes serve under the leadership of a *sacristán mayor* and *segundo*. The cargo of sacristán is not accompanied by a ritual assistant, but because of the manner in which the sacristanes are internally ranked, the mode of assistance between them is stipulated.

The twenty-nine cargos of the Autoridad collectively constitute the body of officers that are assigned specific duties that address the community as a whole and whose responsibilities belong to the public domain. These cargo holders indirectly honor the saints through a vow to assume the burden for the overall affairs of the cult, making each cargo holder in the Autoridad individually and collectively responsible to themselves, the community, and the saints. The sacred responsibility collectively assigned to the twenty-nine cargo holders of the Autoridad is an important aspect of the sacrifice undertaken by these individuals and is directly proportionate to the authority granted their cargos. Juxtaposed to the men of the church, the fifty-four mayordomos are experienced as solitary ritual actors whose ceremonial burdens are directly propitiatory. Their activities center on the household, which effectively removes these cargo holders from the scrutiny of the priest and the community, although their cargos are held in trust for the community. It is for this reason that Chignautecos experience the mayordomos as far more free to make decisions more closely determined by personal inclination. Along with the mayordomos, the men who dance in honor of San Mateo during the months of September through December constitute the largest category of cargos with obligations that pertain to the performance of mayordomias. In this sense, the mayordomos and the dancers are strictly ceremonial in function. However, regardless of the formal duties assigned to a cargo holder, all cargo holders have the opportunity to participate in a ritual performance structurally and functionally analogous to a mayordomía, even though such events are not formally designated as mayordomias.

All ceremonial cargos are accompanied by support personnel. These individuals are formally petitioned to help in the performance of ceremonial duties by the cargo holders to whom they have a specified ritual relationship and to whom they are typically though not always ritually subordinate. The mayordomos are accompanied by their *diputados mayores,* major ritual deputies. The diputados' wives are complementary ritual assistants and are formally addressed as *diputadas mayores. Diputados menores* are minor deputies who contribute goods and labor to the culminating event of a mayordomía. The last category of attendant cargos are the *encargados* of each dance group, who are appointed each year to recruit the dancers who perform in honor of San Mateo. Each dance group also has a dance master, an individual respected for his knowledge of the dance performed by the group he trains. Musicians attached to the dance groups, other specialists such as those individuals with special skill in the preparation of candles, masks, and other types of ritual paraphernalia, assorted kinsmen, and ritual kin make valuable contributions and may or may not be seen as ritual assistants even though what they provide is vital to the realization of the aims of the cult.

Beyond the encompassing distinction between the cargos of the Autoridad and the mayordomos and dancers, that is, between administrative and ceremonial cargos, Chignautecos divide the mayordomias into *mayores* (*grandes*) and *menores* (*chicas*). The literal translation of these terms is close to the meaning behind the bifurcations in Chignauteco thinking regarding the nature of cargos. Mayordomias mayores involve older images and are major events that imply a greater sacrifice and point to the larger quantity of goods consumed by a larger number of participants. Mayordomias menores are minor events in comparison, and are dedicated to images that are less old and revered. The smaller number of participants involved signals the payment of a lesser debt to the saints with a proportionately less burdensome responsibility and sacrifice undertaken by the mayordomo. What is expressed in this distinction is a quality of sacrifice that reflects a balance achieved between what has been provided by the saints and the debt that must be reciprocated. It is for this reason that the sponsorship of mayordomias mayores is associated more directly with authority, leadership, and the status of hueytatoani than are mayordomias menores, even though all mayordomos merit and receive respect for the sacrifices they have made to the saints. In effect, an individual's ritual rank is largely determined by the sacrifice undertaken in serving both the saints and the community of human supplicants. The foundation for such distinctions between individuals is not unlike distinctions drawn among pre-Hispanic Nahuatl peoples who differentiated individuals of rank from the macehualme or landed workers. Dignitaries received the title *tecuhtli* to signify their authority and responsibility and the respect they merited. The office held by the tecuhtli could be passed to a son, nephew, or brother, but only if this and succeeding generations of kinsmen had earned the right to rule (Soustelle 1961).

In order to portray the meaning of sponsorship to Chignautecos and the manner in which Chignautecos select the cargos they do sponsor, I have divided the mayordomias into seven groups. I have amalgamated the basic distinction Chignautecos make between mayordomias mayores and menores and more implicit attributes Chignautecos assign to each mayordomía. What emerges is a method by which each cargo can be assigned a ritual value that incorporates how cargos are experienced as more or less compatible with each other. When Chignautecos experience cargos as compatible or incompatible with each other, they are expressing assumptions about the nature and purpose of sponsorship and the results they expect to achieve by sponsoring cargos in a given order. Grouping the cargos in this manner, I am able to portray both the relative equivalence and relative rank of the mayordomias. Chignautecos conceptualize cargo sponsorship as a sacrifice that is intended to be uplifting. Structurally, sacrifice simultaneously articulates harmony and balance and captures the reciprocal basis of the relationship between gods and human beings as it is experienced in this society. It is therefore axiomatic in the experience of Chignautecos that individuals who undertake a sacrifice to the saints according to their means achieve a balance of favors between that which they have received from the saints and that which must be returned. It is equally axiomatic that certain cargos may be consecutively held while others must not, to avoid undermining the sacrifice of the sponsor. Chignautecos find it appropriate and prudent to sponsor consecutively one or more cargos that I have placed in the same group or to sponsor a cargo demanding an even greater sacrifice than the cargo sponsored previously. Like their ancestors, who believed that a balance of forces in the universe was maintained by their sacrifices, Chignautecos make their sacrifices so that a balanced existence is sustained. However, Chignautecos experience it as unwise to request a cargo that requires a significantly less burdensome sacrifice than a cargo previously sponsored, since these cargos are incompatible and their sponsorship will undermine what sacrifice is expected to accomplish.

Table 1 lists the mayordomias in the groups I have established based on their relative ritual value, compatibility, and relative equivalence in the experience of Chignautecos. The mayordomias of the first, second, and third group are the oldest mayordomias in the system, with the exception of the Virgen de la Natividad, whose relative ritual value and compatibility with

TABLE 1. The Mayordomias Differentiated by Ritual Value

	Mayores
First Group	San Mateo 21
	Primera de Corpus (the Santísimo Sacramento)
	San Mateo 22, 23
	Domingo de Corpus (the Santísimo Sacramento)
Second Group	San Mateo 28
	Virgen de Guadalupe
	Jueves de Corpus (the Santísimo Sacramento)
	Octava de Corpus (the Santísimo Sacramento)
	Virgen del Rosario
Third Group	Sagrado Cuerpo del Padre Jesús
	San Lázaro (Santo Entierro), Virgen de la Natividad
	Señor de la Resurrección

	Menores
Fourth Group	Dulce Nombre de María, Virgen de los Dolores
	Virgen de Ocotlán, Virgen de la Soledad
	San Ramos, Inmaculado Corazón de María
	San Juan Bautista, María Magdalena
	San Pedro, Divino Preso
Fifth Group	San José, Virgen de la Asunción
	Virgen del Carmen, San Antonio Abad
	Sagrado Corazón de Jesús, Santa Teodora
	San Matías, Virgen de la Candelaria
	Niño Dios de los Sacristanes
Sixth Group	San Isidro Labrador, Señor de la Columna
	San Marcos, La Santísima Trinidad
	San Antonio de Padua, Los Santos Reyes, La Santa Cruz
	Santa Cecilia, Cristo Rey (Divina Providencia)
	San Martín de Porres, San Martín Caballero
	Preciosa Sangre de Cristo, Divino Pastor
Seventh Group	Niño de la Cruzada, San Rafael
	Las Animas, Los Angeles (four cargos)
	Jubileo de los 40 Horas, Jubileo de Carnaval (eight cargos)

Note: Mayordomias are differentiated by fundamental ritual compatibility into mayores or menores, then into specific groups by comparable ritual value, and lastly by individual cargo according to ritual value from high to low throughout. Two or more cargos on the same line indicates equal ritual value.

other cargos of the group derives from the association of this mayordomía with the dancers of San Mateo. Just as reciprocity structurally articulates a series of cosmic dualities significant in this cultural system that evokes the presence of cosmic forces, the respect shown the cargo holders signifies their ritual rank and underwrites the quality of sacrifice undertaken. Greater respect is shown cargo holders of the first group than cargo holders of the second or third and so on. Any sacrifice is respected, but individuals who undertake greater sacrifices prove to others that the saints reward those persons who have lived closer to the ideal.

The relative ritual value of the cargos implements the organizing activity of the individual and the organizing principles structuring the conceptual system of these people. The concept of ritual value is a heuristic condensation of many referents belonging to what may be considered an ideological pole of meaning (Turner 1974) containing pivotal, normative values and significant principles of organization. Ritual value, then, represents a structural and ideological coalescence of major elements of the mayordomía complex. The assignment of a relative ritual value to the cargos encapsulates how meanings are clustered in the experience of Chignautecos and how Chignautecos themselves value each cargo differently. The specific attributes clustered together in the person of the sponsor are: the wisdom of age, trustworthiness, and reliability. According to how the sponsor is viewed, the attributes of the sponsor merge with those of the cargo to become publicly recognized characteristics of the cargo: respect, authority, leadership, and rank. These attributes in turn evoke a degree of responsibility and a quality of sacrifice that pertains to the sponsorship. The cosmological matrix from which these attributes derive is centrally organized by reciprocity as the primary implementation of balance and harmony. In this manner, ritual value symbolizes the degree of sacred importance and personal instrumentality of a given cargo.

If a man wishes to become a sacristán or a mayordomo mensajero, it is considered wise to serve first as diputado mensajero. These cargos are not only similar in duties, but are compatible in responsibility and in the nature of the sacrifice undertaken. A sacristán will usually not request an important mayordomía while still serving as sacristán, but he may request a minor mayordomía or serve as a dancer so long as he feels that he can fulfill his ritual obligations. Fiscal primero is likely to be the last cargo a man will hold unless he requests San Mateo 21. Chignautecos firmly believe that the saints become angry if what can be offered is withheld, and such withholding creates imbalance and affects the community as a whole. There is no case of an individual who served as fiscal primero and then held a minor mayordomía. This would be experienced as bizarre. When I posed this possibility to informants, the response was uniform: "No le conviene," it would not agree with him, or would not be suitable, proper, or advisable. "No le conviene" indicates something very dangerously wrong, even though Chignautecos will say that a man is free to serve as his heart tells him. In contrast to the fiscal primero, sponsorship of the cargo of teniente or alguacil is often followed by becoming a mayordomo or a mayordomía mayor or even a diputado mayor of an important mayordomía, since these carry a relatively similar ritual value.

Consecutive sponsorship of incompatible cargos would disturb the balance necessary to achieve the sacralizing effects of reciprocity and respect. Given this constraint, once a man has served in a cargo, he may serve similarly again or he may alter his mode of veneration as long as the saints are shown respect by an appropriate sacrifice. Rarely will a man choose sacristán if he is able to serve as a mayordomo, unless he intends to become a mayordomo mensajero and ultimately fiscal some time in the future.

A man need not hold a cargo of the seventh group as a first cargo followed by a cargo of the sixth group, progressing in ascending order until he reaches a mayordomía of the first group. The choice of diputado mensajero is considered an appropriate initial cargo for a man who believes that in time he will hold the cargo of fiscal, although men who become fiscales often sponsor a mayordomía mayor such as the Virgen de Guadalupe or serve as the mayordomo of the Santísimo Sacramento first.

A man may hold a mayordomía of the third group for a number of consecutive years and then hold a cargo from the second group, but not another afterwards from the third or fourth group. A man who sponsors the Virgen de Guadalupe is not likely to be appointed as the mayordomo of San Lázaro. Even though the Virgen might be requested and granted because of an inherited vow and sponsorship of the Virgen de Guadalupe and San Lázaro are not incompatible sacrifices, the Virgen de Guadalupe is highly valued as a patron saint, and it would be considered inappropriate to sponsor any image afterwards other than San Mateo, who can equally be served by becoming fiscal. It is rare that a man who has sponsored a cargo from only the fourth group will ever hold one from the first group, and individuals may continue to sponsor selected cargos only if they have not destroyed the faith the community has in them to fulfill the sacred duties of office.

Ritual Sponsorship among the Indians

The church with its atrium represents a focal point for ritual affairs. Attached to the church are the priest's residence, a room for the resident sacristanes, and a room set aside for meetings of members of the Autoridad called the *fiscalía*. The barrios of Coahuixco and Tepepan have their own ritual personnel: a complement of mayordomos, sacristanes, and a church commission whose members function analogously to the fiscales but have neither the rank nor the sacred authority of the fiscales of the Autoridad. Coahuixco has fourteen commission members, two sacristanes, and fourteen mayordomos, whereas Tepepan has twelve commission members, two sacristanes, and six mayordomos. Appointment of ritual personnel in these enclaves, however, is still subject to the approval of the three fiscales. Aside from these ritual enclaves, each barrio functions corporately in the sponsorship of several annual ritual events structurally analogous to mayordomias of public concern. As we have seen, the various shrines that represent focal points for the collective identities of the barrios become the sites for annual celebrations held in May in honor of the *Santa Cruz* (Holy Cross), for barrio patron saints, and recently at Christmas for images of the Infant Jesus. These events are sponsored collectively by barrio residents under the direction of an elected committee, or individually by a mayordomo de pila. Although such sponsorships may indirectly influence recruitment by bringing an individual's trustworthiness to the attention of others, once a man has sponsored a parish mayordomía, he rarely returns to barrio sponsorship, even though both are equally valid sacrifices.

The ritual events of the cult are publicly recognized, but aside from the mass and procession for the saint, the majority of activities of sponsorship occur outside the public view. The members of the residential extended family and the nonresidential kin group accompanied by their network of ritual kin perform the actual tasks of sponsorship. For the residential kin group, the household altar serves as the focal point for the performance of mayordomias as well as life crisis events, for curing rituals, in *compadrazgo* (ritual kinship), for the celebration of Todos Santos (All Saints Day), and more recently at Christmas.[2]

The physical premises of the church are immediately associated in the minds of Chignautecos with the Autoridad Eclesiástica and the fiscales. The fiscales assume office at the same time and divide the duties and expenditures of their cargos between them. Each fiscal is responsible for specific duties relating to the church for a period of four months in turn. A ceremonial banquet held in the house of the fiscal concluding his rotation for the fiscal who will replace him marks this transition and acknowledges the respect and reciprocal obligations the fiscales have toward each other. The teniente and alguacil are ritual assistants to the fiscal primero. They carry messages for him and occasionally attend mayordomía masses in his stead. In contradistinction, sacristanes as a group have little formal authority, command relatively little respect, and are less constrained in their behavior, even though they have sacred obligations toward themselves, the community, and the saints.

Highly visible acts of veneration toward the saints are focused around the duties of the mayordomias mayores, those I have placed in the first, second, and third groups in descending order of ritual value. These are the oldest sponsorships in the system, several of which evolved from cofradias. The majority of these cargos have obligations that draw them into the three major communal celebrations held in Chignautla during periods of the year that are marked as particularly sacred and address, in various ways, balance in movement. Day and night, repetitive changes in the seasons, and death and rebirth are themes that occur in the celebrations to which I refer: those held for San Mateo, whose octave occurs at the time of the fall equinox in September, those held at Easter (*Semana Santa*) and associated with death and rebirth and the vernal equinox, and those held in honor of the Santísimo Sacramento during the celebration of Corpus Christi in June. Each celebration symbolically constitutes an octave that begins and ends with a pair of mayordomias, thereby enhancing the significance of balance and reciprocity articulated structurally in these performances while representing an intensification of sacrifice. It is not insignificant that many of the organizing principles that occur in these major celebrations recur throughout ritual events of smaller scale that are not formally designated mayordomias. Every cargo holder is obligated to sponsor directly or participate in the sponsorship of a mass and ritual banquet in a manner that is analogous to the duties of a mayordomo. For example, the sacristanes as a group sponsor a mass and ritual banquet for the image of the Niño Dios, and the fiscales sponsor a mass and ritual banquet dedicated to San Mateo in concert with the dance group ritually associated with them.

The most ritually valued mayordomias are those dedicated to San Mateo. In many respects, the ritual rank and authority of the mayordomos of San Mateo are equal to those of the fiscales, even though they are looked upon differently and the respect they merit has a different quality. The mayordomos of San Mateo are high-ranking cargo holders who become high-ranking *pasados* when they have relinquished their cargos. One or more of the currently serving mayordomos of San Mateo and pasados invariably accompany the fiscales when the fiscales attend other mayordomias. Since the original image of San Mateo was brought to Chignautla long ago, three other images of San Mateo have been placed in the parish church, each requiring its own mayordomía. The oldest and most valued image is celebrated on September 21st, the actual feast day, while the others are celebrated on the 22nd and 23rd and on the octave of the feast of San Mateo, the 28th of September. The mayordomias of San Mateo are celebrated in descending order of ritual value and the rank of these mayordomos provides them with an influential role in recruitment decisions.

The fiscales alone appoint new sacristanes when needed, since sacristanes may leave their cargos for a time and return or may serve for life. Each September, a general meeting of twenty-three members of the Autoridad Eclesiástica is held. Those obligated to attend are the three fiscales, the sacristán mayor and segundo, six sacristanes menores, the four diputados mensajeros, the four mayordomos mensajeros, and the four mayordomos of San Mateo. All decisions regarding the activities and recruitment of the cargo holders are made at this fall meeting. The new fiscal primero is selected in a meeting of the currently serving fiscales, the sacristanes, and the diputados mensajeros. Once the fiscal is appointed, he chooses his teniente and alguacil. It is notable that there is a seeming incompatibility in the ritual value and authority of the cargos that form the Autoridad Eclesiástica. Cargos of great sacred significance are joined with those of relatively little ritual value and authority in the process of selection of ritual personnel. The sacristanes and diputados mensajeros command little respect but are instrumental in recruitment decisions. This seeming contradiction does not alter the system's coherence, and, in fact, it intensifies the significance of constraints characteristic of ritual relations: respect creates harmony between individuals of differing ritual rank whose duties are interdependent.

The ceremonial dancers perform from September 7, for vespers of the mayordomía of the Virgen de la Natividad, until the third Sunday in October, and again in December for the celebrations of the Virgen de Guadalupe. Eight dance groups perform in honor of San Mateo. Two encargados for each group are appointed to call the dancers to practice every Sunday during July and August. The encargados provide the dancers and dance master with cigarettes and *aguardiente,* an alcoholic beverage, during practice sessions and when they perform. They also provide the dancers with ritual meals at the beginning and end of the period in which the dancers perform and pay and feed the accompanying musicians. In Chignautla, dancing in honor of San Mateo is undertaken seriously, with the same intention that compels individuals to request and sponsor mayordomias. Ritual dancing is performed in full view of the population and before the watchful eye of San Mateo. Dancers are chosen from among individuals who are believed to value traditional customs, and who, in their devotion, will not be ashamed to don costumes, wear masks, and enact dramas that have meaning within the Chignauteco experience. Ritual dancing is one occasion when pride is permissible, because it is pride in the collectivity.

Dance performances are sacralizing contexts that evoke, intensify, and revitalize themes of importance in this society and as such are acts of signification. Pre-Hispanic peoples held dances in association with the agricultural cycle and ceremonial battles that were associated with sacrifice to the gods. Dualities important in Aztec culture permeate this mode of ritual expression throughout Mexico and appear in Chignautla's dances as well (Cordry 1980): life-death (the life process); good-evil (morality); day-night (time/space dimension); and male-female (humanity). Dance performances were often clustered around the spring and fall equinox (Vaillant 1962; Kurath 1967). Soustelle (1961) notes that costumes served as a means by which an individual was able to represent the god being worshipped. I believe that costumes also serve as a vehicle of transition between beings of discrepant statuses (mortals and gods) and thereby create a merger between the realm of human beings and the realm of the supernatural beings celebrated, whom the performers also become. After the Conquest, friars introduced dancing as a means of self-indoctrination, especially dances with Catholic themes (Gibson 1964). Dances also developed in Indian communities to commemorate important events in the life of the community and region (Nutini, personal communication). I agree with Ingham (1986) that to understand ritual performances, one must relate the performance to the experience of the actors, so that what is portrayed may be recognized, voiced, and reproduced. I also believe that dance performances provide an opportunity for evaluation and commentary about life as it is lived. Seen in this manner, ritual dances are metaphors of subjective truth expressed through the symbolic structure of these events. Only men may serve as dancers. Young boys who dance grow their hair long, not only as part of their costumes but, more importantly, as part of their sacrifice.

There are five dance groups that invariably perform and three more that perform only periodically at the specific request of the mayordomos of San Mateo. Each dance group enacts a different theme wherein meanings are stratified so that false identifications may be transformed into apt analogies

(Geertz 1973). Of the eight dance groups, the most ritually valued are the Tocotines. Although all encargados and dancers are formally appointed by the Presidente Municipal, who by law must oversee events held in public places and must give his permission for their occurrence, the encargados of the Tocotines are summoned by the fiscales. The Tocotines invariably dance in front of the church, which makes their association with the fiscales and the Autoridad Eclesiástica quite obvious. Before performing, the Tocotines are first to enter the church and pray that their sacrifice made in San Mateo's honor will be accepted. Thirty-four Tocotines perform a dance of military conquest to the rhythm of a drum and rattles. Cortés, his soldiers, and Malintzi do battle against Moctezuma and his soldiers. These three figures are shadowed by children, who are costumed and dance similarly. Given the importance of descent in Chignautla, I believe the presence of children in this dance is a generational statement of reciprocal obligations lineally expressed. Cortés and his soldiers are dressed in nineteenth-century French military uniforms. I suspect this dance commemorates valor and victory as a symbolic condensation of the Mexican victory over the French (a historical theme important in the Sierra) and over the Spaniards during the post-Conquest era. Cortés and his army are beaten and humbled by Moctezuma and his army. Cortés loses his hat, sword, and staff to Moctezuma. Kneeling, Cortés begs forgiveness of the Nahuat hueytatoani. This is history from the Nahuat perspective, in which their own valor, after years of domination, is revitalized through the sacrifice of dancing in honor of San Mateo, their divine leader.

The Santiagos are the second most important dance group and represent a variation of the widespread dance the Moors and Christians first performed in medieval Spain and introduced to the Central Mexican Highlands shortly after the Conquest. Like the Tocotines, the Santiagos carry a standard, but they assume a position in front of the Tocotines in processions. The position of the Santiagos in processions is, I believe, a statement of the value Chignautecos place on wisdom and age, because those who dance as Santiagos are men of advanced age. *Santiago Caballero* (St. James) was the patron saint of the Spaniards who came to conquer Mexico as they had conquered the Moors. In Chignautla, victory implies supernatural favor, which evokes the cluster of attributes that produces a high ritual rank and the status of mayor, symbolically placing the Santiagos in a position mayor to that of the Tocotines. The thirteen Santiagos are associated with the Ayuntamiento Municipal and dance below the portico of the municipal palace, thereby enacting their reciprocal opposition to the Tocotines. A balanced opposition also reflects the traditional relationship between the civil and religious authorities in the community. Implicit within this juxtaposition is a duality embedded in Nahuat cosmology. Flute, drum, and violin furnish the music. The rows of bell straps tied to the dancers' waists and wrapped around their legs provide added rhythm. Of the eight main characters, four involve dual figures. First, there are Romans/Spaniards who wear blond wigs, hats, and large masks of caricatural Caucasian features. These soldiers serve under a *Mayor Viejo/*Pilate figure. The character of Santiago also represents a pre-Hispanic god and Catholic saint and sits astride a white hobby-horse, a carved figure tied to his waist front and back. Santiago leads the remaining dancers, who portray merged figures of Jews/Moors. All carry wooden swords for a battle in which Santiago and the Jews/Moors kill the Mayor Viejo/Pilate. This complex metaphor of restitution revitalizes a layer of self-awareness buried deep within Nahuat identity and affirms the belief in the value of supernatural intervention on their behalf.

The Negritos are a dance group adapted from nearby Veracruz whose performance portrays Negro cane workers brought to Mexico by the Spaniards. The twenty-two Negritos form two lines and dance opposite each other to the music of a violin and standing drum. Their headdresses are adorned with colored foil, feathers, mirrors, and a curtain of black string that hides their faces. Between the two lines a figure wearing a pink sateen dress dances alone. This figure is called the *Maringa,* a derivative of Maruca or María, and is a man who impersonates the Virgin Mary. The head dancer carries a whip and a wooden snake, which, in the dance, threatens to bite the workers who want to kill the snake. Instead, the Virgin holds the snake beneath her foot, rendering it harmless. This dance, I believe, resonates with themes of macehualme protected by the gods, like their forefathers, which makes it attractive to Chignautecos. Interestingly, the Negritos dance on the eastern side of the plaza, perhaps due to a residual connection between east, rebirth, and salvation and an association of the Negritos with the god Mixcoatl (Cloudsnake).

The Guacamayas, alternately called Quetzales, are dressed in the form that has made them famous in Mexico by their association with the Voladores of Papantla, Veracruz. The sixteen dancers wear brightly colored pants and weave in and out in two lines to the music of a flute and hand drum. Between them dances a Maringa, dressed in the same fashion as the Maringa of the Negritos. The Guacamayas' headdresses consist of colorful fanned crowns, roughly four feet in diameter, which create a fanfare of colors as they twirl to the movement of the dancers. The faces of the dancers are partially covered by bandanas, and each dancer carries a brightly colored rattle. This is an indigenous dance incorporating a number of elements from the cosmological underpinnings of Nahuat peoples. The Guacamayas invariably position themselves facing west in relation to the other dance groups. The cosmic direction west is associated with old age and death, just as the guacamaya or macaw is associated with Mictlantecuhtli, the god of death. However, in that the Guacamayas are alternately called Quetzales, they call to mind the god Quetzalcoatl, who is associated with the cosmic dualities east-west and death (night, dry season)–rebirth (day, wet season). Costumed to portray the Feathered Serpent, this dance group may also be associated with the discovery of the artistic use of bird feathers, gems, and precious metals for adornment attributed to the god Quetzalcoatl.

Fourteen dancers perform as Paxtes, whose costumes consist of a covering of a moss called Paxte (Paxtl, Nahuatl). To the music of a bass guitar and violin, the Paxtes dance in a birdlike fashion in two rows, in between which is a Maringa. Some indication of their meaning came from several informants who recounted a legend associated with the Paxtes: When the sun rose for the first time, animals danced in joy because before there had only been darkness. God made the sun so that the animals could live and men could plant their corn. Such statements reveal vestiges of a view of the cosmos in which a duality existed between light and darkness, life and cataclysm. In Nahuatl thought, movement and sacrifice prevented the world from being overwhelmed by darkness, so that life could be sustained (León-Portilla 1963; Soustelle 1961).

The following three dance groups do not perform regularly but will be requested by the mayordomos of San Mateo to add lustre to the dance performances associated with their mayordomias. Chignautecos believe that events designated as "mayor" count more than events designated as "menor." The addition of dance groups to these performances intensifies the sacrifice of the mayordomo and enhances the sacred significance of vows made to San Mateo. The dance group known as the Correos (translated as "couriers") most probably derives from the dance of the Moors and Christians, and represents a variation of the conquest dance from the Indian point of view. Several different types of characters are portrayed by the twenty to thirty dancers performing in this group. Half a dozen or so men, costumed as soldiers in the same manner as Cortés of the Tocotines, fight under the leadership of Martín de Vega and his *caporal*, Hermano Domingo. These two characters are dressed as *charros,* Spanish cowboys fashioned after hacienda ranchers. To the music of violin and guitar, Martín de Vega leads his men unsuccessfully in battle against the soldiers of Cuauhtémoc, who wears a gold crown. Three other characters complete this group: La Reina and María Catarina, dressed as Maringas, and a small boy, masked and dressed as a jaguar ("El Tigre").

The Payasos (Clowns) and the Toreadores—a term taken from *torero* or bull fighter—are dance groups composed of an unlikely assemblage of characters whose derivation, once again, lies in the dance of the Moors and Christians. Accompanied by the music of a violin, the central characters of the Toreadores enact the drama of the bull fight. A man with a headdress in the form of a bull challenges a group of twenty or more toreadores, who are accompanied by several charros, two Maringas, and a clown, who guards the toreadores. The Payasos are led by a Cristiano (Christian) dressed as Cortés and a man who impersonates a female Moro (Moor) wearing an Indian blouse and full skirt in the fashion of a Spanish lady. Each carries a sword to engage in a mock battle in which the Cristiano wins. Other characters include: two clowns who dress like the European harlequin in red and yellow; two mounted fire-eaters called Apaches, who are garbed and painted in red; and a pair of Abuelitos (grandparents), who are masked, dressed in rags, and carry a doll representing their baby. Old and infirm, the Abuelitos constantly faint and are resuscitated by a doctor dressed as a *catrín* (city slicker) with the assistance of his nurse dressed in white. To the music of guitar and violin, the dancers shout and run to create a cacophony of movement and sound. The characters and dances of the Toreadores and Payasos are farcical in a manner that allows them to be associated with carnival, an institution that no longer exists in Chignautla. In this region, carnival typically depicts themes dedicated to the Mexican defeat of the French, who are mocked.

Each dance group, with the exception of the Payasos, is accompanied by as many as twenty to as few as eight *Pilatos*. The figure of the Pilato—a term taken from Pilate—was introduced early in the colonial era with the first dance dramas as guards to the dancers. In Chignautla these characters also guard the dancers and present themselves in a fashion that mocks the Mestizo bourgeoisie. In this sense they function as social commentators. With the exception of several Pilatos belonging to the Correos and Toreadores, these figures are characteristically costumed in dark, vested modern-day suits, but with the jacket tied around their waists, and wear ribbons that indicate dance group affiliation. The Pilato Mayor of the Correos is dressed as a charro and carries a sword and a ram's-horn trumpet with which he summons the dancers of his group. The Pilato Mayor of the Toreadores is dressed in a brown suit adorned with shells and white, barrel buttons. More typical Pilatos are dressed in tall black boots, black hats, and black masks of leather with long white beards to make them dark, unknowable persons. The long whips they carry and crack, the small, desiccated animals tied to their belts, and the stylized walk and laughter with which they taunt the crowds make the Pilatos ambiguous figures, ill-intentioned but not evil. Pilatos announce the arrival of the dancers with their drums and amuse the crowds with lascivious pranks and perfectly coordinated calisthenics, all without speaking a word. The humility typical of the other dancers becomes prideful bullying, which frightens children and adults alike since no one knows their identities.

Unlike the dancers, the Pilatos make a vow to perform for San Mateo for seven years and carry out tasks other dance personnel cannot, such as carrying water and wood at the house of the mayordomo. The Pilatos are invariably ranked among themselves, but they do not merit ritual respect from anyone else. A Pilato told me that he gained nothing for his efforts except a little food, and in fact, lost a great deal of time. But I believe this comment to be only part of the point. A sacrifice made must reflect the good turns received from the saints and Pilatos are typically unmarried men still dependent upon their fathers. Some Chignautecos say that if a vow is not fulfilled, they will go before God as Pilatos with their faces covered to be condemned as unknowns, therefore to be forgotten, a condemnation that removes them from their social moorings as their performance as Pilatos also does. The figure of the Pilato is a contradiction in terms. They act like boys but appear as mature men of means. In mocking the men of the city, they make fools out of themselves. As gentlemen of the city, they symbolize Nahuat suppression at the hands of the Mestizos, while being humbled by their obligation to take care of the Indians who dance. The power they display in exaggerated form is hollow, and as fools, Pilatos are lost between the worlds they metaphorically combine in costume and actions.

The masks dancers wear enable both dancers and spectators to transcend ordinary life by placing the ritual self in the center of attention. Ritual dances are statements about the social order. I believe that the Sierra Nahuat of Chignautla experience themselves as subjugated but not spiritually dominated, a theme played out in dance with note of the possible dangers that accompany invasion, indoctrination, the uncertainties of nature, and the loss of continuity and coherence in social life. These, I believe, are the themes that are unlikely to be experienced consciously by participants in such events but are nevertheless transmitted through them.

In the past, all dancers were unmarried men, but today young married men also dance, and this cargo is especially attractive to those men not yet household heads. Dancers must have endurance to withstand the continuous hours of performing and ritual drinking; they must remain responsible when inebriated, able to retain respect for men senior in ritual rank. The dance groups and their Pilatos are themselves ranked internally and in relation to each other, which is expressed in the positions they assume in processions and the order in which they are fed at ceremonial banquets. The mayordomos whose cargos are associated directly with San Mateo and therefore the dancers or whose mayordomias occur during the months in which the dancers perform have the right and obligation to feed the dancers after the mass and procession, increasing the cost of these cargos. After the encargados are appointed, they appoint their dancers, and Pilatos mayores select the Pilatos menores of their dance group. In an average year, some 170 men may perform as dancers and another 80 as Pilatos. Dancers are either appointed to their cargos or request them, and even though the Pilatos mayores have sizable expenses, these men are not awarded the respect shown to other cargo holders but are valued for their effort and devotion to San Mateo.

Mayordomias are typically costly in time, labor, goods, and cash. The mayordomo is responsible for and organizes all of the mayordomía's functions with the help of his attendants and assistants, who fall into several categories defined by their reciprocal obligations to and ritual relationship with the mayordomo. Most important is the diputado mayor, who commands respect and has authority equal to the mayordomo in his absence. He may stand in for the mayordomo on all ritual occasions except the mass and ritual banquet of the mayordomía. However, unlike the mayordomo, the diputado mayor is respected for his ritual rank only until the year of sponsorship concludes. Since diputados mayores contribute to ritual expenses, they must be trusted, and their selection is cleared with the fiscales. The decision to select a diputado mayor is governed by precedent set for a particular mayordomía. All mayordomos do, however, have a series of from ten to forty minor deputies whose sole obligation consists of contributing a small quantity of corn for the mayordomía banquet and wax that becomes the property of the image.

The mayordomo's retinue, as described above, forms the *acompañamiento* of the mayordomo, whose members are central actors at the ceremonial banquet held after the mayordomía mass in the house of the mayordomo. The central actor in his acompañamiento, the mayordomo is the activating ritual actor for the events of a mayordomía that occur in his household. Analogously, the fiscales are the initiating actors in a mayordomía during the mayordomía mass and procession. The cargo holders who accompany the fiscales constitute the acompañamiento of the fiscales during mayordomias, among whom the fiscales remain the focal ritual actors. The acompañamiento of the mayordomo and the acompañamiento of the fiscales are reciprocal dyads; the acompañamiento of the fiscales represents the collective identity of the saints to Chignautecos, whereas the acompañamiento of the mayordomo represents Chignautecos to the saints. The structural interposition of these groupings achieves the harmony essential to the enactment and successful performance of a mayordomía.

The conglomerate of cargo holders that unite to form the acompañamientos of the mayordomo and the fiscales for a mayordomía is referred to in Chignautla as the cofradía. The cofradía consists of the mayordomo, his diputado mayor, one or more fiscales, one or more of the mayordomos mensajeros, one or more diputados mensajeros, one or more mayordomos of San Mateo, and several other presently serving mayordomos of importance. High-ranking pasados also have the right to attend. Other members of the cofradía are the wives of these ritual actors. The mayordoma and the diputada must be present, and the wives of the fiscales often are. Only for important mayordomias do other wives attend, and when they do, they are treated with respect equal to that of their husbands, since they jointly bear the burdens of sponsorship (Slade 1975). Neither the cofradía nor the mayordomía is complete without at least one fiscal, and there can be no mayordomía without the cofradía. It is the obligation of the mayordomo formally to invite the fiscales to complete the cofradía on the day of the mass and ritual banquet, and for several other occasions during the year of sponsorship. The mayordomía proper represents the central and culminating moment in the annual cycle of ritual activities of the mayordomo and is prototypical for sponsored ritual events in Chignautla.

The Obligations of Sponsorship

Mayordomos are honored during their tenure of office and they must maintain reputations as men who are *formal,* reliable, trustworthy, and responsible. Decorum in all activities and especially formal duties of sponsorship are fundamental to maintaining a good reputation. A sufficient number of adult men are expected to take part in ritual sponsorships during their lives, and most men do participate in some capacity. Although a certain amount of pressure can be brought to bear upon an individual by cargo holders of significant ritual rank, no one serves the saints against their will, nor is an individual asked to go into debt to assume a sponsorship. The men of the church have the right and obligation to deny a request for a cargo if they feel that an individual will endanger communal relations with the saints because of some inappropriate behavior or questionable motives. In the past, a man who lived in a free conjugal union or had a child living in such a manner would not be eligible to hold a cargo, but this custom is no longer followed except for the most ritually valued cargos. A candidate should also have sufficient knowledge of what is expected of him in the performance of ritual duties.

The fiscales have the right to appoint someone if no one requests a cargo, and any man has the right to go to the fiscales and ask to be excused with the acceptable reasons of illness in the family or lack of resources. Most commonly, if a cargo is not accepted a promise will be made to accept the cargo at some time in the future. Cargos may be requested by any individual from six months to several years in advance. There is no limitation on how many times a man may hold a cargo, or how many different cargos he may hold, or the amount of time to elapse between sponsorships. Cargos are held from one to as many as three years consecutively, relinquished for several only to be assumed once again. This is more typical of cargos from within the first three groupings. The exception is the cargo of fiscal primero, which may be held only once and may not be requested. It is not unusual today for a fiscal to retain this cargo for three years.

Presently serving mayordomos always have a say in who replaces them, and the fiscales must be in agreement with the outgoing mayordomo before a new appointment is made. In the past, no one entered church service before the age of twenty-five or was selected for fiscal much before the age of fifty. Today, diputado mensajero and sacristán may be held by men of twenty, a mayordomo of lesser importance by the age of twenty-five, mayordomos of the Santísimo Sacramento and San Mateo by thirty, and fiscal may be held by a man of thirty-five if he has previously served well and can endure the sacrifice required of this cargo. Most men who pursue more than one sponsorship rest from two to four years between cargos, and each cargo is typically held for two years. Sponsoring a mayordomía of significance in Tepepan or Coahuixco would stop a man from sponsoring a minor mayordomía in the main body of sponsorships, just as a man sponsoring almost any parish cargo would be eligible to sponsor Tepepan's patron saint, even though sponsorships in these enclaves tend to be exclusively controlled by those residing there. The cargos of Tepepan and Coahuixco are presented in table 2, arranged on the basis of their ritual value.

Objects of special value accompany all ritual sponsorships and belong to the publicly recognized sacred domain. As such, they are experienced by Chignautecos as being owned by the saints with whom they are associated. The property of an image always includes a replica of the saint called a *demandita* (literally of the vow or promise) that is carried by hand in processions as an emblem of the mayordomo's vow to the saint and a sign of the sacred authority of his cargo.[3] During the tenure of the cargo holder all that belongs to the saint is held in sacred trust by the sponsor. In the minds of Chignautecos what pertains to a mayordomía is experienced differently from the intentions initiating private masses, individual prayer, or the purchase of images destined for placement on the household altar.

The mass is not an unimportant element in Chignauteco religion. A mayordomía mass is more significant and less significant than masses sponsored for other occasions such as personal devotions, illness, the sacraments, or death. On the one hand, holding masses is dictated by the parish priest. On the other hand, the position of the mass in the cult of the saints betrays its local reinterpretation as an attribute of a much broader and inclusive ritual

TABLE 2.   Secondary Ritual Enclaves

Mayordomias of Tepepan	
Mayores	Virgen de Guadalupe
	Virgen de Ocotlán
Menores	Niño Dios
	Padre Jesús
	Virgen de la Asunción
	San José
Mayordomias of Coahuixco	
Mayores	Virgen de Guadalupe (two images)
	Corpus Christi (two mayordomias)
Menores	Niño Dios
	Virgen de Ocotlán
	Sagrado Corazón de Jesús
	Virgen del Carmen, Virgen de la Asunción
	San Isidro, San José
	Las Animas, Los Angeles
	San Rafael

Note: Cargos are listed in descending order of ritual value.

design in a stable, syncretic tradition. For the people of Chignautla, a mayor-domía mass is more significant than other masses because there can be no mayordomía without both a mass and a ritual banquet regardless of the number of individuals that attend. In contrast, a mass sponsored by collection for Mother's Day is invariably well attended.

Nationally or regionally organized religious associations with chapters in Chignautla sponsor periodic masses. For men and younger, unmarried women who cannot obtain a cargo for themselves, these sodalities represent ready means for participation in publicly recognized religious events. Each holds an annual event similar to a mayordomía but without the cofradía.[4] Some associations are quite old and predate the parish, but their events do not compete in importance with mayordomias. Since several associations are devoted to images for which there are mayordomias, the Indian mayordomía will always be held a day before the calendrical feast date, the Mestizo mayordomía on the actual date, and the associations' celebrations one day later. Associations must work in conjunction with the mayordomo who "owns" the image, since they must borrow the image for their celebrations. Members of the associations often assist mayordomos during their mayor-domias and typically attend the mayordomía mass.

The Conduct of Ritual Sponsorship

Chignautecos have well-defined assumptions about interpersonal and human-supernatural relations. What is appropriate and desirable or inappropriate and destructive to maintaining these ties is spelled out in consciously held beliefs about behavior required of the individual within a ritual context or the behavior of individuals who hold a ritual rank. Deferential attitudes and behavior correspond to the respect an individual is owed because of how the individual is evaluated by others. This system of valuation produces a configuration of interpersonal ranking that sustains expectations of reliability among individuals who enter public life. Behavioral expressions of deference are readily observable in all types of interactions in which there is an implicit acknowledgment of superior status similar to the manner in which cargo holders of subordinate rank must defer to cargo holders whose rank is superior to their own: in the way compadres relate to each other and acknowledge respect through hand kissing, in the deferential hand kissing that occurs between godchildren and their godparents and between children and their parents, in the reverential tones with which a ritual specialist or curer is addressed, and in how women defer to men publicly. Respectful attitudes are also displayed in head bowing, in bowing of the body, in silence rather than speech, and in positions assumed in talking, walking, sitting, and being offered food and other items.

As previously discussed, Chignautecos do not rank cargos on the basis of the recognition a sponsor receives, nor does observable deference shown the sponsor correlate with the expenses incurred in sponsorship. Mayordomias menores such as Santa Teodora and Dulce Nombre de María become costly because the dancers must be fed, but these cargos confer comparatively less respect on their sponsors, who have proportionately little influence. The fiscal sacrifices a great deal in serving the saints. A fiscal is an individual who has reached the age of good judgment and trustworthiness, as confirmed by his successful yet humble manipulation of the important social and economic resources that have become available to him during his life. Admiration for the fiscales is not the same as admiration for the mayordomos, cargos that attract different types of men. This is true even for the mayordomos of San Mateo. While men who become fiscales are ambitious, they are also meticulous and reasonable, decisive yet prudent; in short, they are wisely rooted in the ideals of traditional life. Men who pursue the cargo of San Mateo or the Virgen de Guadalupe are also ambitious and successful, but there is a quality of exhibitionism to their expression of devotion to these saints. And indeed, this difference in character partially distinguishes the ritually valued mayordomias and highly respected mayordomos of San Mateo from those of the Santísimo Sacramento, whose character is often similar to that of the fiscales.

While cargo expenses are important to Chignautecos and make it possible or impossible for certain individuals to assume these burdens, ignoring the more subtle expectations individuals hold in requesting cargos deprives us of a wider comprehension of the nature of sponsorship. Verbalized motives for ritual sponsorship are often couched to impress those who pose questions. Answers given reveal expectations in the form of guiding ideals rather than accurate portraits of decisions that emerge from everyday experience. The actors in this system experience their motives as deeply personal, unaware of the cultural bedrock that makes motives recognizable and patterned. Individuals commonly make vows to specific saints. Such vows can be inherited from kinsmen or brought upon an individual through coercive efforts of members of the barrio who have an investment in keeping a cargo circulating among their members. Verbalized motives for holding cargos in a particular manner rest on conceptual givens that operate unconsciously in the ordering of experience, leading actors to the impressions they have about the role of the saints in human affairs.

Idiosyncratic, subjective meanings are anchored to a conceptual system so that the perceptions and experience of the individual are never arbitrary. Chignautecos will state that men who cannot afford to serve are not chosen, and men without good reputation will not be granted cargos even if they request them because to sponsor something valued, an individual must himself be valued. Relative authority follows and is defined here as a legitimate right to command obedience and to make decisions affecting others. Individuals who are granted authority in Chignautla are looked to for information about the nature of living or for confirmation of information that is already possessed. This is not an arbitrary reliance on the authority of men of high ritual rank, but stems from the ability of these individuals to validate beliefs already held. In this sense, Chignautecos employ the authority of the fiscales to confirm their belief in the practices of the cult. Consequently, if a man has not sacrificed what is expected of him for the well-being of the community, he will not be repaid with respect or granted the authority vested in his cargo.

Illness and misfortune are explained as abandonment or punishment by the saints if the saints' favors have not been properly reciprocated. An interesting story told to me illustrates how unconsciously held assumptions become causal explanations, which then validate beliefs. A man had worked very hard and doubled the size of his corn harvest. Believing that he was indeed favored by the saints, he requested the cargo of Sagrado Cuerpo del Padre Jesús, which he served well without incident. Not long after, he was able to buy an orchard and quickly realized a large profit. After some time, the fiscales chose him to sponsor the Virgen del Rosario, but he refused, promising to sponsor the Virgen at some time in the future, even though, in fact, he had pretensions of moving to the Centro, integrating himself among the Mestizos, and ultimately sponsoring the cargo of Niño Dios. But his plans never materialized because he became gravely ill and died. Many came to his wake: candles were lit and the body lay in its coffin before the household altar. Suddenly a wind rushed through the house and blew out the candles. When they were lit again, the body was gone. Knowing that the man had become prideful and cavalier about his debt to the Virgen, everyone assumed that the devil had some role in the body's disappearance, because such events happen only when the saints abandon individuals for their wrongdoing. Frightened, the participants in the wake filled the coffin with stones so that they could have the experience of carrying a body to the cemetery for burial. This story highlights the strength of the assumption that only suffering results from not making a sacrifice for the good turns received from the saints but also makes clear the assumption that the saints have the power to punish those guilty of betraying their wishes, whether or not the betrayal becomes public.

The saints are not experienced uniformly by Chignautecos and there are differences in expectations of responsiveness from them. These differences do not necessarily coincide with those taught by the church, such as the beneficence Santa Cecilia is believed to show to musicians or the special favor shown Mexicans by the Virgen de Guadalupe, the patron saint of Mexico. The Sierra Norte also has a number of miraculous saints important to Chignautecos but these saints are valued by individuals precisely because there is an assumption of reciprocal interest. None, however, are as important as San Mateo. The mayordomos of San Mateo serve a patron saint upon whom Chignautecos depend for their general well-being. The power attributed to a saint, such as San Mateo, underwrites how valuable the saint is believed to be and affects the sacred significance of the celebrations held in the saint's honor.

The Sacred Nature of Respect

All individuals who serve the saints are respected. The quality of deference shown them is relative to the ritual value of the cargos held, which becomes part of an individual's public image. Cargo sponsorship serves as a vehicle for information that belongs to the public domain. The general public does not often know the name of the individual sponsor, but typically, people are able to guess who it might be because of what is known about the cargo in question; the more important the cargo, the more information will be known about its sponsorship. Unlike the situation reported by Haviland (1977) for Zinacantan, in which people are able to establish a who's who by remembering who served which cargo, in Chignautla, if a name is given, this permits a good guess about what barrio an individual resides in, which then allows calculation of which cargo that person might be holding or could have held in the past. This chain of reconstruction operates equally successfully in reverse order. Personal reputation will either facilitate or hamper the chances an individual has to enter the public arena.

I also believe that a distinction may usefully be drawn between respect and prestige, and between an individual's personal reputation and one established by involvement in public life. Respect and prestige are not the same thing, and I, following the Chignautecos themselves, do not see cargo sponsorship as awarding prestige. In Chignautla, *respeto* is a term with many uses, all of which evoke balance, since they all incorporate reciprocity enacted by giving and receiving in contexts that directly or indirectly acknowledge human dependence on the saints.

There is a possibility of gaining respect if the duties of office are performed appropriately, but what must be established is a consistency between public and private reputation and a consistency in the behavior of an individual. Only in this manner can a person's character become credible. Chignautecos believe that the saints will know what others in the community may not know about an individual's character. Therefore, those who select ritual sponsors rely upon an index of credibility established by an individual's consecutive sponsorships, assuming, in this case, that the saints are minding the store. Chignautecos expect themselves to be fallible, but they believe that the saints are not, which is clearly demonstrated in the dream discussed at the end of the introduction. Individuals conceptualize themselves in relation to the saints independently of how they are seen by others and how they will be valued by others. I have heard young men express a wish to be a "somebody" in a world in which it is easy to remain a nobody even though one may be wealthy. It is for these reasons that prestige may be associated with any kind of public recognition but not necessarily respect.

Respect in Chignautla can be either assigned or achieved in actual or potential attributes of reputation. Assigned respect is based on membership in a kin group and barrio. This is one of several factors that make it possible for sons, grandsons, brothers, or paternal nephews of men of high ritual rank to receive cargos of the same ritual value as their kinsmen or members of their barrio regardless of previous service. Thus, a tradition of respect is established and, more often than not, will be reconfirmed with each generation of ritual sponsors. Female kin of these men will receive the same level of respect and must also maintain behavior that merits respect. All other respect shown an individual is achieved by how he or she performs in the various duties pertaining to status as either husband or wife, household head, or cargo holder, that is, in interpersonal and personal-supernatural obligations. Mature men who have retained respect throughout their lives assume a position of leadership and are referred to by the term *tatoani*. Men who have served well in important cargos and are deeply committed to traditional values are looked upon as hueytatoanime, the great and wise men of the community who are highly influential within their barrios and set, and in public activities in general.

Only a small number of men reach this status. The hueytatoanime in Chignautla are not a formally organized group, although their rights and duties are implicit in this status. The hueytatoanime embody all that is valued in the Chignauteco worldview. Their conduct articulates values that have consistently been confirmed in their instrumentality by the very lives these men have led. The hueytatoanime maintain the sanctity of their ritual rank and earn the right and obligation to offer opinions that are considered binding. Their status reflects the degree of balance they have achieved and maintained in their relationship to the saints and to the community.

Deferential behavior, of course, is most extreme in ritual contexts. A mayordomo or fiscal has the option of demanding respect or ignoring his own rank while carrying out routine activities or when entering a local bus or store. If a person offends him, this individual must, as Chignautecos say, "bear the guilt himself, in front of others and the saints." Informants made a distinction between respect for a cargo and respect for an individual. Men who fail to live up to accepted standards of conduct during their tenure as cargo holders are greatly feared, because it is believed that they are placing themselves, their families, and the community in jeopardy of supernatural abandonment. It is also difficult to remove a man from his cargo by overtly discussing his misconduct. This is considered disrespectful; secretive gossip is the only means available for disseminating condemnatory information. Unlike formal Catholicism, in which moral redemption is possible through confession, there is no such redemption in this society. I heard of only a handful of cases of misconduct by men who held religious cargos, and the two who deviated most blatantly from the sacred trust given them by the community left not only the church but the community as well. In effect, they canceled their existence.

Mayordomias of the Mestizos

Mestizos in this community passively affect but do not actively intrude upon Indian ritual practice. What desacralizing changes the Mestizos have brought into the lives of the Indians arrive quietly and are slowly absorbed. Mestizos and Indians participate in exclusive ritual systems with their own images. Mestizo mayordomias are sponsored by mayordomos accompanied only at times by diputados mayores. The fiscales play no part in these activities or in the recruitment of ritual personnel. Instead, the eleven mayordomos of the Mestizos are recruited by public raffle.

There are eleven mayordomias arranged into four groupings, each according to the age and gender of the central actor. Preadolescent girls become the focal actors for celebrations held in honor of the images of the Niño Dios and for the Coronación de la Virgen. Adolescent girls are the actors in celebrations dedicated to the Virgen de Ocotlán and the Virgen del Tránsito. Young men are associated with San Miguel and San Rafael, while adult men sponsor fiestas for the Inmaculada Concepción, the Virgen del Rosario, the Virgen del Carmen, and San Juan Nepomuceno. These celebrations are ranked in value according to the number of guests who usually attend and the lavishness of the display that accompanies the mass and the festivities afterward. Such characteristics combine to create public recognition for the sponsor and do not necessarily represent devotion to the image.[5] These fiestas enhance prestige if they are sufficiently impressive.

Cargos held in the name of girls between the ages of ten and eighteen and of young, unmarried men between the ages of sixteen and eighteen are actually sponsored by their fathers, who are referred to as mayordomos. Young girls become the *madrinas* or godmothers of the image and are the focus of the mayordomía mass and procession. They supply the names for the raffle. A man takes pride in the cargo he holds in honor of his daughter. These celebrations actually function as a social debut for an adolescent woman in Mestizo society. They announce to potential suitors her identity and her family's intentions, with a status confirmed in the elaborateness of the fiesta. The fiestas dedicated to young men function in the same manner. Mestizos say that after serving San Rafael, a young man could be married respectfully, and the vast majority of youths do participate in the mayordomias of either San Miguel, traditionally for young men who are recently married, or San Rafael. At least one mayordomía will be sponsored by each household during the lifetime of the household head, and it is not unusual for wealthy men to have held them all at various times during their adult lives.

The Place of the Civil Cargos in the Cult of the Saints

Respect plays a far less significant role in the administration of public affairs as conducted through civil office, even though some men who hold civil cargos do earn respect for their commitment to the duties of their office. But civil office is believed to corrupt, since there are ample opportunities to act on self-interest through the adoption of values that are contrary to the tenets of Indian society. Although Indians believe that the church authority is more crucial to their existence than the civil authority, both are necessary. This is reflected in the words of an informant:

> God also gave us the civil authority and to show respect for God, you obey the law. If there were no civil authority, how would we live; how would we live without laws? Then we would be like animals. Since the Autoridad has no punishments, how will the people obey? With so many people as there are today, not all will obey God's rules and for this we need the civil authority. But the church is more necessary because in the end, God determines all.

Hence, there is a crucial difference between sacred themes that underlie beliefs about proper conduct and a legal system whose laws, often imprecisely known by Chignautla's Indians, operate from written codes uniformly enforced but not necessarily consensually validated. The authority of the cargo holder is both sacred and legitimate. The cargo holder shares with the saints the willingness, ability, and obligation to preserve all that is essential to an ordered social life.

Aside from the usual officers stipulated by the state constitution for independent municipios, the seven regidores de gasto and their alternates for each section are appointed by the Presidente for one year. The regidores de gasto are men who are already married, even though they reside within their fathers' households. Their obligations involve defraying expenses of a number of civil and religious obligations that involve the entire municipio. The Presidente is responsible for the faena. Every adult man must contribute a day's labor toward the faena once a month for road and bridge repairs or any municipal project. On order of the Presidente, the regidores de gasto inform men in their section when they must report for faena and are responsible for supervising these activities. The regidores de gasto contribute two or three liters of aguardiente in reciprocation for the labor donated by men who are in actuality their kinsmen and neighbors.

Men who serve as regidor de gasto are often taking a first step toward holding more important public office in either civil or religious affairs. This cargo is the only civil office that influences an individual's selection for ritual sponsorship. By serving well as a regidor de gasto, a man demonstrates a mature sense of commitment and responsibility to the community as a whole. The regidores de gasto have specific duties for the celebrations of Corpus Christi and Easter. For the Easter celebrations, they erect five *respaldos,* literally back rests, in the corners of the church atrium and at the main gate to mark the sites for prayer as processions move around the atrium. The respaldos symbolize and spatially denote sacred resting places, not unlike household altars. They are constructed of large boards set atop tables decorated with flowers and ribbons of many colors and fabric adorned with paper figures of angels. Though not very expensive, respaldos are usually made by ritual specialists hired by the regidores de gasto, who also supply the materials used (or they may be bought from past regidores). Carnival has long since disappeared from Chignautla, but when it was held, the regidores de gasto decorated the church atrium with ferns and clothing placed on mannequins around the walls.

The regidores de gasto must supervise preparations for Easter Sunday, which are carried out by the topiles. Each topil is given a day's wages for his labor, a bottle of aguardiente, a pack of cigarettes, and a large meal, toward which each regidor de gasto contributes. Saturday afternoon, the entire Ayuntamiento and the topiles who brought the palms march in procession to the church, where the palms are blessed and distributed by the three fiscales to all who attend. The fiscales then formally thank the Presidente and all officials, civil and religious. A short prayer is followed by a meal in the fiscalía paid for by the regidores de gasto. The regidores de gasto also organize and sponsor a meal of twelve courses representing the Last Supper for the Indians, who portray the twelve Apostles. Finally, for Corpus Christi in June, the regidores de gasto again place their respaldos around the church atrium for the mayordomias held at this time. They supply the materials and build the decorative arches adorning the entrance to the church, supply four oversized candles for these mayordomias, and sponsor a meal held in the courtyard of the priest's residence for members of the Ayuntamiento Municipal and Autoridad Eclesiástica as well as for those who have helped with preparations.

Clearly, a number of cargos with purely ritual functions fall under the auspices of the Ayuntamiento Municipal. According to which authority is held responsible for recruitment, expectations concerning the results of performance of duties differ between these two systems of governance. Those appointed by the civil administration are subject to fines, a form of constraint not needed by the fiscales. The cargo of regidor de gasto entails many expenses. It is not a position of authority, nor does it confer respect; it is often given as a punishment to men who fail to comply with their faena obligations. If a man refuses this cargo, he will be subject to a fine and will be selected again the following year or placed for several days in the municipal jail for all to see.

Engaging in graft is quite common for Presidentes, but it is equally customary for them to endow a project to be completed during their term of office that visibly benefits the community. Mestizo Presidentes who fail to recognize the community retire in shame, while Indian Presidentes similarly remiss are branded as fools who lack the necessary qualities to serve in public office in the first place. The Indians are disillusioned with the civil administration because of corruption and the ineffectual nature of these offices, which contributes to the growing incompatibility in their experience between civil and religious spheres of public life. Regardless of the sentiments of the people, the Presidente has a certain number of obligations dedicated to ceremonial events. He must see to the organization of *fiestas titulares,* public fiestas held in the name of the community that may involve both religious and secular activities. The Indians refer to such events as an *altepeihuit.* An altepeihuit tends to generate greater public participation when associated with one or more Indian mayordomias, such as those held for San Mateo.

The people are always well aware of whose obligation it is to organize particular activities and they are critical when usual standards are not met, just as they are critical when a mayordomo's sponsorship turns out poorly. For fiestas like Octava de Corpus, the Presidente must organize all special events, usually by appointing committees who report to him. Large expenditures will be recorded in municipal records for items such as a band hired for a dance, the liquor and soft drinks provided and sold, the materials used for a horse race, a greased pole and pig, and the paint needed to brighten up the municipal palace. For the Easter reenactment of the Passion of Christ, the Presidente selects individuals to represent the Jews and supplies them with rifles. He chooses and directs the topiles who bring palm leaves for Palm Sunday and sound the large wooden noisemakers that substitute for church bells, which are not rung until Easter Sunday. The topiles supply sky rockets at their own expense for use on Holy Saturday and Easter Sunday. The Presidente also has the obligation to invite ritual dance groups from other communities to join the dancers of Chignautla during the mayordomias of San Mateo. Apart from this, he has other duties involving the celebrations held in honor of San Mateo, the most important being a special fiesta sponsored entirely by the Ayuntamiento Municipal.

The Presidente, fiscales, and mayordomos jointly undertake duties assigned to them during certain events of an altepeihuit. This form of cooperation is, in effect, a series of reciprocal exchanges. For the celebration of San Mateo, the Presidente, ideally accompanied by his regidores, judge, and magistrate, goes to the house of the mayordomo of San Mateo 21. After a ceremonial greeting and meal sponsored by the mayordomo, the Presidente makes a formal request to borrow the demandita and processional platform for the image. Several groups of dancers may accompany the Presidente and his Ayuntamiento, their number dependent upon how much money the Presidente wishes to spend for this event. The Presidente also organizes a meal, fashioned after the ritual banquet of a mayordomía, to which the mayordomo, the fiscales, several sacristanes, and the diputados mensajeros are invited. This meal follows a mass sponsored by the Presidente and the other members of the Ayuntamiento Municipal. No matter who the Presidente is he must go to the house of the mayordomo, and it is his option to make this event elaborate or simple, the latter being more typical of the Mestizos.

Chapter 3

The Economic Dimension of
Sacralizing Activities

Chignautecos believe that a successful life, lived as it should be lived, requires that a delicate balance be struck between social and physical assets and the burdens an individual assumes in maintaining harmonious relations with the saints. Until recently, subsistence practices were not differentiated from other spheres of activity, and the values organizing customary modes of production and distribution reflected priorities belonging to a traditional worldview. Today, modernizing and secularizing influences from the world of the Mestizos have intruded upon traditional assumptions about the nature of existence and have led to the development of certain self-interested ambitions that never appeared before and that direct attention away from the collective good. There is a growing differentiation between means for making a living and other domains of social life resulting from a weakening of the pervasive influence of traditional values. Concerns that never before impinged upon reciprocally organized exchanges within primary relationships have begun to change the character of ritual sponsorship and the sacred premises articulated in these activities.

Milpa cultivation provides the fundamentals of diet and the fundamental requirement for ritual sponsorship. Local specialists—carpenters, masons, bakers, and curers, to name a few—address the needs of Chignautla's Indians. Recently, a skilled and unskilled proletariat has been pursuing full-time wage work locally, in Teziutlán, in migratory labor to the hotlands, in the state capital, and in Mexico City. For these individuals, further integration into the regional and national economy with its associated dependence on larger cash requirements is inevitable. This will alter the value placed on time, land, skills, and money, and will create new differentiations among individuals based on "modern" attitudes, skills, and wealth, rather than on ritual rank, good reputation, and the importance of kinship ties. The traditionally valued tasks associated with the milpa are being relegated to a secondary position by a different perspective on scarce means and alternative ends.

The greatest distinctions between people in Chignautla are those made between Indians and Mestizos, but this in no way implies that Chignautla's Indian population is homogeneous. There are many ways for individuals to distinguish themselves and their families from one another. Individuals do not have uniform access to productive resources. There are variations in size of land holdings, differential opportunities for acquiring skills that would lead to more lucrative endeavors, and positions that offer possibilities to establish a social standing in the community that can be converted into profitable investment. Such contrasts tend to be stable over time since they are often a function of descent group membership and inheritance. Changes in an individual's economic standing may also arise from a willingness to take risks in the context of available opportunities—risks that may focus attention away from traditional patterns of life.

Indians that are seen as poor by Chignauteco standards belong to the most marginal segment of the population. Often owning little or no land, they may rent a house site, which forces them to remain dependent upon subsistence yields and an average annual income of less than 2,500 pesos earned from working in the fields of others.[1] Their limited participation in the mayordomía complex confirms that the saints have not been favorably inclined and costly ritual expenditure would be giving more than what had been received from the saints. Individuals who successfully exploit larger landholdings with diversified crops, or who produce coffee or own cantinas, corn mills, or small shops in the barrios, or individuals who obtain a steady income from wage work, comfortably enjoy an annual income exceeding 20,000 pesos. These individuals will sponsor the more expensive cargos, and through this style of participation in the mayordomía complex, their actions will confirm what is generally viewed as manifest supernatural favor. In contrast to the Indians, most Mestizos are wealthy. Mestizos make their living from local retail businesses and some involve themselves in commercial enterprises that are focused away from the community. Mestizos own all retail businesses in the Centro, the local limestone quarry, and the local bus line connecting Chignautla with nearby towns.

The Productive Use of What the Saints Provide

Chignautecos see themselves as collaborators with the saints in maintaining a good life. They believe they should endure life's struggles without arrogance, greed, or undo exploitation of the land and the people around them. In all activities dedicated to the saints, there is an implicit valuation on how resources of time, labor, and goods are consumed. This form of expenditure is conceptualized as both a burden and a sacrifice in much the same manner as Nahuatlan peoples sacrificed to their gods to ensure their continued favor and participation in human affairs (Carrasco 1952; Madsen 1967; Mendelson 1962). Nahuatlan peoples believed that sacrifice was a sacred duty toward the sun and necessary for the welfare of human beings; without it the world would stop. In his investigation of Aztec cosmology, Soustelle supports his interpretation of this aspect of Nahuatlan cosmology with the following quote:

> As for man, his very first duty was to provide nourishment intonan intota tlaltecuhtli tonatiuh, "for our mother and our father, the earth and the sun;" and to shirk this was to betray the gods and at the same time all mankind, for what was true of the sun was also true of the earth, the rain, growth and all the forces of nature. Nothing was born, nothing would endure, except by the blood of sacrifice. (1961, 97)

These words are remarkably similar to the speech given by the fiscales to mayordomos at ceremonial banquets held on the culminating day of a mayor-domía in Chignautla.

The Instrumental Value of Milpa Cultivation

Cosmological notions concerning the milpa can be inferred from beliefs regarding the relationship between the land, the saints, and human beings who are dependent upon the milpa to provide minimum requirements for living. Beliefs about what is appropriate and respectful in how one cultivates the milpa persist among older generations who are concerned with young men who do not respect the land or its use. However, while the communal lands of the municipio are still largely viewed as held in trust for the saints by all Chignautecos, privately owned land remains the most vital ingredient for successful participation in social and ritual obligations. The land most commonly conceptualized in this manner is devoted to milpa, implicitly associated with the production of corn and beans, which remain staples of the Indian diet in the Sierra Norte and whose successful exploitation represents social and economic stability. Households without sufficient milpa to produce an adequate yearly corn and bean harvest lack a most basic means for extrahousehold commitments. "A sense of security lies in our rich land, in our milpa, even though our dependence upon it imprisons us," is an expression I often heard, revealing to me the conflict Chignautecos experience between the old and the new.

Among the Mestizos, land is readily sold if another source of income becomes available. Mestizos disdain working in the milpa and will utilize Indian labor for this purpose. Among the Indians, the land of one's natal barrio is most reluctantly sold. Ties to patrimonial land are closely associated with expectations of reliable assistance among core members of a kin group who continue to reside in a specific barrio, and through whose assistance an individual negotiates the obligations of ritual sponsorship. Thus, the barrio becomes the point of convergence for resources, both human and supernatural, and establishes the rights an individual may have to the sponsorship of particular cargos commonly sponsored by residents of a given barrio. Rights in land, therefore, are carefully guarded by preferences regarding inheritance of land and vows made to saints among successive generations of the residential and nonresidential extended family. In effect, the social boundaries of the barrio are typically drawn by reliable participation in events requiring reciprocal assistance. It is in this manner that the barrio comes to represent both a territorial and a religious unit within the social structure, making meaningful the Chignauteco saying that "saints watch over the land and the barrios watch over the saints."

Ideally, one's household is surrounded by sufficient milpa for household needs. An assortment of plots will be owned elsewhere in the community, and, if an individual has been fortunate, in the nearby hotlands as well. While acquisition of land has never been a primary economic goal, if a plot becomes available it will be purchased. Private ownership of land and domestic animals is customary and is seen as an indicator of wealth among Chignautecos and other Nahuatlan peoples (Madsen 1969). To cultivate the milpa is a sacred act, but an individual of high ritual rank will never work the land of another for a wage regardless of the amount of monetary compensation offered. Productive land devoted to milpa is unevenly distributed throughout the municipio and is typically cultivated in unmechanized ways, leaving uneven yields subject to what is interpreted as the capriciousness of the saints and human inclination. Chignautecos will, at times, cultivate cash crops for sale in the market in Teziutlán on land that offers above average yields in corn and beans. The production of temperate climate fruits also offers the potential for high profits from established orchards in the drier, more sandy soil Arriba, even though the higher elevations Arriba carry a greater risk of frost. Vegetable cultivation is consistent and successful in the warmer, well-watered environment Abajo, but profits from the sale of vegetables are lower than are the potential profits from the production of fruit in larger quantities.

Strategies for the productive use of land result in either meeting direct consumption needs of the household, generating a cash profit, or generating an immediate cash return. Production for profit in fruit, vegetables, or coffee invariably involves the use of a *regatón* (a type of trader), who collects, bulks, and transports these goods. In contrast, production aimed at generating immediate cash for a specific purpose typically involves the sale of smaller quantities of goods that are produced with household labor and sold by piece in local markets. In local usage the term *regatón* derives from the verb *regatear,* to haggle, bargain, or sell at retail. The meaning of *regatón* is best captured in English by the word *middleman,* a trader who buys commodities from producers and sells them to wholesalers, retailers, or even directly to consumers. In that these traders are often women in Chignautla, I have avoided the term *middleman.* Women travel daily to Teziutlán to sell small quantities of fruits and vegetables, the eggs they have collected, or the tortillas they have made, and they will spend the cash they earn on other items needed for the household. Similarly, a man might buy a young pig for 100 pesos, fatten it for three months, and sell it locally or in Teziutlán for 300 pesos, viewing the 300 pesos as profit. This type of economizing is actually a form of exchange, a ready means for generating, storing, or banking liquid capital for future expenditures.

Both men and women begin participating early in life in this type of exchange. Adolescent boys will raise a pig or two and adolescent girls will raise a number of chickens. Unlike investments made for profit that enhance the economic standing of the individual, production for immediate cash returns establishes and maintains a productive capacity that can be periodically inflated for extraordinary expenditures without endangering the productive base. Individuals expect to enhance their standard of living during their adult years and many do, successfully absorbing extraordinary expenditures such as ritual sponsorship without altering productive means or reducing an established level of wealth. Level of wealth is typically defined materially in land, socially through extensive networks of kin and ritual kin, and symbolically in the manner in which the saints are celebrated.

The concept of money becomes meaningless when it is stripped of its contextual moorings. *Money* and *wealth* are terms with complex denotative and connotative meanings. *Money* serves as a concretization, condensing a great deal of content into a single verbal utterance, and in this sense money is a symbol with a wide range of meanings. In Chignautla, if a man has money, he is attributed with successfully using productive resources within normative standards of behavior and will be considered *muy trabajador*, a hard worker. Or, conversely, he may be attributed with failing to live up to these standards by being overly concerned with the accumulation of money. In this latter sense, money is associated with ambition, and carries a negative connotation, especially when viewed in isolation. Being successful is closer to assertiveness in our sense, a quality of forcefulness when decisiveness is valued, especially when utilized to generate a positive reputation through serving the saints in a decision-making capacity. And given the Chignauteco value on humility, a conspicuous display of what money can buy to impress others would never be rewarded, whereas the expansion of an individual's productive base definitely would. Thus, it is considered reprehensible and dangerous to incur monetary rather than social debts in service of the saints.

Resource management is not insignificant, and several writers have reported that part of the means for ranking cargos in relation to each other is the amount of time consumed in these activities (Haviland 1977; Chick 1981). This does not clarify the precise meaning of "wealth" consumed in cargo sponsorship. In Chignautla, the concept of wealth entails both social and material resources. The family is viewed as the most valued resource, with land following close behind. In fact, one's network of kin and one's land are inseparable requisites in meeting the burdens of ritual sponsorship. In very general terms, not only must a man have a certain amount of productive land, but he must be married and hold the position of household head. These requisites are interdependent: a man must reside in his own household to be a household head, and to support a family a man must own land, which, in turn, becomes possible only after marriage, since a son typically receives an inheritance in land only after he has established a family. However, the position of household head and the possibility for cargo sponsorship is not determined by gender. The two women who have become high-ranking cargo holders in their own right owned sufficient land to bear the expenses of sponsorship and were also household heads. They were, therefore, unmarried. Wealth, defined as it is in Chignautla, can be used to influence recruitment only if the individual also merits respect.

Socioeconomic success is associated with successful management of resources. Good management not only is considered a valued skill that earns respect, but provides confirmation of the role the saints are believed to play in favoring those who maintain their level of living and are able to assume the burdens of sponsorship as well. In Chignautla, ritual sponsorship does not strip the household of its primary resources. Rather, sponsorship stimulates efforts that lead to the expansion of resources in order to meet the requirements of cargo sponsorship. Therefore, accumulation of wealth, as defined above, is activated and guided by these efforts. Successfully managing the routine demands of life and the extraordinary demands of service to the saints are conceptually and experientially linked so that there is never doubt about causality. However, there is a distinction between unexpected and expected good fortune. Unexpected good fortune is conceived of as an instance of *suerte* (luck), which carries no supernatural implications and may befall any individual at any time. This is also true of spontaneous occurrences of bad luck as they may occur to an individual and will be accepted as a natural part of life. What results from bad luck does not include instances of illness, crop failure, death of a kinsman, loss of one's house through fire, flood, or strong winds, or loss of animals that are part of a household's primary resources. These misfortunes are invariably attributed to supernatural punishment for failure to live up to the dictates of belief and imply that the individual has a central role in influencing personal fate. This mode of thinking also reflects unconsciously held assumptions about the reciprocal nature of human-supernatural engagement, in which the actions of one affect the actions of the other. Consequently, within the interpretive framework typical of Chignauteco thought, that is, within their organization of experience, continued success in endeavors throughout the stages of an individual's life and intergenerationally signals the participation of the saints. Unless an individual takes advantage of unexpected good fortune and is able to convert what is singular and momentary into something durable and long term, the character of the individual rather than the saints is held to blame. It is therefore not inconsequential that individuals who sustain a good reputation throughout their lives are also the individuals who maintain the economic bases for sponsoring cargos from either the same conceptual grouping or from a more ritually valued grouping. It is the lives of these individuals that establishes the subjective truth of beliefs about the appropriate way to be, which includes a consistent concern with repaying the saints for their favors. It is an absolute truth for Chignautecos that if unexpected wealth is not utilized to live a righteous life, which must include celebration of the saints without undue pride or ambition, then what was gained will be lost: wealth, respect, and reputation. This is clear in a statement made by an informant:

Filomeno is known because of his wealth, but we see that he is not a good man. A person with a lot of property and corn is a hueytatoani, but the true meaning of the term is Don Benito, who was fiscal, mayordomo of the Santísimo, Presidente Municipal two times. But then there is Juan. He got rich and served San Mateo 21 but he became poor afterwards and had to work in a way not befitting a pasado. Fiscales make their own harvests but not in the fields of another.

Corn is the only crop that has social significance because it is an essential ingredient in reciprocal transactions between kinsmen and ritual kinsmen and because a sufficient amount of corn is a requisite for ritual sponsorship. The productive capacity of the milpa determines to large degree the nature of participation in ritual activities. In contrast to Brandes's (1988) study of Tzintzuntzan, I found that no one in Chignautla sells land to serve the saints, nor do people borrow money to meet the expenses of a cargo. Land may be used for collateral, rented, or sharecropped. Renting land in Chignautla or in the nearby hotlands to produce extra corn is typical when an individual knows in advance that he will require a greater quantity of corn than his own land can provide. There is a disparity in land ownership throughout the population even though Mestizos do not own a disproportionate amount of land in relation to their number. Approximately 10 percent of all households from the more than 250 sampled during a general census of the municipio own more than four hectares of land. The majority own less than one hectare. Table 3 presents a sampling of land holdings from a cross-section of house-holds within the municipio.[2]

Fragmentation of plots through partible inheritance and a growing facil-ity for buying and selling land has produced a pattern of plot dispersal. Land cultivated within the territorial domain of one's barrio is preferred because ties of kinship and ritual kinship assure safety of crops not continually at-tended. If a milpa is owned or rented at a distance of more than four hours' walk from the household, a small shelter will be built so that a man and his family may remain to accomplish agricultural tasks requiring more than one day's labor. Roughly 25 percent of those who cultivate land also own parcels of land for corn or coffee cultivation in La Garita, one day's walk from Chignautla in the municipio of Hueytamalco. It is not uncommon for Chig-nautecos who own land in La Garita to sponsor the mayordomias for the handful of images in La Garita's chapel. Owning a number of small, widely dispersed plots is not viewed as a blessing. Even so, it is rare for a man to turn down property offered for a reasonable price regardless of its distance from his household. If a man needs more land but does not have funds available for such a purchase, he will borrow the money on credit and plant corn to fatten his pigs for sale to repay the debt.

Household economy revolves around the strategic manipulation of milpa yields and animal husbandry. The requirements of household production and consumption are often balanced without large sums of cash: without land there is no corn, and without corn there can be no animals, which are needed for other investments. Cultivation of the milpa follows a predictable pattern dictated by seasonal changes and by the time needed for the corn to mature. Corn and beans are seeded together in February and again in March after the fields have been prepared. While there are several bean harvests, the fields are carefully fertilized and weeded so that the average yield of one to two ears per stalk is not diminished. Milpa is cultivated with a hoe, a horse-drawn plow, and a digging stick, and the mature plants are doubled over to dry in October so that harvesting and stacking of the dried ears may be completed by early December. Nothing is wasted. Dried corn is stored inside the house compound and ground daily to make dough for tortillas. The beans are hung to dry from the rafters until eaten, and the dry cornstalks are fed to the animals. The milpa is regularly blessed by burning incense at the edge of the fields in March when the first growth appears.

Cultivation of the milpa is expensive and laborious, and unless a man owns less than three-fourths of a hectare and has one or two sons who help, it is imperative to rely on reciprocal exchanges in labor or to hire laborers. Everyone is familiar with the tasks and expenses of milpa cultivation. Women and small children help in spreading fertilizer and in harvesting. When Chignautecos convert their time and labor into its monetary value, this conversion is calculated on the basis of milpa cultivation, which serves as a standard of value for relative costs in general. Costs are calculated in terms of the number of men needed to accomplish a given task in one day, the common denominator being one man per *tarea* (twenty tareas equal one hectare). Thus, it would take one man twenty days to prepare one hectare for planting or ten men two days at the payment rate of ten pesos a day, or two

TABLE 3.   Sample Distribution of Landholdings

Hectares	Households
0 to under ¹/₄	1
Over ¹/₄ to 1	128
Over 1 to 2	61
Over 2 to 4	43
Over 4 to 6	5
Over 6 to 10	8
Over 10	4
	250

hundred pesos. Each step in the cultivation of the milpa requires a different amount of labor and time, and not all milpa is of the same productive quality. Plots on hillsides, *barbechos,* require more labor than open and flat fields, *solares,* and yield far less. The number of men employed also depends upon the speed with which a particular task must be accomplished and the capacity of the employer to afford such assistance. Labor is usually calculated on the basis of either one man or five men, that is, by tarea. A man who needs assistance will hire a friend or neighbor but never a ritual kinsmen because this type of request is not compatible with the respect maintained between ritual kinsmen. Kinsmen will offer such assistance with an expectation of reciprocation some time in the future, even though today hired labor is displacing the importance typically given this system of labor exchange. In contrast, labor offered to assist a ritual sponsor never involves a wage because favors exchanged in this context are sacred.

Corn is far more expensive to buy than to produce with hired labor, and the productive use of the milpa determines both wealth and options for further investments. As can be seen from table 4, the land Arriba yields less than the land Abajo and far less than land in La Garita. It is imperative that a man be able to anticipate his corn yield so that he may allocate seed for the following year's planting, adjust to changing consumption needs of his family, or determine the propitious moment to request a cargo. Land owned or rented in La Garita is a valuable asset. The hotlands produce two corn and three bean harvests annually. These harvests correspond to periods of scarcity in Chignautla when corn prices peak, reaching 1.40 pesos per kilo in October. A low price of 90 centavos occurs just one month later because of the harvest, and the price rises steadily again throughout the year. Yields and the fluctuating price of corn directly influence the cost of ritual sponsorships. Most Chignautecos who own land in La Garita devote some portion of their plots to coffee cultivation, making possible a yield worth as much as 4,000 to 5,000 pesos from half a hectare of good land.

In general, a family consisting of a man, a woman, and four children will consume at least 1,300 kilos of corn a year. Household labor is not always pooled, and if a woman owns the land her husband works and insists upon using the profits as she wishes, she must pay him for his labor or hire someone else. The residential kin group is usually an extended family. The nuclear families within it may or may not share a household budget. Dependent sons may keep a portion of their earnings just as a woman or daughter may keep the money earned from the production and sale of vegetables she produces. Apportionment of income depends upon ownership rights and the needs of household members. A man must carefully plan for ritual sponsorship, buying materials and setting aside the corn he anticipates he will need to fatten animals and to feed those who assist in and attend the activities of sponsorship. Others will lend a sponsor corn in quantities of fifty or more kilos, for which no interest will be collected, but a return in kind is expected. Men with little or no milpa will not generally be appointed to sponsor even a minor mayordomía. And it is just as improbable that a man will be asked to sponsor a cargo if he has insufficient corn for household use (the exception being those men with a steady income from employment who make it known that they wish to serve in this capacity rather than as a diputado mayor or dancer). A sample of the amount of corn consumed by typical households is presented in table 5, along with the land that is cultivated by these families.

Secondary Productive Resources

The Sierra Norte is known for its excellent fruits—plums, peaches, pears, apples, and apricots. A sizable profit is possible from the production of fruit if sufficient land is available for an orchard of reasonable size. Profits from less than half a hectare of orchard range from a high of 8,000 pesos to 1,800

TABLE 4. Average Annual Yield in Corn and Beans

Area of Municipio		Corn		Beans	
		Bultos	Kilos	Bultos	Kilos
Arriba					
Barbecho	$^1/_4$ hec.	12	600	$^1/_4$	15
	1 hec.	48	2,400	1	60
Solar	$^1/_4$ hec.	18	900	$^1/_2$	30
	1 hec.	75	3,750	$1^1/_2$	90
Abajo					
Barbecho	$^1/_4$ hec.	15	750	$^3/_4$	45
	1 hec.	60	3,000	$3^1/_2$	210
Solar	$^1/_4$ hec.	20	1,000	1	60
	1 hec.	80	4,000	4	240
Coahuixco					
Barbecho	$^1/_4$ hec.	10	500	$^1/_4$	15
	1 hec.	43	2,150	1	60
Solar	$^1/_4$ hec.	12	600	$^1/_4$	15
	1 hec.	50	2,500	1	60
Hueytamalco					
	$^1/_4$ hec.	18	900	7	420
	1 hec.	72	3,600	28	1,680

Note: These are figures for average or slightly above average yields in normal years. Bultos are gunny sacks used to store ears of corn in their husks.

pesos annually, depending on the fruit grown. Muscatel plums are harvested early and bring top prices when shipped throughout Mexico, but success depends upon the weather since these trees bloom when the risk of frost is highest. Fruit trees have recently suffered from a blight and yields have fallen significantly, making production more uncertain, but people remain reluctant to replace their orchards with milpa. Because Teziutlán is a major regional bulking center for fruit, a relatively large number of Indians have become regatones and a significant number of these are women. Small producers sell directly to regatones and receive payment immediately. Those who produce in large quantities ship directly by truck to markets or jam factories in Puebla or Mexico City. There is much competition, and prices fluctuate in response to prices in the major markets of Mexico. Yet, in a good year regatones are able to realize a profit of 400 or more pesos a week for the season.

For many Chignautecos, producing fruits offers a means for defraying the price of corn as it rises until the new harvest, or the price of fertilizer and the expenses incurred in household celebrations like Todos Santos, in ritual kinship, and at Christmas. For this reason, nearly every household has several fruit trees and the fruits are sold to vendors in Teziutlán. Since Chignau-

TABLE 5.   Sample of Milpa Utilization and Corn Consumption

Occupants	Animals Kept	Annual Corn Supply (in kilos)	Land Cultivated (in tareas)
Household 1: Arriba 8 adults and 5 children	3 pigs, 1 mule, 1 turkey, 4 chickens	3,120	42.5
Household 2: Abajo 6 adults and 2 children	3 pigs, 1 mule, 2 turkeys, 8 chickens	4,250	30.0
Household 3: Coahuixco 6 adults and 5 children	3 mules, 30 chickens, 7 turkeys, 14 pigs	4,380	60.0
Household 4: Arriba 3 adults and 4 children	1 pig, 1 turkey, 3 chickens	1,300	10.0

Note: 1 hectare = 20 tareas.

tecos believe it is inappropriate to buy corn to finance cargos, an individual's intention to cultivate fruit or any other cash crop will depend upon the alternative use of both land and labor. Preference for one productive strategy over another, of course, follows from the perceived certainty of outcome. In a sense, a man's social reputation and his potential ritual rank are known by his cultivated milpa. There is a close association in the minds of Chignautecos between cultivation of the milpa, an essential activity that maintains life, and the results of that activity, which is sacred in itself. A man will take risks with cash crops only if he has sufficient corn; he will never risk having to buy corn because of a cash crop investment.

The people of Arriba and Abajo are interdependent in many ways but nevertheless have persistent squabbles over access to water, women, and cargos. This rivalry has intensified with population increase and new sources of economic enhancement. It is not difficult to understand the advantage of those living Abajo, whose expansion into the hotlands provided the opportunity for a double corn harvest and coffee cultivation. People of the major barrios of Abajo feel that they have been favored by the saints, and their mode of participation in the mayordomía system clearly reflects this belief. Individuals who live Arriba feel similarly favored because of their successful fruit production, resulting in competition between Arriba and Abajo over the distribution of cargos among their constituent barrios, which shifts with economic fluctuations within the community.

Animal husbandry and horticulture are also significant. The climate in Chignautla is excellent for vegetable production. However, the only way an individual can generate a profit by producing vegetables, as opposed to a small cash return, is to act as a regatón or to sell wholesale in markets that are free of competition. Women typically produce, sell, and act as vegetable regatones. Even a small garden will provide a means for earning a little cash that can be used independently of a husband's or father's authority. Potatoes grown Arriba and cabbage grown Abajo are the major crops. Potatoes can yield as much as 6,000 pesos per hectare, but cabbage is needed for ceremonial banquets and is therefore more valued than potatoes. Domestic animals are important secondary resources and most households cannot meet their production and consumption needs without them. Pigs, chickens, and turkeys are essential ingredients in ritual banquets, and trade in pigs is nearly universal. It costs approximately two to four pesos daily to maintain a pig. Pigs mature at six months, having been fattened sufficiently in three months or less to be ready for sale or slaughter. Pork and lard are dietary items that are especially important for ritual occasions. Raising pigs also serves an important banking function. A cash surplus will invariably be used to purchase one or more pigs to enhance the productive base of the household.[3]

While there is always a market for pigs and chickens, larger animals such as horses, mules, and cows will be raised to defray the cost of unexpected events such as illness or ceremonial events planned for the future such as weddings, baptisms, and funerals. Many factors influence price, including regional fairs and religious fiestas and the price and availability of corn. Regatones purchase animals cheaply in other markets of the Sierra Norte and transport them for sale at a profit in the Friday market in Teziutlán. Chignautecos agree that families who are unable to afford to raise chickens, one or more turkeys, and at least one pig are poor indeed because they are bereft of the means to defend themselves adequately against contingencies.

The type of food offered at ceremonial meals and banquets is rigidly defined by custom. Mayordomias attended by more than fifty persons include a ritual meal of cabbage soup with lamb. Mayordomias menores typically include a meal of colored rice followed by mole served with either pork or chicken. These are foods important to sacralizing contexts. Cooked turkey and chicken presented during ritually designated circumstances, whole or by piece, symbolically confirm relationships of respect between the individual who offers this gift of meat and the individual who receives it. These special portions of meat are given to the central actors in mayordomias and other occasions involving cargo holders, and they are given to the central actors in compadrazgo. Live turkeys serve as obligatory offerings in initiating relations of ritual kinship, and presentations of cooked turkey or chicken are made in any context in which a relationship of deference must be formally acknowledged. The use of animals in rituals forecloses their use for alternative ends.

Sacralization in Economic Endeavors

Patterns of reciprocal exchange in labor, goods, and assistance in the performance of important activities traditionally played an instrumental role in the lives of Chignautecos. Today, the principle of reciprocity continues to structure interpersonal relations, but surfaces most boldly as an interpersonal ethic in ritual contexts to which the evocation of balance and harmony is central. Obligatory reciprocal exchanges continue among members of the nonresidential kin group and underwrite the interdependence of these individuals. It is revealing that Chignautecos distinguish between different contexts, the tasks involved, and the individuals chosen for such assistance. In cultivation of the

milpa, kinsmen, neighbors, and ritual kinsmen (in descending order of preference) will be asked for assistance. In ritual contexts, the order of preference
is kinsmen, ritual kinsmen, and finally neighbors. This preferential rear-
rangement reflects latently held assumptions of compatibility between certain
tasks and certain persons with whom obligatory respect and expectations of
reciprocal assistance are determinant. Immediate kinsmen are obligated to
assist in all endeavors regardless of context and they feel bound by these
obligations. Ritual kinsmen are readily asked to assist in preparations for all
types of ritual events and ceremonial occasions and feel both honored and
respected by these requests.

In Chignautla, men and women have mutually supportive roles in all
activities. By custom, men are concerned with productive efforts outside the
household, especially in cultivation; women do the marketing, cook, tend to
children, and care for the animals as well as cultivate vegetables important
to the diet. Since the advent of the electrically powered corn mill, women
have been released from hours of grinding corn for tortillas, enabling them
to pursue nontraditional means of generating a cash income. Unlike the
customary contributions of women to household maintenance, women today
sell their labor, grow cash crops, or become regatones and realize their own
profits to be used as they wish. Men who lack special skills move from one
job to the next in patterns of seasonal, migratory labor or in construction.
Pay is comparatively high for jobs outside the region, and money earned in
this fashion is creating a new category of successful wage earner. Such
occupations disturb the general pattern of life, since these individuals will
be absent from the community for longer periods of time than ever before.
However, with readily available capital, they will be able to sponsor expensive mayordomias earlier in their lives than could their fathers, who had no
access to such opportunities. But these men cannot serve as sacristanes,
mensajeros, or fiscales or even as the mayordomos of San Mateo because
cargos of this type require a great deal of time throughout the year.

Occupational specialists, like curers or masons, tend to be clustered
within specific barrios, their special knowledge passed to younger generations of kinsmen living nearby, consolidating the wealth and standing of
these barrios. It is interesting to note that while fiscales have been local
masons, none have been employed as factory workers in Teziutlán or by the
Federal Highway Commission since such occupations are incompatible with
this type of ritual rank. Average incomes from a variety of occupations are
listed in appendix 2 and appendix 3, along with their associated landholding
and ritual sponsorships. From these tables it is clear that there is a coales-

cence in traditional means and ends in living the Chignauteco version of the good life. Men are usually at their peak productive capacity between the ages of thirty-five and fifty, which correlates directly with the years of most intensive involvement in ritual sponsorship. This is a direct result of the existence of opportunities not available to Chignautecos in years past. Other factors related to mode of sponsorship are intricately tied to traditional occupations and the developmental cycle of the residential extended family. In the past, before the age of thirty or thirty-five, a man would have had little chance of being economically independent of his father. Even though men who are wealthy tend to assist more in their sons' move toward independence than men who are less wealthy, they remain more heavily dependent upon this ready source of labor and are unwilling to lose it. Assistance between fathers and sons is mutual and obligatory, but either may benefit or suffer from the contractual aspect of this primary kin tie.

I know of only a few men who held top cargos before the age of twenty-five and the vast majority will not fully involve themselves in ritual sponsorships until the age of at least thirty. Wealthy men who themselves held important cargos create in their offspring not only expectations regarding appropriate modes of ritual engagement with the saints, but predetermined choices of sponsorships by leaving unfulfilled vows to specific saints that are typically inherited by sons, grandsons, and paternal nephews and are carried out in exchange for the inheritance of a house, other property, or some other valued good. This custom places the individual generationally and intergenerationally in relationships of respect and reciprocity. Today, there is a trend toward younger and younger men holding highly valued cargos. The fear the hueytatoanime have regarding these young cargo holders stems from the sense of danger generated by the individualistic ambitions and prideful displays characteristic of young men anxious to pursue their fortunes who forget the wisdom of protecting the interests of the collectivity through obedience to the saints.

Certain occupations make it possible to increase income in preparation for sponsorship by carefully manipulating investments in animals and by inflating corn production. The impetus to strive toward improvement is captured in the words of an informant:

> I plan to make a promise of sponsorship to give thanks, and with another to give thanks again. They say that a man shouldn't serve only to slide back. We must work to improve our respect and responsibility through success. We cannot simply sponsor a cargo and stop working, thinking

that God will do it all and everything will be easy from now on. After a cargo we must work even harder.

Poor management not only ruins a sponsorship, but erodes the uplifting quality of sponsorship. A joyful sponsorship is one in which the sponsor willingly and successfully makes a sacrifice to the saints for himself and the community, from which only good can follow.

The Sacralizing Effects of Reciprocity

Two forms of interpersonal assistance may be identified. The first is called *ayuda,* help solicited for mundane tasks and often requiring monetary compensation except between members of the residential kin group. The second form is makwis makepis, which Chigautecos shorten to the term *makwis.* Makwis refers to an interpersonal ethic whose constraints intensify within contexts in which obligatory exchanges are enhanced by respect. This form of reciprocal assistance is evocative of the sacred premises central to social life in this society. The most intense expression of the sacralizing influence of reciprocity occurs in the performance of acts directly dedicated to the saints, making pivotal the achievement of common goals. The most binding forms of reciprocity invariably occur in conjunction with obligatory respect. Both reciprocity and respect are vehicles of sacralization: they create a pattern of interaction that evokes the sacred yet pragmatic contract between saints and human beings and intensify the value placed on interdependence in interpersonal and personal-supernatural relations.

The conceptualization of social life captured in the term *makwis* depicts a mode of interaction in which each partner is bound by the actions of the other. Makwis exists in a variety of unstated forms, such as the help a daughter might give her father in expectation of receiving a gift of land, or the help a son gives to his father knowing that he is likely to inherit his father's house. A major motive for requesting mayordomias is also a form of makwis, specifically the inheritance of unfulfilled vows and more generally the sense of debt to the saints to whom success in life is attributed.

Among members of the residential extended family, makwis is simply assumed in the tasks of daily living. Makwis will be activated for certain occasions between members of the nonresidential kin group, between ritual kinsmen, and often between members of a barrio who live close by when more labor is needed than a household can provide. These are interactions that are constrained by the ethic that is implied in voluntary obligations. Such patterned interactions are inherently sacralized. This contrasts with situations in which ayuda obtains. Divorced from a sacred content, ayuda is overtly and immediately delimited and carries no implications for future interactions. It is for this reason that ayuda is not seen as reliable and is typically ensured by a monetary compensation. It is clear that ayuda is a mode of assistance that is the desacralized counterpart to makwis, bearing witness to a gradual transformation of interpersonal attitudes in a context of increasing monetization of the economy. New demands for cash limit makwis to certain contexts in which help is given for a short period of time in the form of contractual labor or monetary loans.

Makwis must be directly solicited when it involves persons beyond the household. An individual may be "invited" to help; willingness to comply is the favor given. To insure assistance in preparations for ritual events, a sponsor must request the assistance he expects to and will receive. Those persons approached first are always members of the nonresidential kin group, followed by ritual kinsmen with whom relations are dependable and intimate. Neighbors encountered in the street might also be invited, but they are not expected to help even though it is considered appropriate to volunteer. In ceremonial contexts, assistance given between individuals carries no specific time in which reciprocation must occur. Participants have entered an unspoken, enduring agreement to which they are morally bound. To activate such contributions, the primary sponsor must formally *pedir favor,* literally request a favor. Even among members of the nonresidential kin group, formal requests must be made because they enact the respect essential to reciprocal ties between individuals related by blood or ritual kinship. When a couple goes to the household of individuals of whom they wish to ask a favor, the household head will speak for himself, as will his wife. Men generally offer their labor while women offer to lend something they know will be needed, such as dishes, pots, and other kitchen utensils. Ideally, a man at harvest time will put away the estimated amount of corn needed for the celebratory events of his cargo, but if the date of the event is long after the harvest, he may find that he has an insufficient supply. The people of the barrio, knowing that he is serving the saints, will offer fifty kilos or less of corn interest free, a gesture of respect that occurs only in this context since the giving of such a gift is sacralizing in itself.

Even before kinsmen, ritual kinsmen, or close neighbors are formally invited to attend a ritual celebration, everyone within the barrio will be well aware of what event is occurring and the work it entails. Those invited will be told when to arrive to "accompany" the sponsors and will be told what to do once they arrive at the sponsor's house. People arriving to help are guests, the *invitados*, individuals invited to join in an event of sacred significance. Invitados are expected to contribute either labor or goods, for it is rare and inappropriate that a person invited to accompany a ritual sponsor simply attends without demonstrating support. In mayordomias, members of the cofradía, though invited, are referred to as *los que vienen,* literally those who come to the house. These individuals are not invitados but designated ritual actors and do not contribute to preparations. Similarly, in celebratory events initiating compadrazgo, the ritual actors who come to the house do not contribute to preparations since they are themselves the objects of celebration.

The provision of meals in Chignautla implies respect by offering something of value in reciprocation for the help provided. Invitados offered food at ritual events are obliged to receive it ceremoniously, whether it is consumed at the fiesta or taken home to be eaten later as is commonly the case. Obligations are fulfilled in the corresponding acts of giving and receiving, confirming the sacralizing property of reciprocal engagements among individuals who demonstrate respect for each other. Pragmatically, reciprocal engagements are social and moral investments a person makes to insure help when it is needed. Mayordomias always demand greater amounts of goods and labor than a single household can provide. It is a rare occasion when a man tries to "make it on his own" in sponsoring a cargo, for no man is expected to reduce his assets to do so. Any invitation to assist in a mayordomía is an invitation to enter *makwis.* For mayordomias, preparations are often carried out well in advance, and the sponsor may hire helpers for a wage for more strenuous tasks such as chopping wood, fixing a roof or patio, or slaughtering animals. For example, it is common for ritual sponsors of important mayordomias from Abajo to hire helpers to chop wood from the small forests of the communal land Arriba where fallen trees and branches are available to all Chignautecos. Men who help in this fashion will be paid except on the day of the celebration, when they will work for free as a sign of respect to the mayordomo, whose sacrifice is for the good of all.

Chignautecos do not like to feel obligated and try to maintain a balance of favors in interpersonal relations. Even the most secure and wealthy individuals strain under the feeling that they have not reciprocated favors done them, believing, as they say, that "one cannot be free if one's time or goods belong to someone else." In effect, by entering an interaction that is organized reciprocally, an individual is able to remain at least partially in control of his destiny.

The Pragmatics of Ritual Sponsorship

Much of what has been presented thus far concerns the pragmatic attributes of Chignauteco religion. The remainder of this chapter is devoted to addressing how Chignautecos translate what they believe into what they do, and how the actions Chignautecos take affirm what they already believe to be true about their world. In effect, this chapter has been devoted to the teleological dimensions of this ritual complex, the physical expression of beliefs central to it, and the ideological basis for the practices that follow upon beliefs.

All ritual activities have a substantive basis in the material conditions of life. The practice of the cult in Chignautla involves a wide range of expenditures in time, labor, and goods. While cargo costs are important, the actual cost of cargos is not a topic of casual conversation unless an individual is planning to request a cargo or a cargo holder has overextended himself and has encountered difficulties in meeting ritual expenses because of poor or careless planning so that he is left with less than what he had before sponsorship. In fact, most cargo holders prepare well in advance so that they already have the means to meet expenses before they are actually needed. It is for these reasons that differential cargo costs do not, in and of themselves, determine the ritual value of cargos or the deference shown the sponsor.

People are generally not well informed as to the cost of specific cargos, but they do know the general range of expenses. A man will be familiar with costs only if he has had personal experience either in sponsoring a cargo or in helping someone else. The duties of sponsorship are standardized to a large degree, and fairly accurate estimates can be made on the basis of which individuals determine their ability to hold particular cargos. Interestingly, I found that men focused more on formal ritual expenses, whereas women were able to estimate more inclusive costs. Records of expenses are not kept, but individuals remember much of what is consumed or bought. Chignautecos do not generally consider items produced by household members in the cash requirements of sponsorship, although they are certainly included in expenses. Distinctions are made between cargos that demand large expenditures for one occasion and those that require continuous expenditures over a year's time, bringing into focus how time, labor, goods, and cash are valued and experienced separately. Ritual sponsorships involve the expense of a mass, rockets, and a ceremonial meal as central ritual acts. Mayordomias mayores require a minimum of five hundred kilos of corn, while mayordomias menores require one hundred kilos or less. During the months devoted to honoring San Mateo, all mayordomias call for the use of special rocketry. Hundreds of small rockets set upon a wooden frame in the form of a bull (hence the name *toros*) are carried by an individual so that when one rocket ignites, the rest ignite in rapid succession. Toros cost approximately 450 pesos and it is usual to burn two toros following vespers for the mayor-domía the following day. The burning of the toros is a special event. Three or four *coyoleras* (from the term *coyote*, a shyster or trickster) are engaged by the mayordomo to amuse the crowd with antics while the individual carrying the toro runs through the streets. The coyoleras are men dressed as women in flowing skirts, sombreros, and shawls crossed over their chests. They carry small noise makers to alert the crowd to the approach of the toro. Toros call attention to the role the mayordomo plays by his sacrifice toward collective aims that underwrite these celebrations.

Chignautecos estimate the burden of sponsorship in a number of ways. Routinely available resources like the quantity of corn produced annually and the domestic animals routinely maintained by the household are differentiated from those items that require a cash outlay and must be purchased outright. Time and cash are ingredients of sponsorship that Chignautecos experience as threatening and will partially influence which particular cargo an individual is willing to request. In contrast, basic resources such as the amount of land devoted to milpa form part of the considerations taken into account by the fiscales in determining whom they will accept or reject for sponsorship. For both the fiscales and the individual sponsor, the cost of the mass is an issue of concern since the mass constitutes the largest single cash expense of sponsorship and must be "bought" from the priest. Aside from the expected benefits of the mass in terms of repayment for a debt owed the saints, the cash spent in the mass cannot be recouped. For specific details regarding the ways in which these costs are met for different cargos, see Slade 1973.

The costs of cargos in Chignautla vary widely and limited comparisons of cargo costs are listed in appendixes 4,6,7,8, and 9. Individuals who intend to pursue sponsorship carefully accumulate what is needed according to a system of priorities in which cargos are neither first nor last. This pattern of accumulation is illustrated by the words of an informant who has successfully sponsored three ritually valued cargos:

The harvest was good; and because of whom? God, and for this, I make another vow. I think with what am I going to give thanks to God, always with the mass. Then after the cargo, if there is something left over, I will invest it in my work. If I know I have a sufficient corn supply and there is still something left over, I will buy animals. If people know that

I have a profit from my harvests, they will come to the house to offer land and animals for sale. If there is still money left over, I will fix up my house. It is a sacrifice made to God and we are expecting his continued favor. I didn't do it so that people will respect me.

No Indian pays for cargo costs out of cash on hand since cash is not stored in this manner. The essence of good management requires a balancing of production and consumption so that actual expenses are met without going into debt, reducing assets, borrowing money, or altering a given style of living. Large amounts of corn are generally not purchased for sponsorship. However, men who are engaged in steady wage work are the exception. These individuals may rent land and hire laborers to work it or purchase corn outright, thereby altering the traditional correlation between size of landholdings devoted to milpa and the type and ritual value of cargos requested and received. Requests for cargos are not taken lightly and are implicitly aimed toward insuring further success. Thus, a young man does not request, nor will he be granted, a cargo until he is economically viable, and young men who receive an inheritance of land in Hueytamalco often begin sponsoring cargos sooner than most.

Chignautecos value restraint. More secure investments are preferred to potentially high-profit but risky ventures because such investments might have a disastrous result. Yet, preparations for sponsorship are themselves not free of risk. If a man spends a great deal of money in purchasing pigs, and if they die, the cash investment will be lost as will the corn used to fatten them, placing the success of the celebration in jeopardy. Once a man feels successful, he will not make further investments until he has given thanks to the saints by requesting a cargo. A man will choose the most ritually valued cargo he can afford from among those for which he has a personal preference. There will always be a balance between the cargo an individual receives and his ability to absorb the economic burden.

At the departure of the fiscales from the house of the mayordomo after the central mayordomía banquet is held, the fiscales make formal speeches that address the aims of sponsorship. The first fiscal turns to the mayordomo, stating in Nahuat the following:

We give thanks to God so that He might entrust us with more in order that we may give Him more. God gives us more and we give more. God protects us more so that we might give more. With God, we lack nothing nor shall we be lacking. With the mayordomía neither are we lacking, nor have we too much. We do not lose anything nor shall we have too much nor shall we be lacking, because you made your sacrifice that we accompanied you with this day.

It is important to note the meaning behind the use of the term God in these statements. God, *Tata'tzin* in Nahuat or *Diostzin,* an amalgamated term, refers to *Dios,* the term in Spanish for God. The saints collectively are referred to by the term *tatiotzitzin.* These terms have shifting referents, including meanings presented to Chignautecos from formal doctrine of the church as taught by priests and reinterpretations that incorporate traditional meanings from their indigenous past. God and the saints are terms used in the singular and plural interchangeably since the saints and God hold ambiguous cosmological positions in Chignauteco thinking. In mayordomias, the ritual activities that occur in the church and involve the priest usually result in a more formal Catholic usage than may be heard during events that occur outside the church, where Nahuat is spoken. Use of the term *Dios* during the mass will refer more strictly to God conceptualized in this context as having supreme powers, while at other times, the term *Dios* will refer to the collectivity of saints who are believed to be equally powerful and directly influence the lives of individuals. In a similar fashion, when Chignautecos speak of the church, *tiopan,* or the cargo holders of the Autoridad Eclesiástica, *tiopawemini* (literally the work between us all for the saints), they are referring to many things: to the pantheon of saints believed to reside in the church, to the Catholic church with its allegiance to powers beyond Chignautla, to the Christian God, and simply to the place where the priest and the saints live. It is this conceptual ambiguity that allows Chignautecos to interpret a diversity of events and symbols, uses and purposes behind ceremonial activities in a coherent way, allocating meaning to what is important at that moment of time in their existence.[4]

If a man with little property and few animals approaches the fiscales to request a cargo, they cannot refuse him outright, especially if he is a man of good reputation. He will be asked to return in a week, when he will be questioned as to how he intends to manage the sponsorship. If they determine that he is overestimating his capacity, he will be offered a less costly cargo. If the members of the Autoridad believe that he is dangerously ambitious, they will simply ignore his request, since the fiscales do distinguish between the single-minded pursuit of self-enhancement and the type of self-enhancement that derives from good works. While commitments to serve the saints must be made willingly, holding back nothing, an equally potent constraint requires a proper attitude of humble respect that will predispose the saints to listen. The fiscales must find an individual who is economically viable, not simply an individual with available cash or animals, for these can be dissipated before the mayordomía celebration is held. The fiscales, of course, have access to this kind of information through the observations of the sacristanes, who reside throughout the municipio.

Plans and preparations may be made several years prior to requesting a cargo, and usually this is a time of economic expansion. Or individuals simply proceed with life, but if they become successful, they will begin to focus on sponsoring a cargo. Once a cargo is accepted, the goods to be consumed are purchased slowly and less expensively in the markets of the Sierra. Shortly after receiving an appointment, a mayordomo will seek his diputado mayor, purchasing a liter of aguardiente and a pack of cigarettes to add to a small basket of selected items traditionally accompanying requests for favors. The basket and its contents is called the *chiquihuite de pedimento*. The chiquihuite is an acknowledgment of a reciprocal transaction, an offering given in return for forthcoming assistance. Giving a chiquihuite also acknowledges the respect that invariably accompanies reciprocity by compensating for that which will be given, thereby sacralizing the agreed upon transaction. A chiquihuite is required in any *pedimento* or ceremonial request, whether it pertains to ritual sponsorship or the rituals of compadrazgo.

If a man accepts the position of diputado mayor, a meeting is planned with his and the mayordomo's wife to decide what will be consumed, what type and how many rockets will be used, and the division of the burden that will be shared between them. Ideally, the diputado mayor lightens the burden of the mayordomo by sharing expenditures: if five pigs will be needed, the mayordomo will contribute three and the diputado two, or a mayordomo might contribute eight sheep and his diputado five. The mayordomo always pays for the mass and the diputado for the rockets set off at mid-mass. The mayordomo alone supplies the rockets for vespers and those needed for the mayordomía procession the next day. The mayordomo will buy twenty-five liters of aguardiente and the diputado twenty, the mayordomo four cartons of cigarettes and the diputado three, and so on. A mayordomo who wants a diputado mayor knows in advance that he is actually increasing the overall cost of sponsorship since the relationship between the mayordomo and his diputado requires celebration in specific events dedicated to this purpose. Yet, the support offered by the diputado is significant in the management of activities and in the contribution of time that frees the mayordomo to do other things. It is not uncommon for a mayordomo who works in Teziutlán to select a diputado whose occupation leaves him free to remain in the municipio to use the time the mayordomo does not have to fulfill the obligations of the cargo. Serving as diputado mayor is service to the saints and personally meaningful, but these men are rarely remembered by the general population years after their contribution. Accepting this role is an act of respect for the mayordomo; the diputado mayor will stand by the mayordomo through the difficult year leading to the culminating fiesta of the mayordomía. In turn, the mayordomo assists his diputado in requesting a cargo when it is his turn to petition the fiscales.

Cargos are most commonly held for two-year terms, the second year requiring fewer expenditures than the first. For an initial year, a *recibimiento* or acceptance ceremony will be held, improvements will be made on the mayordomo's house, new items of clothing will be bought for the image, or property of the image will be replaced or enhanced. A lesser charge is made for the mayordomía mass the second year and there is ample time for the mayordomo to breed his pigs so that his stock will not be depleted for his second year of sponsorship or after relinquishing his cargo. Nevertheless, the mayordomo is invariably assisted by his kinsmen and ritual kinsmen and members of his barrio, whose contributions include needed goods and labor and especially valued emotional support.

The Sacrifice of Sponsorship

A commonly told story reveals Chignauteco notions of what constitutes proper conduct and attitudes necessary to serve the saints successfully and to reap the benefits of sponsorship. A man, having failed repeatedly in his efforts to enrich his life by converting his milpa to orchards, beseeched the fiscales to offer him the mayordomía of San Mateo 28 when it suddenly became available. The fiscales cautioned him against overextending himself but gave their anxious approval since barely four months remained before the 28th of September. They reminded him of the commitment he was making to himself and to the community, a commitment that should be made with a pure heart. These admonitions incorporate the significance of a balanced and respectful sacrifice undertaken in sponsorship. Disregarding the difficulties and implications of such a short preparation time, the incumbent sold his orchard, borrowed money, and planned an elaborate fiesta. The people who went enjoyed the music the band from Teziutlán played throughout the culminating events of the mayordomía, but they gossiped about what appeared to be the mayordomo's excessive expression of devotion to the saint. Predisposed to question the mayordomo's intentions, no one was surprised that within six months of the fiesta, the mayordomo began drinking heavily. His wife had become ill and under stress from her illness, he worked less and drank more. After he nearly killed a man in a cantina quarrel he fled from the municipio.

It is clear that the individual in this case was compelled to request this cargo because he was seeking social and material restitution as well as psychological compensation for his experience of failure in the economic venture that led him to endeavor to tap into the power of the saints in the first place. To interpret the motivation of this man as essentially based in prestige or people's gossip as based in envy would miss the point. Rather, it was his desperation combined with his blind ambition that made those who came to his fiesta suspicious of his actions and not surprised when bad fortune befell him. The nuance in this story is culturally determined and would not be understood if detached from its cultural context, which is what I believe is often done by writers who assume that prestige is invariably a motivation in cargo sponsorship. The interpretation I have made is close to what Chignautecos themselves make of this story, and differs from interpretations perhaps epitomized by Cancian (1965) in his book *Economics and Prestige in a Mayan Community,* who relies heavily on the inevitability of prestige to explain the nature and operation of religious cargo systems. Prestige seen in this light, I believe, is distinct from the status enhancement depicted in pre-Hispanic cultures of this region in which the offering of a sacrifice and the sponsorship of celebratory rituals was an important component.

While expressions of self-enhancement were rarely verbalized in reference to cargo sponsorship in Chignautla, fantasies of self-enhancement were definitely present in the minds of certain individuals when they considered requesting specific cargos. However, such inclinations remain hidden because they detract from what is considered an appropriate attitude, one that allows an individual to appear worthy of respect and enables him to be granted this form of sacred trust by the community. Self-seeking motivations are experienced by Chignautecos as a distraction from appropriate intentions, and an individual who hopes to have an impact on the general population rather than quietly serve the saints would have to disregard what would commonly be expected to occur from coercing the saints. On the one hand, the Indians fear that certain individuals who become wealthy will refuse a sponsorship, thereby making the character of these individuals suspect. On the other hand, managing a sponsorship without undue hardship is a consciously held ideal. A man must neither hold back nor overextend himself in order to maintain a balance between supernatural favor received and the sacrifice of sponsorship. Chignautecos will state that one must fulfill the obligations of sponsorship "as if it were nothing," an ideal realized in the manner in which cargo expenditures are actually managed so that a cargo holder does sponsor his cargo without becoming impoverished and consequently demonstrates to himself, his family, and everyone else that all that is believed is actually so about the role of the saints in human life.

There is no way to prove objectively that supernatural disfavor is a response to the actions of certain individuals. What is inferred from observation and interpretation produces a conceptualization of the ideology of a people that specifies causal relationships between beliefs and their outcomes. But if explanations are offered in specific terms, we are led to pursue specific beliefs that tie a conceptualization about the nature of the world with particular behavior and notions of cause and effect that are embedded in organizing assumptions within the people's experience. When Chignautecos relate a legend about how powerful San Mateo is they are telling us something about their most basic truths. A story was related to me about a parish priest who did not believe in the power of San Mateo. He wished to teach Chignautecos that San Mateo was a saint whose life and good deeds should be admired and inspirational, but not confused with the power of God, who could not be touched or seen. In his resolve to bring what he viewed as their pagan beliefs into greater conformity with Catholic theology, the priest insisted upon proving his point by demonstration. He inserted his knife into the image of San Mateo and, to his surprise, the image began to bleed. Chignautecos love this story and delight in telling that the priest eventually became insane and fled the parish, a clear sign of what happens to individuals who fail to believe in the power of San Mateo to punish those who transgress in thought or deed.

When people live up to the dictates of belief and become successful in their economic endeavors and in the cargos they sponsor, others generally value their efforts. Failure in and of itself does not ruin a reputation, but failure to remain humble invariably makes an individual a target of gossip and not only may ruin a reputation, but also cause personal, familial, and communal calamity, as these are readily attributed to supernatural disfavor. This indicates the existence of meanings that lie on the deeper layer of assumptions that organize experience. I have found that envy (*envidia*) tends to occur between neighbors who are very familiar with each other, rather than between individuals of greatly discrepant status who know each other only slightly. This is similar to what has been reported by Romanucci-Ross (1973) in her work in Morelos. She interprets envy as a form of status assertion that fosters competition with the intention of invalidating the gains of the envied person and thereby reducing his or her status. She finds that envy does not necessarily follow success but may, in fact, award respect. It is when success disregards collective interests and is accompanied by self-interest, pride, and presumption that success becomes the object of envy. She also found that the greater the status differential created by successful endeavors, the less envy is attached to the success. I believe this to be equally true in Chignautla. I have heard Chignautecos say over and over again that if a man is called upon to serve in the church and refuses on the grounds that he does not have much money, he will only end up by having to spend the same or more on medical bills and other difficulties. These injunctions are not only normative but actually do result in compliance as reflected in the words of a fiscal about his struggle after sponsorship:

> Some men after holding a cargo just stop working. Instead of bettering their condition they make it worse. While I was fiscal, older men advised me not to become lazy, to continue to plant my milpa. This may happen because of the amount of drinking a man must do in his cargo. A man is not supposed to become poorer; just the opposite, to do business with the seeds of blessing. Before I entered fiscal, we bought a lot of corn; I didn't have the desire to work hard. I felt that life was just going on and I didn't have any obligations to work, nothing. But with the cargo, I found a spirit to work. Now that I have served as fiscal, I continue to have this spirit. With my orchards, I improve my situation. Now with my harvests, I have something to live on.

Chignautecos believe that immediate choices should enhance one's fortune while one's long-range plans must never disregard the saints. In a general way, which cargos are sponsored indicates to all an individual's relative degree of success in life. I have never attended an important mayordomía in a house not made from stone, whereas many of the minor mayordomias are sponsored by men whose houses are made from wooden planks, only to be replaced with stone before or shortly after they request and receive mayordomias of greater ritual value. The economics of ritual participation may be summed up as follows. If a man is diligent and achieves success in his endeavors with something left over after all household expenses are met, then he requests a cargo for which he need not alter his productive capacity. He then rests for several years, investing in animals, equipment, more land for milpa, or an orchard. In effect, he employs his wealth capitalistically. A ritual sponsor will have the corn he needs and enough money to pay for the mass and rockets, three of the major considerations in ritual sponsorship.

While there is a historical, ideological, and behavioral relationship between success and sacrifice, ambition and humility, the Chignauteco view of the cargo as a sacrifice and burden is not grounded in the facts of sponsorship and, in fact, contradicts what is viewed as the appropriate manner in which sponsorships should be and are accomplished. The terms *sacrificio* and *promesa* (vow or promise) are used interchangeably with the term *cargo,* meaning burden, position, or duty. The distinction between an economic sacrifice and an economic success regarded as a sacrifice does reveal the interplay between ideology and structure in this complex. Sacrifice is an evocative symbol. When it is associated with cargo sponsorship, and it invariably is, the power of this vehicle of sacralization is intensified, confirming the instrumentality of normative standards as they apply to the use of productive resources that then become associated with the position the saints hold in experience. "Burden" refers to something borne with some degree of difficulty, whereas sacrifice refers to a substantively potent gesture of entreaty in which there are reciprocal implications: something of value is exchanged for something of greater value in a context of discrepant statuses.

The rituals of the cult represent the most significant sacralizing vehicles in Chignauteco religion and serve as a model of what all rituals should be. Ritual sponsorship is believed to imbue the mayordomo with the sacred attributes of his cargo and creates a sacred bond between all individuals who contribute what they can to serving the saints. Through ritual sponsorship, interdependence is transformed from accepted fact to sacred aspiration. The dependence of primary ritual actors upon those who assist them (and who will be primary ritual actors themselves at some time in the future) becomes uplifting, validating the Chignauteco assumption that relationships thus sacralized are the only ones of value.

Chapter 4

The Sacralization of
Interpersonal Relations

I have conceptualized ideology throughout this book as organizing individual experience according to a specific design that is recognizably Chignauteco. This normative dimension of experience embodies ideals for conduct that dictate explicit rights and obligations between individuals in a given relationship to each other allowing individuals to anticipate what will occur upon marriage, what is expected from inheritance, and what assistance will be forthcoming from kinsmen or ritual kinsmen.

Themes of harmony and balance imbue the Chignauteco conceptualization of descent with a content that creates the basis for standards of interpersonal conduct between individuals whose relationship is established by common ancestry. The structural significance of affiliation through patrilineal descent allows us to grasp the importance of kinship in this society, and the manner in which kin ties are intensified and extended through ritual kinship. On the one hand, the reciprocal implications inherent in a shared ancestry in the patriline are realized in the nature of residential choice, inheritance, the giving and receiving of assistance, and the fundamental sense of mutuality that exists between these kinsmen. On the other hand, deferential conduct invariably occurs in conjunction with engagements that are inherently reciprocal, since respect is entailed by reciprocity in this cultural system. Respect maintained between close kinsmen is the conscious acknowledgment of the reciprocal patterning of their interactions. That is, *confianza* is an experiential attribute of the bond between primary kinsmen. When Chignautecos use the word *confianza*, they are emphasizing the reliability, intimacy, and trust characteristic of relationships safeguarded by norms of respectful conduct. Lack of respect between primary kinsmen truncates the support made available through these bonds. This type of loss is the structural analog to the sense of jeopardy generated in Chignautecos when they note disrespectful attitudes toward the saints. Therefore, it is the confluence of descent, reciprocity, and respect that brings significant cosmological premises into play in the experience of the actors to indirectly intensify the importance of collective aims that sustain harmonious relations between individuals dependent upon each other and proper conduct toward the saints.

The Instrumental Nature of Kinship

The social universe for individual Chignautecos consists of people who are kinsmen, *compadres,* intimate neighbors, others living in the barrio, individuals living in adjacent barrios, the residents of Arriba, Abajo, or Coahuixco not personally known, and all others who share an identity as Chignautecos but with whom there is little significant contact. Chignautecos distinguish between intimate neighbors and ritual kinsmen, between ritual kinsmen who are *compadres de fé* (that is, those contracted for the sacraments of marriage, baptism, first communion, and confirmation), and between other ritual kinsmen. Neighbors, of course, when they are neither kinsmen nor compadres, share barrio affiliation, making them more indispensable than other Chignautecos. For example, the confianza that exists between a mayordomo and a neighbor chosen to serve as his diputado mayor will be heightened, or a certain degree of familiarity will develop between men who are members of the cofradía in any given year. Friendship within Chignautla remains a fragile institution. Indians do establish friendships with other Chignautecos and with Mestizos of Chignautla or Teziutlán. These friendships are eventually formalized through ties of compadrazgo or they tend to fade away. Compadrazgo created in this manner guarantees that the respect necessary to preserve the relationship becomes intrinsic to it, even though the forms of compadrazgo initiated between Indians and Mestizos will not be of the most significant type.

The Principle of Patrilineality in the Reckoning of Descent

Within the more immediate social network of the individual, *parientes* (kinsmen) are differentiated as either consanguineal or affinal kin. Parientes whose relationship is established on the basis of patrilineal descent are differentiated from other parientes with whom there is a consanguineal bond.[1] A strong sense of connection and belonging occurs between individuals who share descent from a remembered paternal ancestor, typically great-great-grandfather, and includes those persons related up to the third degree of collaterality. In the absence of a functionally significant concern for ancestors in Chignauteco culture, acknowledgment of ancestry in this fashion produces a group of living individuals among whom interaction is intensive and organized reciprocally. Affiliations established by patrilineal descent allow for distinctions within the larger grouping of an individual's parientes wherein group sentiment is valued although not necessarily enacted. The importance of patrilineal ties typically results in patrilocal or patrineolocal residence, which creates the nexus of a shallow descent group that is primary in the social and religious life of this community but does not meet the criteria for lineage organization that would ultimately produce clans. Patrilineal affiliation results in the configuration of residential units and kinship groupings interpositioned between the household and the barrio by specifying the group of parientes with whom there is an intimate relationship and with whom reciprocal obligations are imperative.

Parientes políticos, affinal kinsmen, are also important. During the developmental cycle of the family, significant affinal kin are typically present within the household compound. The nature of relationships between consanguineal and affinal kin who are members of the residential kin group depends upon the internal complexity of the extended family as it differentiates into nuclear families who eventually obtain some degree of spatial and economic autonomy by establishing independent households. Relations between affinal kinsmen sharing a residence are characterized by formality and deference when they involve spouses of immediate consanguines of ascending generations, but the degree of intimacy that exists between the larger grouping of parientes políticos is often dependent upon whether or not they live close by.

A categorical distinction Chignautecos make between consanguineal kin related through father and those related through mother is accentuated by the importance given such relationships in carrying out social, economic, and religious activities. According to Chignauteco thinking, closeness of relationship is determined by blood ties unbroken by a cross-sex linkage, making parientes who share the same blood primary, patrilineally related consanguines. The reckoning of closeness of relationship among these agnates is based on the degree of shared blood; in effect, the degree of relationship to father, grandfather, great-grandfather, or great-great-grandfather, since beyond the fourth ascending generation such connections tend to become vague. This makes genealogical reckoning strikingly paternally skewed with a noticeable lessening of genealogical awareness for similar relatives related through mother in both ascending and descending generations. In reference to parientes related through mother, it is not uncommon to hear expressions like "no son nada mios" (they are nothing to me) and "no llevamos la misma sangre" (we do not share the same blood), reflecting the lack of involvement with individuals belonging to related but distinct blood lines even though they are acknowledged as *parientes.*

Interactions between patrilineally related kinsmen up to and including the third degree of collateral relationship are strongly governed by normative expectations articulated as consciously held ideals, which readily translate into conduct between individuals who share a paternal surname and residential proximity. Reciprocal engagements between these kinsmen will diminish or increase relative to the reckoning of connection to a common ancestor. Ideals for conduct do not always translate into behavior. But given the degree to which these ideals are realized in residential preferences, in the reliability of reciprocal exchanges between certain parientes, and in normative patterns in inheritance, it is clear that the reckoning of descent among Chignautecos functions to establish social entitlement and results in a definite alignment of kinsmen. This aggregate of kinsmen forms the core membership of the extended family, the traditionally most important social and residential unit in this society. These individuals also constitute the nucleus of the nonresidential extended family, a kinship grouping based on ties between household heads who are related collaterally as brothers or lineally as fathers and sons and who typically live near each other.

The functional and conceptual importance of patrilineally related kin appears in the Spanish kin terms that have replaced or are used interchangeably with Nahuat kin terms displaying idiosyncratic Chignauteco usage: primary, secondary, and tertiary kin in the patriline are called *parientes carnales,* kin of the same flesh, a term never used for matrilateral kin. *Primo hermano,* first cousin, is accompanied by other terms expressing the same lineal emphasis: *tío hermano,* father's brother as distinct from mother's brother, simply *tío; tía mamá* for father's sister rather than *tía* for mother's sister, *tataabuelo* for father's father rather than *abuelo* for mother's father, and so on. The principle of bifurcation emerges in these terms: maternal and paternal aunts and uncles are distinguished from each other and from mother, father, and grandparents. This bifurcate collateral kinship terminology attests to the importance of a single line of descent confirmed in patterns of interaction between kinsmen important to each other.

A most striking contrast is seen in relations between an individual and sons of *tío hermano* and *tía mamá.* Sons of *tía mamá* will rarely be invited to help with the expenditures required in ritual sponsorship, nor would these individuals automatically participate in life crisis events and compadrazgo rituals as is expected of closely related consanguines. Expectations individuals have toward patrilateral kinsmen not agnatically related are decidedly lower. Chignautecos hesitate equally in asking the sons of tía mamá or a close maternal kinsman such as mother's brother, mother's sister, or maternal cousin for assistance, even though they might live close by, since there is no justification for doing so. Favors from matrilateral parientes are often in the form of ayuda, although it is not entirely uncommon for great affection to develop between a man and his mother's brother in the absence of paternal uncles, or for a woman to become especially close to a maternal aunt. The manner in which an individual relates to matrilateral kin is largely dependent upon personal inclination rather than a sense of duty. These kinsmen would be asked to attend a fiesta, but they would not be invited to help with preparations since such ties never have equal weight in recruitment for assistance.

Father's father and father's brother are important kinsmen from whom an individual is likely to receive an inheritance that usually will be activated by a reciprocal exchange. Caring for these senior kinsmen will be acknowledged with a gift of real property: a house, a house lot, or land for milpa or coffee cultivation. Both tataabuelo and tío hermano are able to step into father's or older brother's place, assuming the role of father in offering all forms of supportive assistance. Father, tío hermano, and older brother may act as formal representatives for an individual in formal ritual contexts, for initiating compadrazgo relationships, and in wedding negotiations. Among female secondary relatives, it is father's sister who steps into the role of mother as a representative of the patriline, a position mother could not assume since she remains affiliated with her own patriline regardless of her marital status. Although strong ties may develop between individuals and paternal aunts, this is more likely to occur between women related in this manner.

Relations between brothers are usually strongly developed, and only if half-brothers share a father will they feel a bond of kinship. Although conflicts may develop over work allotments and inheritance possibilities as sons mature, relations between brothers can be extremely intimate. Brothers prefer to live near each other to facilitate the give-and-take nature of this bond, which is fundamental to their interdependence and the viability of the nonresidential kin group. When a residential shift to another barrio occurs, the intensity of the interaction between brothers diminishes, although attending funerals remains obligatory, as do reciprocal exchanges in labor, time, and goods needed for the sponsorship of cargos. A patrilateral parallel cousin is a kinsman who is most likely to assume the role of brother in the absence of actual male siblings, and it is this kinsman who is called *mi carnal,* a term of reference also used for brother. Female paternal cousins often do not involve themselves in this manner. They are considered to be less bound to contribute since upon their marriage their primary responsibility is transferred to their husbands and children, persons belonging to another descent group. Along with the wives of her husband's kin, a wife of a household head invariably calls upon her sisters and the wives of her brothers to help with food preparations and other tasks falling to women in ritual activities.

Apellidos, paternal surnames, represent distinct bloodlines and serve as the most significant bar to marriage. Men and women retain both surnames so that an individual's affiliation with a patrilineal descent group is recognized. If individuals who belong to distinct descent groups with the same apellido do marry, it is often a topic of ridicule because of its suggestion of incest. When people refer to persons with the same apellido, they are often pointing to a group of individuals who live near each other and are bound by mutual obligations and collective interests, and who are attributed with common traits believed to be passed down from generation to generation.

Descent traced patrilineally is a critical means by which people establish entitlement to kinship prerogatives and to the help expected from others. A man is responsible for his offspring, who will bear his surname. Parientes carnales, Chignautecos say, are individuals who respect their kinsmen and who can be trusted to respond to a request for help by lending goods, securing services, providing opinions in decision making, or offering emotional and public support. For baptisms, weddings, funerals, and ritual sponsorship, patrilineally related consanguines and their wives are always invited to assist regardless of where they live, and it is unusual for them to refuse. Refusals generate a strong response best captured in the statement "he no longer wishes us to be kinsmen." I consistently observed adult siblings and their spouses, father's siblings and spouses, and most of father's brother's sons and their spouses in attendance at these affairs as participants who were, as Chignautecos say, invited to help. Those unable to attend usually send contributions of corn and meat or at times money. In sum, these are the relationships that are most strongly regulated by ideological injunctions and their importance in social life establishes descent as a sacralizing vehicle in this cultural system.

Patrilineality and the Residential Alignment of Kinsmen

Given the importance of patrilineal descent, it is not surprising that patrineolocality predominates. Strong attachment to patrimonial land in the context of initial patrilocal residence and positive group sentiment sustains the cohesion of the membership of households whose heads are related collaterally through brothers and lineally through fathers and sons. The availability of these individuals during routine tasks of daily living and the sense of give and take that develops between them prepares the members of the residential extended family for interactions that will occur among individuals who, in the future, will be members of distinct households. The residential extended family gives rise to future constituents of the nonresidential kinship grouping, from which future generations of extended families emerge. Relationships between core members of the residential extended family and the nonresidential kin group are defined by common descent and a history of dependable exchanges in labor, goods, and services that facilitates the pooling of resources for marriage ceremonies, funerals, and the elaborate rituals of compadrazgo and cargo sponsorship. Interactions between members of these two structural units overlap, but are subtly differentiated. Assumptions that guide daily interactions between individuals who reside together are implicit and taken for granted. In contrast, interactions among members of the nonresidential kin group contain explicit expectations that produce patterns of interaction that are value-laden, holding the members of the nonresidential kin group together once residential unity is lost.

The respect between generations of parents and children, between brothers and their in-marrying spouses, and between younger siblings and older siblings and the help one offers any other kinsmen living within the household are facts of life. Relations between fathers and sons are highly constrained and what occurs between them is never taken for granted. Sons ideally owe their fathers respect. A son's respect for his father is enacted by his obedience to his father's wishes. His respectful obedience acknowledges his father's gift of care in guidance and protection since birth and the promise to fulfill specific obligations a son contracts while approaching maturity. Ideally, a father is obliged to sponsor the sacraments of baptism, confirmation, and marriage and provide an inheritance in land and perhaps a dwelling for his son to raise a family. This ideal is compelling. There are readily shared tales that highlight the misfortune befalling sons who fail to respect their fathers and equally pointed tales of misfortune befalling fathers who disregard their children.

Chignautecos use the term *casa* to refer both to the enclosed house compounds dotting the landscape and to the physical structure housing the extended family whose members are called *familia* or *familia de la casa,* verbally noting the distinction made between these kinsmen and those closely related parientes carnales who reside in other casas. A compound is usually surrounded by a fence or wall with one entrance to the street; its complexity depends upon the social composition and wealth of the extended family residing there. Households of independent nuclear families are simple structures. Within a surrounding wall, an open patio with a trough for collection of water and perhaps animal pens will be positioned in the center of two or more rectangular buildings of one room each, the largest used for living quarters and entertaining while the smaller serves as a kitchen. Each household invariably has a steam bath or *temazcal* of stone. A compound of poorer residentially independent nuclear families may consist of a tiny room made from wooden planks to which a kitchen room is attached, surrounded by a fence of dry corn stalks. Households vary in style. Those made of cement block or locally quarried limestone are built to sustain a second story so that newly married sons can be accommodated without sacrificing land needed for milpa.

Nearly all older house compounds in Chignautla contain within their surrounding walls a series of rectangular, contiguous rooms whose doorways open to a large courtyard where domestic animals are penned, the number of rooms increasing with the maturation to adulthood of new generations. Usually directly across or to the left of the courtyard entrance is the oldest structure, once the dwelling of the original household head and now the compound's focal point. Dwellings are rectangular rooms that are sparsely furnished with beds or sleeping platforms, several chairs, long benches, and a table or two. A household altar is typically positioned on the north wall of the dwelling room of the household head, centrally displayed along the wall to the right of the entrance. All entertaining and ritual events will occur in the open space in front of the altar. However, if a son who continues to reside within the compound has achieved independence in production and consumption for his nuclear family, his dwelling room will have its own altar and a cooking hearth set aside in the kitchen announcing the son's engagement in a social network independent of his father's. The number of altars and cooking hearths indicates the various phases of the developmental cycle of the residential extended family as it internally differentiates into dependent and independent nuclear families, only one of which generally remains within the parental household. The others disperse to form the component nuclear or extended families of the nonresidential kinship grouping.

Household altars are set upon small tables adorned with a tablecloth and flowers. The wooden table serves as the altar base, upon which a variety of sacred objects are placed. Three or four images of saints, representations of Jesus and the Virgin Mary in framed prints, and calendar pictures encircled by plastic floral decorations enhance the altar and give it a characteristic look. Several images of saints in wood, plaster, or plastic, a cross or two and a crucifix, incense burners, rosaries, and a variety of personal religious paraphernalia used on ritual occasions occupy the table altar. In this sense, the altar is structurally and functionally analogous to the altar in the parish church or any altar in any chapel or elaborate shrine located within the community. During mayordomía masses, the image of the saint celebrated is placed just below the main altar in the church and to its left is the demandita. During the ceremonial banquet of a mayordomía the demandita is centrally placed on the household altar of the mayordomo to remain throughout the mayordomo's tenure. The presence of a demandita on the household altar publicly acknowledges the special relationship between the mayordomo and the saint he serves. The household altar is also a focal point for Todos Santos, for funerals, and for compadrazgo rituals. The larger a residential extended family is, the more complex the household altar becomes as it incorporates the particular devotions of each family member.

Indian households are typically situated in the midst of the milpa so that they are virtually surrounded by cultivated fields owned by the household head and perhaps by one or more sons who have established conjugal unions and have received a portion of their inheritance. The yearly corn supply produced with household labor is stored within the compound and its division is a sign of internal differentiation. Residentially dependent nuclear families that have achieved partial autonomy are said to be living *gasto aparte,* living on a separate expense budget. When all members of the casa participate jointly as a single unit in social, economic, and ritual activities, they are living *gasto junto.* Sons who live gasto aparte continue to owe their fathers respect and will contribute their labor and some portion of what they produce toward activities of the group as a whole. Living gasto aparte is only one phase in a much longer process for a son en route to becoming a household head, a process that may take years and will depend upon the father's willingness to let go of his son's labor and meet the expenses of his son's wedding. Formal marriage necessitates division of the patrimonial estate, which many household heads attempt to put off for as long as possible. With a promise of a good inheritance later on, grown sons will not move far away. Their wedding may simply be followed by building an extension onto the house compound with its own entrance to the street. Once married, a man is under great pressure to accumulate more land as close as possible to his household so that he may not only live up to the ideal but maintain the integrity of his milpa. As in ritual sponsorship, those individuals able to plan well and successfully balance the imperatives of kinship obligations with production and consumption are valued and rewarded in this society: intergenerational mutuality is the key to success.

The residential extended family among Chignautla's Indians commonly consists of from two to three and at times four generations, and, at its greatest generational depth, contains a household head and his wife, his elderly father and mother, one or more sons with spouses and children, and unmarried sons and daughters. Conjugal unions usually begin when a young man of seventeen or eighteen not yet independent of his father and without announcing his intentions "robs" a woman from her natal household and brings her to live with him in his father's house. Nearly all marriages evolve from this type of elopement without the formal pedimentos or marital petitions that lead to betrothal. A wedding includes a mass and three days of intense activity sponsored in part by the groom's parents, in part by the bride's parents, and in part by a couple who has been chosen to be the godparents or *padrinos* of the wedding by the groom's parents. Perhaps another couple or individual will be asked to sponsor the music for a dance at the house of the groom. These individuals and the baptismal padrinos of the bride and groom participate as the central actors in an elaborate series of events that involve ritual exchanges that occur between significant consanguineal and affinal kin, between compadres, and between individuals who will become compadres through these rituals. Each of the main actors has the opportunity to assume in turn the position of "one who gives," creating an obligation to receive and reciprocate, thereby formalizing the respect that must obtain between the most important affinal and consanguineal kinsmen of the families of the bride and groom and the compadres of the wedding party. This ceremony is called the marriage *xochitis*.

A marriage is not formally recognized without a xochitis, which marks the *cumplimiento* or ceremonious fulfillment of one of a series of obligatory rites. A xochitis always accompanies the sacraments of baptism, confirmation, and marriage and sacralizes the relationship between compadres. The xochitis is a sacralizing vehicle that initiates ritual kinship through a series of reciprocal exchanges between the central actors. While a ritual called the xochitis is commonly present in Indian communities throughout the Nahuat region, the xochitis in Chignautla clearly expresses the importance of patrilineal descent. It includes an exchange of items of symbolic significance followed by a stylized dance called the *xochipitzahuac*. In other areas of the Sierra Norte, the xochipitzahuac is danced individually or in a circle, with no particular design to selection of partners. In Chignautla, this ritual is performed by two lines of individuals who dance opposite each other, each line consisting of a core of agnates with their spouses. After the xochipitzahuac is performed, there is a further exchange of material goods. The xochipitzahuac and the exchanges before and after it allow ties of ritual kinship to be extended to include significant parientes carnales of those who dance. In the experience of the Indians, the xochitis and xochipitzahuac have always been performed. Today they are performed out of a sense of duty to tradition, even though such traditions are problematic because they are ethnic markers. However, the xochitis remains sociologically important because it intensifies the significance of indigenous elements that embody ideological tenets that affirm traditional values.

Weddings are major social events and are very costly. Aside from the contributions made by all members of the residential extended family, weddings prototypically activate reciprocal rights and obligations for assistance between parientes carnales who are members of the nonresidential kin group. An abduction requires that an agreement be reached between both sets of parents so that the woman who has been robbed may obtain the consent of her parents. An initial accord is accomplished by less formal pedimentos than those needed to set a date for a formal wedding, which may occur years later. Pedimentos directly addressing the wedding also include a discussion of residential options for the couple, although the first three nights of marriage will be spent in the household of the groom's father. Residence may be a moot issue if the young woman abducted is already living in the groom's household with her belongings. Typically, both sets of parents know each other, since young men often choose women who live quite nearby and whose parents may not know the boy, but will presume to know him through the reputation of his father. Pedimentos can become belabored, continuing weekly, biweekly, or monthly for up to three years if there is great resistance by the bride's parents. Resistance diminishes once a child is born.

Initial pedimentos exclude the future bride and groom. The groom's father enlists the aid of his own father, his tío hermano, an older brother, or a compadre to act as his representative, preferring to ask a kinsman of high ritual rank who can speak with authority. Pedimentos must always be accompanied by a chiquihuite, which for marriage is not inexpensive and contains bread, sugar, coffee, meat, soap, candles, chocolate, rice, cigarettes, and aguardiente, and sometimes a small amount of corn. Only after the first pedimento will the prospective bride and groom be present, accompanied by their baptismal padrinos and both sets of parents. It is customary to have at least three pedimentos. Only at the third, when the bride makes *atole,* a corn gruel, to demonstrate her fitness as a wife to the boy's parents, will a decision be made. The young woman will be asked if she indeed chooses this man for her husband. If the answer is yes, her parents then state how long they require the pedimentos to continue.

The traditional wedding includes numerous ceremonial banquets and elaborate exchanges of goods. The initial day is reserved for formal preparations in the church. Compadres of the central actors have been invited to help because of their right to ask them and their obligation to respond to their compadres' request. The next two days are occupied by an early morning mass followed by household rites, at the center of which is the xochitis. The xochipitzahuac is followed by ceremonial banquets, the giving of presents, formal presentations and speeches offering advice, and *agradecimientos,* highly stylized expressions of gratitude.

The household festivities begin with a special breakfast of sweet rolls, coffee, *xole* (a corn gruel sweetened with chocolate), and a stew of tripe (sometimes replaced today by mole served with pork, turkey, or chicken) offered at the house of the padrinos of the wedding. The parientes carnales of the padrinos with their spouses are busy assisting in making the *xochikoskat* or ceremonial leis of orange leaves, flowers, and three or four sweet breads, which are exchanged in the xochitis before dancing the xochipitzahuac. The xochikoskat are referred to in Spanish as *rosarios de pan,* rosaries of bread, and must be prepared in the households of the bride's and groom's parents. The xochikoskat will be exchanged after the wedding mass, during a series of exchanges that follow the *encuentro* or ceremonial greeting of the bride at the groom's house, and the groom at the bride's house. The xochitis and xochipitzahuac of the wedding involve an exchange of xochikoskat between the padrinos of the wedding, the baptismal godparents of the bride and groom, the bride and groom's parents and, by extension, primary parientes carnales and spouses of all the above couples. All who exchange xochikoskat become compadres and must dance opposite each other in the xochipitzahuac. In any xochitis, the presentation of the xochikoskat occurs in a manner dictated by custom. The xochikoskat is placed around the neck of a corresponding participant, who returns the gesture if he or she intends to assume a reciprocal position of equal ritual status. In doing so, the following words of agradecimiento are offered: "Allow me, *compelitzin* [or *comaletzin*], to do this, because we will now become compadres, now and forever in the eyes of God."

At the groom's house, the padrinos of the wedding are given two live turkeys and the *nacatzontet* or special serving of meat that is invariably present at a ceremonial banquet. For a wedding, the nacatzontet consists of one cooked turkey. The nacatzontet is presented as a gesture of respectful reciprocation for the sacrifice made by the padrinos in ritually sponsoring the wedding. At the bride's house, the padrinos of the wedding receive a nacatzontet of one-half cooked turkey or two whole chickens followed by a shoulder of pork served on special rice. Exchanges in a wedding begin with the pedimento of the padrino by the groom's parents for which a chiquihuite is required. This gift creates a debt that requires reciprocation. Upon acceptance, the padrino assumes the position of "one who gives," able to elicit further reciprocations. The position of "one who gives" is important, since this individual may extend ties of compadrazgo to any individual within the multiple kinship networks participating simply by placing the xochikoskat around his or her neck. The xochitis serves, then, as a means of intensifying or extending interpersonal bonds that will be constrained by respect. Individuals placed in the role of giver tend to be chosen carefully, even though the individuals who receive have the option to accept the xochikoskat in their hands, a gesture that respectfully signifies unwillingness to enter a relationship of balanced intensity. Such a refusal is unlikely for the principal actors at a wedding, but common among others who have been invited to attend because their assistance is needed—that is, those present primarily because of patrilineal ties, secondarily because of affinal ties through patrilineal kinsmen, or because they are already ritual kinsmen.

Chignautecos say that a xochitis is never just giving, but is giving and receiving, thereby demonstrating how people should respect each other. Reciprocal relations entered in this manner allow the xochitis to serve as a sacralizing vehicle by making respect obligatory and mutually binding. The meanings evoked in the structure of the xochitis are also evoked in the structure of the mayordomía. These rituals function analogously in the sacralization of interpersonal relations and, in so doing, replicate the Chignauteco image of a balanced and harmonious universe.

The wedding, without which a son cannot become a jural adult, legitimates a son's right to demand residential independence. Today, land scarcity is forcing young men to take jobs in Teziutlán. With a cash income, land may be purchased independently of an inheritance from their fathers. Young men are also more willing to live in the natal household of their wives until they build a house of their own. These factors contribute to a growing number of independent nuclear family residences built on smaller and smaller plots of land. Yet, nuclear families with residential independence are never self-sufficient, and remain dependent upon assistance from members of the non-residential kin group.

Several nonresidential extended family groupings have quite a large membership, with nearly a dozen household heads. Wealthy in landholdings and successful in other profitable ventures, such families have developed a characteristic mode of ritual sponsorship over several generations. The mutual support available to these men not only facilitates this mode of sponsorship, but guarantees a say in decisions regarding recruitment for the future, virtually assuring selection according to their interests. Influencing recruitment is one aspect of the corporate functions of the nonresidential kin group, a fact of life readily comprehensible to Chignautecos: general well-being and success can be expected if interpersonal relations are as they should be, guided by tradition and used in service of the saints. It follows that the greater the degree of reciprocal assistance provided within this social grouping, the more efficacious the ideological foundation of reciprocal engagements appears to be to the actors themselves.

A young woman robbed by a dependent son will be treated kindly, but she must be completely obedient to his senior kinsmen, making this a difficult period in her life. Frequent visits to her mother ease the strain. Cross-set conjugal unions are generally unpopular because if she comes from Arriba but now resides Abajo, relations with her family are greatly diminished. Especially tense relations exist at least initially between a dependent son's wife and his parents. She can remain in this ambiguous status for more than five years, during which time several children will be born for whom rites of baptism and confirmation are provided by the household head. Should the conjugal union dissolve, a woman has rights to her children only if they are still nursing. If a woman with young children loses her conjugal partner, she will return to her father's house, leaving her children behind since she would not wish to remain, as Chignautecos say, "living among strangers."

A daughter does not generally bring a conjugal partner into her father's household because such an arrangement is not congenial. The position of her conjugal partner will be problematic, since his allegiance will be split between his parientes carnales and parientes políticos and their respective households. Uxorilocal residence accounts for only a small percentage of households in this community, generally when a man lacks land or is an orphan, or if his labor is useful to his wife's father. It is rarely the basis for an extended family, since this form of residential alignment is generally incompatible with traditional patterns of reciprocal assistance, succession, and inheritance. The derogatory expression "a man who is acting like a woman by making atole for his wife" refers to uxorilocal postmarital residence. Unless residential independence can be established within a reasonably short time, such arrangements tend to be ephemeral or fail altogether. Men who live in households owned by their wives are nominal heads who must fulfill the faenas imposed for their section without the benefits awarded de jure heads of households. It is also unlikely that such a man is able to pass the house on to a son, since his wife retains her rights of ownership. She typically passes it to a daughter or a paternal cousin, a relative within her patriline. Unless he owns land elsewhere, the man will have little or nothing to offer his sons.

Parents have liens on whatever is earned by dependent offspring and their spouses. Women have the duty to obey their husbands and his parientes carnales and spouses. A wife will contribute what she can to make the extended family household a viable unit, just as husbands who are dependent sons are obliged to invest their efforts in household needs before investing in personal needs. Fathers and daughters, mothers and sons living together have a close, affectionate relationship in marked contrast to the restraint characterizing relations between fathers and older sons, young women and their husbands' mothers. The social identity of a dependent daughter is bound by her father's reputation, and she will be known outside her household and barrio as the daughter of so-and-so. Daughters of men of high ritual rank are treated with deference. They gain more experience assisting their fathers during ritual events than do daughters of men of lower ritual rank. Such a young woman will not marry a man who has never held a cargo, nor will she allow herself to be abducted.

Subtle forms of antagonism between in-marrying women and their affinal kin diminish when a marriage is held or an independent domicile established. Brothers-in-law typically have a warm, joking relationship that is commonly formalized through ritual kinship. If good feelings do not develop, cooperative efforts will be experienced as an imposition and obligations will be discharged as unceremoniously as possible. The close bond that brothers normally feel at times deteriorates when their father dies and one son takes his place, especially if the father has been reluctant to provide for each of his sons adequately. If a man goes to speak with the fiscales, he will always be accompanied by an older brother, his father, or his grandfather, and brothers are often chosen to carry the image in mayordomía processions. Sons, fathers, and brothers may take each other's places in most ritual contexts, and any close patrilineal kinsman may act as an assistant, even though diputados mayores are seldom chosen from within the household. Situations do develop when conflicts occur between a mayordomo's brother and his diputado mayor over the right to make decisions in the absence of the mayordomo that concern an activity occurring in the mayordomo's house. Brothers actually have the right to decide in their brother's stead, but this right conflicts with the authority of the diputado mayor. This would not be true for ritual kinsmen whose rights and duties to the mayordomo are far more circumscribed. In comparison to patrilineal kinsmen, compadres have no formal obligations concerning the duties of cargo sponsorship. Out of respect they assist by contributing a kilo or less of wax for candles and invariably assist in the preparation of ceremonial meals.

Men engage most actively in ritual sponsorships when adult sons and their wives reside with them. Ideally, household heads are chosen for ritual sponsorship, although both dependent sons and sons living gasto aparte have been appointed. The appointments are never coterminous, especially for ritually valued cargos. This is not an issue of ritual incompatibility. A son living gasto aparte may become a sacristán, a diputado mensajero, or even a diputado mayor while his brother is a mayordomo and his father a fiscal. Marriage is an important institution in Chignautla. It is the couple rather than the individual who participates in all social, economic, and ritual activities, even though each partner creates a personal reputation that can affect the other. A wife's inappropriate behavior can have disastrous effects on her husband's chances of receiving a cargo. Women are not passive participants in the lives of their husbands, even though they may act in this fashion in public view. Women exert a powerful influence over the choices made by their husbands for they are truly partners in every sense of the term. A woman cannot accept or reject a cargo appointment for her husband, nor would a man make a decision to sponsor a cargo without first consulting his wife, for he cannot meet ritual obligations without her. Women always accompany their husbands to meetings of cargo holders, either in the fiscalía or in the barrio, and women have equal access to ritual knowledge. In fact, there is no facet of life from which women are absolutely excluded except socializing in a cantina.

Women and men hold complementary roles in ritual activities, but neither an unmarried man nor an unmarried woman would be denied a sponsorship because of gender. A woman would depend upon a brother, tío hermano, or primo hermano just as a man would rely on kinsmen similarly positioned, even though a man's female kinsmen will be divided in their allegiance far more than a woman's. As I have already mentioned, a woman who is a household head has an equal right to sponsorship. For example, one of my most knowledgeable informants was a woman who was the preferred child of a man of some wealth whose two sons left the community to find their fortunes in the lowlands, where the eldest ultimately died. Always close to her father, she remained unmarried, caring for him until his death. In reciprocation, she inherited his house with over ten hectares of land in the barrio of San Isidro, Arriba. Part of the reciprocal agreement between them involved her fulfillment of his vow to sponsor the cargo of mayordomo mensajero held in honor of the Santísimo Sacramento. Some twenty years after his death, she requested the cargo, and with help from her parientes, compadres, and neighbors, carried out the obligations of sponsorship. She chose her diputado mensajero carefully and avoided activities that were dangerous to her as a woman of her ritual rank, especially those involving heavy drinking. She took her place in the Autoridad Eclesiástica and participated in all decisions made regarding church affairs, fulfilling the vow she inherited without incident. She was granted this cargo because there was no basis upon which she could be refused. If a woman becomes a widow while her husband is holding a cargo, she is expected to complete the obligations of sponsorship. A widow may also request a cargo in the name of her deceased husband.

In Chignautla, gender relations reveal the value people place on balance, reliability, and respect. The lives of men and women become increasingly interdependent as they move toward jural adulthood. Descent and marriage determine their positions in the broader activities of social life, which, in turn, define the manner of their participation. What men gain in public life by marriage, however, women generally tend to lose, since there can be only one household head. Men need wives to function adequately, whereas marriage for women diminishes the range of activities in which a woman can engage without encountering a conflict of interest with her husband. A wife's public role in the mayordomía complex is neither muted nor disguised. The mayordoma manages the elaborate preparations for ceremonial banquets, greets the members of the cofradía who arrive at their house after the mass, and presents them with the nacatzontet. The wife of a mayordomo is the mayordoma, even though the mother of a mayordomo remains simply the mayordomo's mother.[2]

The Principle of Patrilineality in Inheritance

In Chignautla, there is no proscription as to which son should inherit the parental house, even though there is a preference for either the eldest or the youngest son if one proves respectful and willing to care for his father in old age. Men are generally grandfathers before the age of forty and become independent long before inheritance decisions are made and titles formally transferred, but one son is inevitably chosen over the others. Inheritance is structured in the same manner as relationships reckoned by descent, in which the give and take of favors is clearly delineated and predictable.

All material goods are individually owned. Individuals have an inalienable right to dispose of gains from their productive efforts. Women do not customarily receive land as an inheritance because their relation to the patrimony is undermined by marriage. Daughters do not generally press for an inheritance in land since to do so labels them as greedy. If a man is wealthy, he will give a daughter a portion of the patrimony, which she is then free to pass on to her children. A man may encourage a daughter to bring her husband to reside in his house, offering the couple a promise of an inheritance of significance such as a store or corn mill. Husbands and wives become joint owners of all property if they are civilly married. Civil marriage is less common among the Indians than among the Mestizos because the Indians are aware that property ownership and inheritance as stipulated by law erodes the continuity of the patrimony. Patrimonial land is important to men because it provides a basis for attaining a dominant position within the nonresidential kin group by assuming ownership of an established house compound and of the prime lands surrounding it. Sons may also inherit land from a paternal grandfather or tío hermano, particularly if these men lack viable offspring of their own, but again this will occur in reciprocation for special favors rendered. Assuming the financial burden of caring for senior consanguines during illness or any other life crisis or paying for their funerals merits a plot of land or a small house site.

A son becomes responsible for the unpaid debts of his father. Not only must financial debts be assumed, but all unfulfilled ritual obligations and vows made to the saints become part of these debts. Vows to saints are not taken lightly and return to mind when the individual is close to death. Individuals who fall gravely ill and then recover make a vow to a saint in reciprocation for having survived. However, many such promises made remain unfulfilled and are passed to a close kinsman in exchange for an inheritance. Spiritual debts are binding and most often fall to parientes carnales by verbal agreement in much the same manner as promises are made to transfer real property. As an extra measure of security, Chignautecos feel more comfortable asking a primary kinsman, a wife, son, or daughter, a grandson, brother, or tío hermano, to respond to this type of favor, knowing full well that these individuals are most likely to carry out their wishes.

Compliance with a request to fulfill a vow is buttressed by a belief in the *alma en pena*, or wandering soul. Chignautecos believe that souls of individuals who have fulfilled their duties to kinsmen, their barrio, and the community and served the saints for the beneficence they received during their lives pass over the river separating the living from the departed, who watch over close kin left behind for several days after death. Individuals who lived improperly, however, will suffer an improper death. People may not be aware while the individual is alive, but impropriety is signaled just before, at the moment of, or shortly after death by strange occurrences attributed to the presence of the devil waiting to snatch the soul. Wandering souls of deceased kinsmen who wish to alleviate their suffering communicate their requests as apparitions or verbally in dreams. Or they might contact anyone to fulfill such a vow or carry out some form of vengeance in exchange for pointing to buried treasure. No one wishes to encounter a wandering soul, who may cause accidents or illness from severe fright.

A large percentage of requests for cargos result from inherited vows. These are referred to as *dejar dicho* from the manner in which they are contracted, that is, by an agreement whose contents are literally "left spoken." To receive an inheritance through the operation of dejar dicho is compelling. An individual is given a gift for which he or she owes a return whose nature has already been stipulated. This transaction is reciprocally organized, in the same manner that favors are believed to derive from the saints, who must be thanked adequately. In both cases, the indeterminate nature of transfer between the giver and the receiver, who is then obligated to give again, creates an unspecified sense of debt with a fear of loss that is expected to follow from failure to comply. Vows to the saints contracted through dejar dicho may take a person an entire lifetime to fulfill, long after the inheritance has been received. But the fact that they inevitably are fulfilled attests to the strength of the beliefs upon which this form of exchange rests. The incentive of receiving an inheritance in return for assuming the burdens of ritual sponsorship is supported by the operation of three constraints: fear of disapproval from the saints, who are believed to know if an individual holds back what is owed; the danger associated with encountering wandering souls; and the fear of the fate that befalls an individual who refuses to fulfill obligations in a relationship that is already sacralized. The close association in the minds of Chignautecos between good fortune and sacrifice guides the selection of men who sponsor cargos: a man should not offer what does not belong to him in reciprocation for the saints' good will, since this is believed to be coercive and dangerous. Accordingly, people do not sponsor cargos until the need arises. These sentiments are captured in the words of an informant:

> The old man didn't have enough time before he died so he left it spoken that the house would be inherited if the promise were fulfilled. Grandfathers and fathers always do this. They arrange many things for us because the majority leave some commitments pending when they die. They don't think to do it when they are young, but they remember when they are old. They came into this world and didn't do anything for God. It should have been done, but by then, they couldn't, so they leave their promises to us. When we have the fortune to earn a lot, this also has a meaning. One should, before anything else, give a mass to San Mateo or to Santo Entierro or Padre Jesús.

Inheriting vows has a number of important sociological consequences. First, dejar dicho must be viewed as a form of balanced exchange between significant kinsmen. Dejar dicho serves to maintain the generational integrity of the core of the descent group. Members of the nonresidential kin group are lineally tied to each other through descent and inheritance as makwis binds members collaterally to each other. These are the sacralizing ingredients that are explicit in formal ritual contexts. Dejar dicho also allows genealogical connection to generate choice in what cargos are sponsored, creating a pattern for cargo sponsorship that is solidified by its genealogical depth. Initiating dejar dicho guarantees that individuals who share membership in a descent group will continue to select sponsorships of a particular type and ritual value, ultimately resulting in an association between a characteristic mode of participation in the cult of the saints and a given patriline.

The Sacralizing Context of Compadrazgo

Compadrazgo in Chignautla is taken seriously. Individuals who enter ritual kinship are pursuing intentions at once pragmatic and sacred, personal and social. The events that initiate compadrazgo are symbol-laden and enhance the sacred meanings incorporated in these formalized relationships. The sacralizing significance of respect between compadres evokes both harmony and balance, core themes in the cosmology of these people. The sacrifices undertaken in becoming padrinos makes compadrazgo a sacralizing vehicle that intensifies but remains subordinate to kinship. Compadrazgo functions largely as a secondary source of material and social support. Chignautecos choose for compadres individuals known to them through ties of kinship, through cooperative activities in the barrio or in public life, or because they are compadres of kinsmen and have proved themselves worthy of this sacred bond. Individuals whose status is ritually or socioeconomically vastly discrepant will not be chosen as compadres, nor will individuals with whom there is a potential for conflict.

Compadrazgo is established contractually and requires a specific object or occasion for its initiation. The most important occasions for entering compadrazgo are overtly sacramental, but combine elements of formal Catholicism with indigenous practices without obliterating their distinctiveness in the experience of Chignautecos. That is, Chignautecos consciously recognize those aspects of the rituals initiating compadrazgo that pertain to the church and those of indigenous origin, even though they do not consciously recognize the syncretic basis of the complex as a whole. The xochitis, in its several variant forms, provides a means for fulfillment of sacred obligations without which this institution does not achieve its central purpose. The most intense expression of compadrazgo occurs in those types contracted around baptism, confirmation, and marriage. First communion has only recently been added to this list.[3]

Petitions to prospective padrinos are formally made by presentation of a chiquihuite de pedimento or informally by simply asking a favor. There is little chance of refusal; refusing a request to become a compadre is considered in very poor taste. Moreover, such refusals risk engendering supernatural disfavor similar to that which results from refusing to serve the saints when asked. This type of refusal conflicts with one of the main sacralizing goals of compadrazgo; that is, to contribute to making the world safe for existence by doing one's part to sustain harmony and balance between human and supernatural forces through respectful attitudes and conduct.

The ritual sponsors for baptism, confirmation, and marriage are asked to become compadres de fé, a relationship requiring the most elaborate ceremonial initiation. Once padrinos are petitioned, the amount of sacrifice they are willing to undertake signifies the strength of the bond that will be established, the quality of respect that is obligatory, the type of favors compadres will have the right to ask of each other, and what can be expected in terms of reliable assistance. These obligations are activated by rituals that, by themselves, have sacralizing implications.

The forms of compadrazgo present in Chignautla are relatively limited, which is not unexpected given the nature of kinship in this society, and may be grouped as either optative or obligatory. Obligatory forms are experienced by Chignautecos as necessary burdens that require a formal chiquihuite de pedimento and confer the right to ask and refuse favors, to extend ties of respect to others in the kin group of the compadres, and to demand the most elaborate form of xochitis. Limited to baptism, confirmation, and marriage, all of which strongly invoke sexual prohibitions, this form of compadrazgo contains a number of obligations: a meticulous avoidance of conflict, the use of formal terms of address, and large ceremonial expenses, which may be left pending to become available for inheritance by patrilineally related kin. The xochitis is essential to the ceremonial realization of these forms of compadrazgo and includes a ceremonial banquet, the exchange of xochikoskat and other items, the nacatzontet, and the xochipitzahuac, usually followed by a secular dance. Optative forms of compadrazgo carry less normative expectations, although certain types require Catholic sacramental rites that are generally not considered optional. For these, formal pedimentos are unnecessary and respect serves only as a behavioral ideal, making the bonds between these compadres available as a means of social enhancement. Choice in terms of address is again optional although formal terms are preferred. These types of compadrazgo rarely involve a xochitis and do not include the right to extend respect relationships to a wider range of individuals. Instead, a simple exchange of xochikoskat is followed by an elaborate meal. First communion remains an intermediary type of compadrazgo, involving an amalgamation of characteristics that have been added to what was once simply a matter of carrying out the duties of a Catholic rite. Today, however, first communion typically includes a xochitis with all its implications, even though it continues to be contracted without a chiquihuite.

Some of these forms of compadrazgo serve to intensify bonds between compadres that already exist and include specific obligations between compadres distinct from those used to initiate the relationship. Of these, baptism is the most important: the padrinos of the wedding serve as the baptismal godparents of at least the first three children of the couple for whose wedding they served as sponsors. This custom allows these individuals to move from a relationship that anticipates compadrazgo to its formal actualization. A wedding xochitis creates ties of ritual kinship between a large number of generationally related couples who share in the sponsorship of children. This insures obligatory respect between sets of compadres and consanguineal and affinal kinsmen who have relatively intensive contact and who will be able to offer reliable supportive assistance to each other. Through the xochitis, baptismal padrinos of the groom and the bride enter the highest grade of compadrazgo with the padrinos of the wedding, who then serve as the padrinos of baptism of the children of this couple. Thus, weddings ritually link generationally several sets of parents and children. It is also believed in Chignautla that a couple chosen to be padrinos of confirmation of one's child may fulfill the same ritualistic functions as those chosen to be baptism padrinos if necessary, and are often the same individuals for the first three children a couple have, so that they assume multiple roles in the lives of their compadres.

Not surprisingly, intensification of established compadrazgo continues around the duties that padrinos of baptism and padrinos of confirmation assume, if they are different, for the wake of a deceased compadre. Ideally, two sets of compadres are required, but the funeral masses that would become their obligation are not customary except for individuals of public renown. Invariably, compadres are obliged to purchase funerary candles and provide a series of crosses, one cross for the ninth day of the *velorio* or wake that begins after death, one for a wake held on the eightieth day after the funeral, and a third for a velorio held at the end of the first year. These individuals must also buy a cross of wood or metal for the cemetery to mark the completion of each year for three consecutive years. At the end of this period, a cross or an image of a saint is purchased and placed on the household altar of the deceased in his or her memory.

In a wake, the body lies wrapped in a shroud before the household altar. Out of respect, compadres are not asked to wash the body. If the compadres have not carried out a cumplimiento they will place the xochikoskat around the neck of the deceased or around the coffin, a gesture signifying completion of obligations (but without a xochipitzahuac, since dancing is prohibited in the presence of the dead). This act entitles these compadres to put on emblems of mourning, a right reserved for compadres who have participated in a cumplimiento. Once the coffin has been buried, a *zempoalxochit,* marigolds arranged in the form of a cross, takes its place before the household altar. A zempoalxochit is reconstructed for the wake of eighty days and for the end-of-the-year ceremony. The compadres are obligated to offer the formal *despedida* or farewell speeches in Nahuat to the deceased. On each of these occasions there is reference to the symbolic cumplimiento represented in the xochikoskat given to the deceased. At the last velorio, the armbands and ribbons of mourning are ceremoniously removed by the compadres from each other and from the parientes of the deceased, who were invited to assist in the funeral as in a xochitis.

Velorios occupy most of the day and night, during which several special meals and breakfasts are served, specialists are paid to chant prayers and mourning songs, and specific games are played during the long vigils. I recorded seven games played during wakes in Chignautla. Of these, two were overtly sexual in nature and were played only by men. All involved, to one degree or another, the hitting and humiliation of one player who is punished for not knowing the answer and therefore the rules of the game. This is behavior extraordinary for Chignauteco culture and the humor involved is quite different from the humor used by the Pilatos during the celebrations of San Mateo. I agree with Bricker (1973) that humor, especially expressed in these games, is a type of abstract moralizing. Funeral games create a context in which joking, hitting, or humiliating takes place between individuals whose relationships demand formal respect and appropriate distance. I also believe that a velorio, a component event within a funeral, is a transitional moment in space and time: expectable patterned behavior is interrupted only to be reinforced metaphorically in the games that are played. This contrasts markedly with the highly regulated activity of the entirety of the funeral itself and the explicit enactment of rights and duties activated by a death. Funerals are expensive, and the nonresidential kin group supplies some portion of the labor and goods while neighbors contribute a few kilos of corn and money to lighten the burden. Funeral obligations between compadres provide a means to do God's will, a saying also associated with the agradecimiento offered to those who assist in ritual sponsorship celebrations held in honor of the saints.

Unlike the significance of ties between compadres activated for a funeral, less significant forms of compadrazgo occur around occasions that celebrate joyful events through which friendship or a kin tie may also be celebrated by granting the relationship a quality of respect. It is customary to bless a new house or store with the purchase and raising of a cross on top of or beside the house. Padrinos are chosen to purchase the cross. A celebratory meal will be given them, which may involve an exchange of xochikoskat between the principal actors to demonstrate a respectful agradecimiento. Purchase of a truck or any new object of importance also provides an occasion for initiation of this form of compadrazgo. The padrino sponsors a blessing by the priest and perhaps some decorative item for the truck, after

These three Santiagos affirm Nahuat identity by metaphor in their ritual dances.

The bravado shown by this dancer underscores the social commentary made by the Pilato.

Under a shower of flower petals, two saints' images bow in greeting amid a crowd of Easter celebrants.

The ritual dancers enact history from the Chignauteco point of view.

The main characters of the Tocotines. *Left to right:* Malintzi la chica, Cortés, Cortés el chico, Moctezuma, and Moctezuma el chico.

A barrio shrine adorned with an arco de lujo for celebration of the barrio's patron saint.

The ornate façade of the church reflects the influence of the Franciscans, who also left their mark on the ritual dances performed in Chignautla.

Seen against the skirts of Mount Chignautla, the dance of the Paxtes in the church atrium celebrates what nature provides.

Behind the standard held by Cortés of the Tocotines, San Mateo 21 is carried high for the procession held in his honor.

The mayordoma and her acompañamiento await the arrival of the cofradía during the mayordomía for the Virgen de Guadalupe. The capilla of Coahuixco is in the background.

The fiscal primero, his wife, and his granddaughter by the entrance to the
central dwelling of their house compound.

The Spanish grid pattern is clearly visible in this view of the Centro of Chignautla.

Women of the household and those who come to help in preparation for the ceremonial banquet of a mayordomía.

A procession dancing toward the household of the mayordomo.
The Guacamayas and Negritos are visible.

Against the backdrop of Mount Chignautla, five saints are marched in
procession during the pageantry of Semana Santa.

Prayers are offered for the deceased before the household altar to conclude a year of mourning.

The special rocketry of the toros on display in front of the municipal palace.

Waiting to begin the xochipitzahuac to initiate compadrazgo.

Two crosses of marigolds before the household altar during a wake.

An Indian family.

Specialists preparing cacalas for a xochitis.

A ceremonial banquet in fulfillment of the obligations of compadrazgo.

The large quantity of corn to be consumed in the culminating event of the mayordomía for the Virgen de Guadalupe.

The embrace following the exchange of xochikoskat between individuals who will forever be compadres de fé.

Labrado de la cera in the house of the mayordomo.

The cofradía being served aguardiente by the diputado mayor as prelude to the ceremonial banquet of a mayordomía.

Procession of the twelve apostles during Semana Santa.

Reverence is shown the demandita as it is carried by the fiscales from the church to the house of the mayordomo.

A masked Santiago in procession en route to the house of the mayordomo.

Devotion to one of four images of San Mateo, here adorned with xochikoskat, is a heavy burden.

which a celebratory meal and exchange of xochikoskat is given in return. A birthday or saint's day may be utilized similarly, but involves a three-year commitment by the padrino during which he hires musicians to play early in the morning of the saint's day at the house of his compadre, who will offer those attending a simple meal in reciprocation. The third year, the padrino purchases a small image of a saint for his compadre's household altar followed by a meal for immediate kinsmen of both parties, accompanied by an exchange of xochikoskat.

Minor forms of compadrazgo utilize the occasion of purchasing a small image of a saint in celebration of a particular devotion, for curing illness, or for the bedding of an image of the Infant Jesus at Christmas entered by two adolescent girls who then become *comadres,* alternating in the role of madrina for three consecutive years. Forms borrowed from the Mestizos that are still relatively rare among the Indians are those surrounding a graduation from primary school or a celebration of a fifteenth birthday for adolescent girls. These celebrations provide entertainment and creative expression without initiating formal ties of compadrazgo since the exaggerated respect maintained during the fiesta will fade rapidly.

Non-Catholic rituals associated with compadrazgo contain a number of significant activities, nearly all of which are expensive, requiring large quantities of goods and labor that can be equally held in reserve for a mayordomía sponsorship planned for the future. However, while a mayordomía banquet cannot be delayed beyond the feast day of the saint, a cumplimiento is typically delayed for many years. Acceptance of sponsorship is binding once promised, although the date of a xochitis remains the right of the padrinos. The cumplimiento for a baptism, for example, is not necessarily held coterminously with the rites of the church. For the church ceremony, the padrinos must dress the child and provide whatever else pertains to the Catholic rite such as compensating the priest for the mass and offering small change to those who attend the formal baptism. There is a tendency to wait until three children are born to the couple whose wedding was sponsored so that the padrinos will have to provide only one cumplimiento. This is also true for confirmation and first communion when several children will be sponsored. Such decisions depend upon the resources available and the respect they have for those from whom they have asked this favor.

For confirmation and first communion, the child or children must be dressed and given the appropriate ritual objects: candles, rosaries, and prayer books. After the rites of the church are completed, the padrinos return to the house of the child's parents, their arrival announced by a small number of

rockets fired in the street. After a ceremonial greeting and serving of cigarettes and aguardiente, the principal actors exchange xochikoskat. The exchange of xochikoskat always occurs in the same manner: from padrino to
compadre, madrina to comadre, padrino to comadre, madrina to compadre,
and so on, extending to ascending generations of kinsmen and to brothers of
the compadres and their spouses, all of whom then dance the xochipitzahuac.
As already noted, the xochipitzahuac is danced in parallel lines after the
xochikoskat have been placed around the necks of participants. Participants
stand in order of ritual importance, beginning with the principal actors, who
are positioned next to the household altar. In descending order of ritual
importance stand the compadres, the parents of the padrinos and compadres,
then down the line of the patrilineal kinsmen of the husbands and their
spouses and possibly a series of the brothers and spouses of the madrina and
comadre. The padrinos and those who accompany them represent *los que
vienen,* those who come as sponsors of this event. This group of related
individuals is faced by members of the household of the compadres who are
referred to as *los que esperan,* those who wait for the padrinos.

If the ritual exchanges terminate in a xochipitzahuac, this event will be
considered a *taxochiwal,* an intermediary xochitis creating compadrazgo but
leaving certain obligations for a cumplimiento to be held at a later date. In a
taxochiwal, the xochipitzahuac is followed by a simplified ceremonial banquet given to those who come by those who wait. This event begins with a
formal presentation of the nacatzontet, in this case, half of a cooked chicken
for each godchild, one given to the padrino and one to the madrina. The
meal consists of colored rice followed by mole, and much drinking all
around. If part of the ceremonial obligations remains incomplete, the principal actors consider themselves to be compadres and must act accordingly,
but leave the date for the final cumplimiento up to the padrinos. This is a
mere shadow of the xochitis that represents a cumplimiento, which is called
a *hueyxochit,* or great xochitis, and may be years in coming.

A cumplimiento is experienced as an interpersonal and sacred (personal-
supernatural) obligation. Its sponsorship is associated with the moral character of the couple. A couple who has had some measure of success in life is
likely to contract hundreds of compadres during adulthood, even though the
majority of couples who reach middle age have not yet cosponsored a
hueyxochit, which may remain pending when they die. However, while the
relationships between compadres who have completed their obligations and
those who have not do not differ markedly in the quality of respect maintained between them, there are some experiential distinctions. The level of

confianza and the formality of respect will be tempered by a deep sense of caring and intimacy, making compadres who have cosponsored a hueyxochit more likely to expect and rely upon an enduring pattern of interchange of favors and support. It is these comparatively few compadres from within a potentially larger network of ritual kinsmen who appear to act toward each other in much the same manner as close parientes carnales do. These compadres are invariably invited to help at ceremonial events of the life cycle and the mayordomía complex.

Above the level of behavioral conformity, the implicit rather than explicit distinction between compadres who have or have not cosponsored a hueyxochit reveals differences in levels of compliance with ideals of conduct, since the beliefs surrounding them are never uniformly translated into behavior. In this case, the respect that evokes harmony and the reciprocal exchanges that evoke balance imply a fundamental importance given to compadrazgo that regulates this behavioral complex. The difference, however, in choice of cumplimiento is not unlike the ritual value that underlies the different conceptual groupings of ritual sponsorships dedicated to public veneration of the saints. Central and unifying ideological and cosmological themes are shared with compadrazgo and may be interpreted in the following way: the greater the gift, the greater the sacrifice, the more binding the commitment becomes, leading to an assignment of greater ritual significance that is confirmed in the exchanges that reinforce the enduring character of relationships regulated by obligatory respect.

The hueyxochit begins similarly to a taxochiwal but many more rockets are fired. The godchild or godchildren are dressed once again and a special type of large basket, the *canastilla,* containing bread, meat, sugar, chocolate, coffee, soap, and candles is given. It is this second gift of clothes and goods that allows the terms *xochitis, canastilla,* and *cumplimiento* to be used interchangeably in reference to this event. An exchange of four xochikoskat per godchild per compadre follows. Xochikoskat may be given to whomever the padrinos wish, allowing these individuals to further extend ties of respect to tios hermanos, primos hermanos, and their wives. Such extensions may include all other parientes and compadres who have been invited to help even though they do not dance the xochipitzahuac. The placement of xochikoskat in their hands makes this group of individuals *compadres lejanos* or simply distant compadres. It is considered appropriate to maintain respect for a compadre lejano because of the respect maintained with the intermediary compadres. If people chosen to be compadres reside in the same barrio, which is often the case, those living in a barrio develop multiple relational ties with each other, all of which are regulated by the sacred, contractual bases upon which compadrazgo rests.

The nacatzontet, which evokes bonds of respect and expectations of reciprocity between the giver and receiver, is far more elaborate in the hueyxochit. The nacatzontet consists of a pair of live turkeys per godchild, each representing the padrino and madrina, offered as an agradecimiento whose explicit purpose is to defray the burden of sponsorship. Symbolically, this exchange brings into balance the differential costs obligatory for these compadres. Food for the ceremonial banquet of the hueyxochit is special and brandy supplements the customary aguardiente. The xochikoskat may be more elegantly made of expensive bread and flowers set between orange leaves. A secular dance with a large band may conclude what is by now an extremely expensive affair, costing up to five thousand pesos or more for one godchild. If one of the parents or spouses of the compadres is deceased, a candle will be wrapped in a xochikoskat to represent the individual's presence in the xochipitzahuac. In the meal, the padrino and madrina are given the usual half of a cooked chicken per godchild and a cooked shoulder of pork set on a bed of rice with unusually large breads to accompany xole made expressly for this occasion. The live turkeys will be adorned with xochikoskat before being ceremoniously presented to the padrinos. The xochipitzahuac will commence afterward and is danced twice for each godchild for whom the event is held.

The xochipitzahuac is replete with symbolic statements that express more immediate cosmological themes. Those who wait for and upon their padrinos are requesting that a sacrifice be made for them, and on behalf of their children. The xochipitzahuac is one expression of an exchange in which individuals give and receive, only to give and obligate a response once again. Compadres bestow honor and respect upon the padrinos in this event of agradecimiento. In the xochipitzahuac, givers and receivers dance together in a harmonious fashion, balancing the burdens of sacrifice with respect and gifts. An aspect of balance is also achieved by empowering the padrinos with the right to extend their ties of compadrazgo to other individuals related to their compadres, but a compadre also has a right to refuse.

Chignautecos do not consciously conceptualize these relationships in terms of obligations (what must be done), but rather in terms of rights (what should be done, because it can be done), since binding obligations only pertain to parientes carnales. It is in this sense that compadrazgo implies options that kinship does not, especially options regarding who will be asked to be a compadre.[4] Informants state that it is very common for a hueyxochit to celebrate at least three but not more than five godchildren, since this would involve an offering of five pairs of turkeys and an exchange of twenty xochikoskat per bond. The exchange of xochikoskat defines and activates specific attitudes of a sacred nature and is one of the central acts in a xochitis. The xochitis and exchange of xochikoskat occur in a variety of sacralizing contexts in this culture. Each gives shadings to its intrinsic meaning as an agradecimiento that regulates behavior by establishing relationships of respect. Individuals who have exchanged xochikoskat greet each other in the street in formalized ways that acknowledge respect, such as bowing slightly and inquiring politely as to the other's health. Xochikoskat will be placed around the neck of the image of San Mateo during the mayordomias held in his honor. They will be exchanged between the fiscales and Tocotines, between the dancers and their encargados, and between Pilatos mayores and menores. Among these ritual performers, discrepant ritual ranks and positions in the system are sacralized to ensure harmonious relations.

In sum, the sacralizing context of compadrazgo, like the ritual contexts of cargo sponsorship, sacralize interpersonal relations. As the patterns of life change and the latent meanings in many of these events become desacralized, compadrazgo will also change in its structural design. Compadres will be chosen less frequently from among those who are comfortably alike than from among those who might contribute to social enhancement in a society diversified by wealth, levels of sophistication, and dedication to national culture.

Chapter 5

The Design of Ritual Sponsorship

The composite events of the mayordomía embody collective aims that imply a fundamental truth about the balance that must be maintained between favors given and received. In the performance of these rituals, routinely accepted facts of life are available for affective elaboration. When a man plants his milpa or fixes his house, or when a woman makes tortillas to feed her family, these activities do not immediately call attention to human dependence on the saints. But within the context of the mayordomía, such labors take on great significance because their meaning and instrumentality is transformed and made sacred.

Mayordomias are very important to Chignautecos. They are direct venerative statements that serve a propitiatory purpose. Ritual occasions demand strict adherence to ideals of conduct as dictated by belief. Part of the potency of the composite events of the mayordomía derives from the evocation of sacred themes that otherwise recede to the background of concern. The mayordomía is a sacrifice enacted by the mayordomo through his vow to serve a specific saint in the celebration he sponsors, a sacrifice that is acknowledged by the people in the respect shown the mayordomo and his acompañamiento. Mayordomias also bring the significance of rank to the center of attention. Motivated by a sense of indebtedness, the mayordomo reciprocates the favors rendered him by the saints as he would a kinsman from whom he has received assistance or from whom he expects to receive an inheritance. Chignautecos do not assume the burdens of sponsorship simply because they are taught by custom to venerate the saints in this manner. Rather, as individuals, they are compelled to make their sacrifice to the saints so that the good turns received from the saints will continue, only to necessitate a sponsorship once again. These activities share an inclusive ideological foundation that, as long as the system of belief to which it refers remains sacred, denotes and intensifies the values basic to Chignauteco social life.

Mayordomía sponsors assume a sacred trust and are expected to carry out the duties of their cargo with meticulous care, passing through the taxing sequence of events that constitutes a mayordomía as if it were nothing. Mayordomía sponsorship activates rights to request and receive contributions in labor and goods from a network of individuals to whom the mayordomo is related in clearly defined ways. Mayordomias activate the cofradía. The mayordomo offers a celebratory banquet to the cofradía so that the saints will feel celebrated. The structural design of the mayordomía is a microcosm not only of the cult of the saints as a whole, but of the fundamental truths articulated throughout the domains of this society.

Inclusive and Exclusive Sacralizing Contexts

The immediate directives to action presented in the introduction encapsulate what is formulated more precisely in injunctions that regulate ritual performance. These directives specify what is required of the ritual sponsor for the saints to appreciate a sacrifice. In summary form, saints must be approached properly through processions, ceremonial banquets, prayers, masses, and offerings made to individuals who assist the sponsor and to those who represent the saints by their sacred offices. All forms of ritual sponsorship, regardless of the context for their occurrence, share the same aims and means and utilize ritual paraphernalia whose symbolic and socioreligious significance either latently or explicitly expresses core assumptions. Activities become sacred when they are distinguished by formalized expressions of giving and receiving, offerings of special foods in exaggerated portions that express appreciation and respect, stylized greetings that overstate welcome, speeches that elevate the importance of humility, and processions that insist on distinctions in rank. These acts are set apart by abandoning daily tasks to the firing of rockets, the burning of candles and incense, the adorning of rooms and paths with pine needles and flower petals, and the above-average consumption of aguardiente and cigarettes. The occurrence of these markers denotes a sacred time, movement, and space. What they express relates diverse aspects of experience to one another on the basis of a single generalized pattern according to a logical design, allowing those not directly participating to become aware that crucial rites are being carried out for them.

Despite interference from various parish priests, mayordomias continue to be performed regularly in Chignautla. Not a week goes by without the church bells ringing for a mayordomía mass or without the firing of rockets to indicate what manner of event the bells are announcing. For mayordomias, the bells are rung in a distinctive fashion and the rockets used are of a special type. While Chignautecos maintain that mayordomias concern the entire community as presented by the sponsor to God and the saints, they do not themselves need to witness these rites. The majority of collective activities of a mayordomía occur at specific locations outside of public view and among discrete groups of individuals. The mass sponsored by the mayordomo, of course, is open to all who wish to come, as are the processions that follow in the atrium. Chignautecos distinguish between celebratory activities held in the name of the community and those held in the name of a saint for the community.

The personnel needed to achieve the purpose of a ritual event constitutes the acompañamiento of the central actors. The acompañamientos of significance are the juxtaposed groupings of those who come to the house and those who wait at the house to greet them. The reciprocal transactions of the personnel who form these acompañamientos fulfill the sacralizing purpose of a ritual sponsorship, whether for a godchild or for a saint. Structurally opposed in this manner, each acompañamiento engages the other in an enactment of rights and obligations. Giving and receiving in a ritual context demonstrate the place of reciprocity and rank as organizing properties in this system, and of respect and sacrifice as encoded ideals. In Chignautla, one does not simply attend a ritual event, and unfavorable gossip follows an individual who enters the compound of the mayordomo without rightfully being there. Such persons will be suspected of attempting to get without having first given. Those invited to attend are given this right when their assistance is petitioned in a manner befitting their relationship to and with a participant. Some petitions require formal pedimentos, while others do not. The juxtaposition of those who come to a house to enact their sacred intentions and those who wait for them to confirm these intentions is a sacralizing process.

All propitiatory acts with collective aims occur within the context of the duties of formally appointed cargo holders, and all ritual events occur within a circumscribed domain. The most exclusive contexts for propitiatory enactments take place within the individual household for compadrazgo, velorios, and Todos Santos and involve the immediate network of kin, ritual kin, and neighbors of the central actors. On the other extreme, the mayordomias of San Mateo and Corpus Christi draw large crowds and visitors from nearby communities who enjoy the festivities. Between these extremes are events such as the mayordomía for the Niño Dios. No longer guided by tradition, all Chignautecos may attend some of the events at the house of the mayordomo who may be either Indian or Mestizo.

I have categorized barrio celebrations into two types. These events either replicate an altepeihuit, as do the celebrations for the Holy Cross, or they replicate a mayordomía. Barrio celebrations have retained much of the structure of the early cofradias. Under the direction of a mayordomo who bears the majority of expenses, barrio residents corporately sponsor events held in honor of their patron saint or in honor of an image housed in a barrio shrine. For the Holy Cross in May, wealthier barrios now hold horse races and other recreational activities along the barrio's main street. These are well attended by young men and women who take advantage of the situation for courting. In barrio celebrations resembling a mayordomía, the site is adorned with an *arco de lujo,* an arch made of wood adorned with dried hearts of palm woven into an elaborate design. Prayers are recited and a celebratory meal is offered as an agradecimiento by the mayordomo to those who contributed goods and labor. Depending upon the size and wealth of the barrio or the ability of the mayordomo, these events may cost from 500 to 2,000 pesos and may include rockets and music. Arcos de lujo mark sacred sites. They are used to adorn the portal of the parish church for important mayordomias and invariably will be placed on the portals of the chapels in Tepepan and Coahuixco. Once erected, arcos de lujo remain until the palm disintegrates, indicating to all who pass propitiatory rites that have occurred or will occur.

The proliferation of ritual forms is, I believe, an evolutionary process not unlike the developmental cycle of the residential extended family or the formation of new barrios from lugares as discussed in chapter 1. Barrio fiestas were increasing in number and size in the 1970s and have continued to increase in number and complexity, but under the direction of a chosen committee or a mayordomo rather than a mayordomo de pila, a position whose function will become extinct when all barrios develop systems for potable water. Population increase, availability of wage labor, and increased wealth in the absence of a concurrent increase in the number of available formal cargo appointments is partially resolved by augmenting the range of sponsorships available without altering their central purpose. On the one hand, the more circumscribed the ritual context, the more likely it is that a ritual event will include elements of national culture and will, by definition, conform more closely to Mestizo practice. On the other hand, the more public an event is, the more it will include elements of public entertainment and will bear the earmark of a secularized religious fiesta, as does the alte-peihuit today in Chignautla. It is also noteworthy that the focus of an alte-peihuit is toward the world beyond the community, whereas the focus of other celebratory events is limited to the community itself regardless of overtly secular events appended to a ritual occasion.

It has been estimated that ceremonial events occupy approximately one-third of the year in this type of community (Reina 1967), an estimate that would be correct for Chignautla if we were to include only the culminating events of mayordomias, i.e., the mass and procession followed by the ceremonial banquet in the house of the mayordomo. Each image housed in the church and chapels of the barrios requires a day of celebration. A number of images are duplicated. To accommodate these conditions, certain mayordomias are not held on the appropriate Catholic feast date. The priest must also be willing to officiate at events requiring a mass.[1] There is also a wide range of activities pertaining to sponsorship that require many more days of preparation. Thus, it is not incorrect to say that some form of ritual event occurs almost daily in Chignautla. Even for minor mayordomias, component activities are spread over the year from the day of formal appointment to the moment the cargo is formally relinquished. Viewed in their entirety, the activities of sponsorship can be realized within a two-month period for the mayordomias menores, or they span an entire year's time for the fiscales, mayordomos mensajeros, their diputados, and the mayordomos of San Mateo.

The cost of a mayordomía mass is higher than any other individually sponsored mass. To the Indians, such expenses are an imposition on their sacred purpose and create a false and irrelevant distinction between cargos based on expense. It is equally significant that while the mass is integral to the mayordomía, this Catholic rite is far more central in the mind of the priest than it is in the minds of the Indians—reflected by generally poor attendance at Sunday mass. For Chignautecos, the mayordomias of San Mateo provide a welcome opportunity for recreation, socializing, and gossip among the crowds that fill the Centro. This is not unusual in a folk religion, nor is it antithetical to the sacred premise of the mayordomía. Only the mayordomos and their immediate families suffer the burden of responsibility for the management of complex and highly specific events; only the Pilatos' stylized antics relieve the tension of constant dancing, masses, processions, and ritual drinking. One does not see, however, the abandon that at times characterizes the fiestas reported elsewhere (see especially Brandes 1988). Mayordomias offer the opportunity to share information, and it is at major celebrations that prospective sponsors communicate to men currently holding cargos their desires for particular mayordomias or their intentions not to serve in the future.

The Sacralizing Context of the Traditional Mayordomía

Venerative activities dedicated to the saints are always set apart from the routine of daily life. Not all religious practices equally demand the rigid adherence to form characteristic of the mayordomía. Idiosyncratic interpretation of religious belief and individual preference in the practice of certain rituals does occur, as we have seen for the xochitis in compadrazgo. Personal choice responsive to practical contingencies may alter the order and elaboration of the component structural elements of the mayordomía, but little will be added or deleted that would alter the traditional configuration and undermine its purpose. Nor would such additions or deletions be condoned by others. The structure of the mayordomía remains clearly delineated and mayordomias are managed with great care with reference to standards dictated by custom. The mode of performance of the mayordomía becomes the benchmark of tradition testifying to the continuity of Chignauteco ideology within the organization of individual experience.

Organizational Principles of the Mayordomía

There is a ritual order that determines how people walk in relation to each other in processions, how they will be seated, how they must greet each other, and how food, alcoholic beverages, and cigarettes will be served. The food prepared for ceremonial banquets is designated by tradition rather than according to what is favored or readily available, since all that is consumed has a sacred purpose and meaning. There are no proscriptions regarding what is worn, but ritual sponsors and their company attempt to present themselves in clothes that express humility rather than elegance. Presenting oneself in a conspicuous manner is seen as prideful, an attitude incompatible with sacred aims.[2] The formality with which individuals address each other and what they can or cannot say expresses a well-established ritual etiquette. Low tones of voice, serious facial expressions, and bowing gestures are overdetermined. These are intended to communicate respect and activate rights and duties necessary to the activities of sacralizing contexts.

In the myriad obligations ritual actors have toward each other, respect, rank, and exchanges are performed in a balanced order. What become consciously held rules of conduct must be taught to entering ritual actors, even though when they are children they unconsciously absorbed this form of behavior accompanying their parents to these events. Breeches do occur and are always interpreted as a lack of respect. If, for example, the dancers are kept waiting too long to be fed at the house of the mayordomo, or the members of the cofradía are not invited in the appropriate manner or in the proper sequence, the ritual order will be disturbed. If the mayordomo has failed to manage his affairs and cannot offer the nacatzontet to the top-ranking members of the cofradía, the purpose of the mayordomía will not be achieved for himself or for the community. When these breeches occur, they must be acknowledged. The mayordomo will go as quickly as possible to the fiscales with a bottle of aguardiente and cigarettes or even a chiquihuite to accompany his petition for pardon. Once pardoned, the breech must be corrected as soon as possible.

The composite of events necessary to a mayordomía demonstrates the operation of organizational principles whose ideological-structural convergence makes this form of ritual expression the most significant vehicle for the sacralization of interpersonal relations, intensifying beliefs and affirming assumptions regarding the role the saints have in the lives of these Indians. Indeed, the purpose of the mayordomía is to state in a variety of ways that which is already subjectively true in the experience of Chignautecos. As we have seen, the mayordomía is incomplete without the cofradía, whose members form the acompañamiento of the fiscales, the highest ranking officers of the Autoridad Eclesiástica, the body of cargo holders ultimately responsible for relations with the saints among the entire array of ritual sponsors. The acompañamiento of the mayordomo waits in his house to greet the acompañamiento of the fiscales in such a manner as to demonstrate respect for their ritual rank. Those who accompany the fiscales show their respect for the mayordomo by their participation in the cofradía, and in doing so share in the sacrifice of the mayordomo. Further symbolic acts evoking balance and harmony can be observed in the disposition of the food required for a mayordomía or any other ritual event in this cultural system. Food in proportions appropriate to ritual rank must be given and must be received, whether or not it is eaten during the event. It is for this reason that guests invariably eat only a token amount of what is served at a ceremonial banquet. Women bring jars with them in which they carry home what was respectfully given and respectfully received. These patterns are replicated throughout the events of a mayordomía and highlight the interplay of ideology and structure.

The Composite Events of the Mayordomía

A mayordomía consists of a structural sequence of fifteen distinct events. This sequential arrangement is not consciously noted by Chignautecos. Each event is experienced as a moment in time wherein a sacred duty is carried out. These duties require specific preparations, personnel, and paraphernalia organized by specific beliefs about what must be accomplished and what should not be done. When an event concludes, participants are relieved, unaware of what connects these events to each other as constituent elements of a mayordomía. When Chignautecos refer to a mayordomía, they are most often making reference to the purpose and duties of sponsorship and the associated expectation of continued supernatural favor. In effect, any one event may stand for the mayordomía as a whole, explaining why in everyday speech one may hear the terms *misa* (mass), *comida* (significant meal), *promesa, mayordomía, sacrificio,* and *compromiso* (in this sense obligation) used interchangeably.

The mayordomos, their diputados, the diputados mensajeros, and the sacristanes work together with the fiscales to ensure that appropriate respect and humble obedience characterizes interaction between individuals in situations that by nature engender stress. The more demanding a cargo, the greater the subjective potency of the symbols incorporated within it. All duties of sponsorship of a mayordomía require the presence of the mayordomo, the mayordoma, the diputado mayor and diputada mayor, and other members of the mayordomo's acompañamiento. A mayordomo may on some occasions allow his father, a brother, a son, or a tío hermano to take his place. Each of the composite events of a mayordomía is a sacralizing context. What becomes paramount throughout is the interdependence among ritual performers and the complementarity of their positions as they enact necessary exchanges that evoke important cultural themes. The central activities of a mayordomía include initiating and terminating events, as do all intermediating ceremonies that form components of the mayordomía as a whole. Initiating and terminating events structurally replicate each other. Replication insures continuity of experience and coherence in the meaning behind giving and receiving and demonstrates the circularity of reciprocal engagements. Ultimately, the mayordomía serves to integrate individual and collective aims so that Chignautecos can safely anticipate the goals of their venerative actions.

What follows is a description and analysis of the mayordomía, a chain of events to which Chignautecos refer when they use this term.

1. The *nombramiento* or formal appointment to the cargo is an initiating event. Appointments to cargos are ritually and socially binding and are noted in the book of the fiscales, in which records of all transactions by the mayordomos are kept. For the individual requesting a sponsorship, a pedimento must be made to the fiscales in the fiscalía. A bottle of aguardiente and several packs of cigarettes are offered to the fiscales as an acknowledgment of their rank and as a gesture of return for the favor about to be asked. A man who wishes to serve the saints does not approach the fiscales alone.

Accompanied by his wife and a senior kinsman of the highest ritual rank possible, the prospective sponsor will approach the fiscales on any occasion when they are available in the fiscalía. Bowing and offering salutations, the prospective mayordomo presents the chiquihuite of aguardiente and cigarettes and states his request after briefly commenting on the weather and the milpa. The fiscales respond to the request by emphasizing the seriousness of such a venture and by questioning the petitioner about his plans for meeting the obligations of the cargo. The fiscales do not give their answer during the first pedimento, and a prospective sponsor will usually make two more pedimentos before receiving the nombramiento to confirm the appointment, which arrives in the form of a letter signed by the fiscales and carried to the house of the candidate by a sacristán or diputado mensajero. The attitude with which the petitioner conducts himself in the pedimento offers the fiscales an opportunity to determine whether or not the petitioner will be capable of serving the saints appropriately. The fiscales already know a great deal about the man's situation and the history of service to the saints in his patriline. If his request is based on dejar dicho, the fiscales need a powerful excuse not to consider his request seriously.

Formal notification of appointment to a cargo may arrive without warning, reminding and admonishing the individual to comply with his sacred duty for his own benefit and for the welfare of the community. Whether or not plans have been made to accept the cargo, appointees must present themselves to the fiscales within three weeks to give an answer, offering a bottle of aquardiente and cigarettes as an agradecimiento. In the past, refusing an appointment to a sponsorship was very difficult. Today, it is not so startling when appointments are returned by a child, even though this demeans the authority of the fiscales and indicates a weakening of fears that traditionally generated compliance. By this I mean that experience over the last decades has not consistently validated the expectations that were based on the association of supernatural punishment with lack of respect for men of high ritual rank. Assuming the burdens of a cargo for which one is chosen by the fiscales makes it more difficult to sponsor a desired cargo at some time in the future. Refusals must be justified by acceptable reasons, and if they are accepted, the fiscales are forced to secure another sponsor. The longer this takes, the greater the pressure on the fiscales to make a selection and on the individual they finally convince to accept the cargo. At times mayordomias remain unsponsored. This is not common, but a combination of the right circumstances will result in a cargo vacancy. The more important the mayordomía, the more difficult it will be to accept on short notice and the more anxious the new sponsor will become over the requirements of sponsorship. In all cases, a vacant cargo generates fear in proportion to the ritual value of the cargo and sometimes desperate choices are made in the selection of a sponsor that would not be made under normal circumstances.

2. The pedimento of the diputado mayor is the first official act of the mayordomo. Once a mayordomo is named by the fiscales, he will make a decision regarding a diputado mayor in consultation with his wife. A diputado mayor must be selected with care. Mayordomias menores may not necessitate such assistance whereas the mayordomos of the Santísimo Sacramento absolutely must have their diputados mayores. Diputados mayores are usually chosen from among individuals who are known to be of good reputation; they are rarely kinsmen or compadres, but they must be able to work cooperatively with the close kinsmen of the mayordomo. Other factors are also considered. A man with many mature brothers may not wish the assistance of a diputado mayor because his brothers will offer adequate and reliable assistance. There is a preference for choosing diputados mayores from within the barrio, but this may not be possible, and a selection will be made from an adjacent barrio. A diputado mayor must be a household head who is financially able to make this sacrifice at the time he is asked and whose occupation allows him to remain in the municipio. He must not hold a ritual rank as a pasado incompatible with the ritual value of the mayordomía in question or with the status of diputado mayor. No man will become a diputado mayor if doing so interferes with his plans for future sponsorships even though such plans may be facilitated by the respect he earns and the support he can rely on from his mayordomo when he requests a cargo for himself.

Soliciting a diputado mayor necessitates a formal pedimento of cigarettes and aguardiente and the presentation of a chiquihuite containing bread, chocolate, coffee, meat, sugar, and salt. Once the chiquihuite is accepted, the contract is binding, and the favor requested is partially reciprocated. Within a week, the mayordomo and his diputado confirm his selection with the fiscales, since no individual can serve the saints without their approval. The mayordoma invites the diputada to her house so that she will become accustomed to the mayordoma's kitchen and will be better able to direct others who come to help. This invitation activates the diputada's right to attend to the ritual personnel who will come to the mayordomo's house during the ritual events of the mayordomía. The mayordomo and diputado, in consultation with their wives, arrange the date of the recibimiento to transfer the demandita and other property of the image from the house of the outgoing mayordomo to their house.

Within the next several months, the diputados menores will be selected. Formal pedimentos without a chiquihuite are made to those individuals from among compadres and neighbors who are invited to assist in the mayordomía. Usually thirty or more agree to contribute one or two kilos of wax, to take the place of the mayordomo in faenas called by the fiscales, and to assist in adorning the mayordomo's house and church. Sponsors rely primarily on the dependable assistance of others with whom makwis makepis obtains. Compadres de fé also contribute, for it is their right to involve themselves in these ceremonial activities. More often than not, they feel obliged to respect their compadres' wishes, making their participation both a right and an obligation. The performance of a mayordomía intensifies the implications of balance and harmony, whose efficacy can be seen throughout its composite events and in its regulatory effect on relations structured differently between the individual *and* the group, between the individuals *in* the group, and between the individuals *of* the group.

3. The *recibimiento,* or transfer of the sponsorship and its belongings from the outgoing to the incoming sponsor, is the first formally constituted event of a mayordomía. The recibimiento necessitates participation of individuals of differing ritual rank who have central roles in a series of institutionalized enactments that serve as vehicles of intensification for more encompassing statements incorporating human-supernatural relations. The composite rituals of the mayordomía are carried out in such a way as to enact exchanges that balance the positions of individuals of differing ritual rank. Such exchanges facilitate these relationships: rank is accorded respect, which encodes balance, since these exchanges are invariably and implicitly reciprocal and are aimed toward the activation of rights and obligations that are mutually binding. This is a ritual system in which rank is an important dimension, and exchanges between people of differing rank create harmony because they highlight respect between those who give and those who receive. There is an obligation to receive from the person who has the right to give, just as there is an obligation to give so that what is needed is received.

Potentially elaborate and costly, the recibimiento is held in the household of the mayordomo and replicates the main events of the culminating day of the mayordomía. The mayordomos of San Mateo, the Santísimo Sacramento, and the Virgen de Guadalupe must have a recibimiento that is separate from the events of the culminating day and is usually held during the first months of sponsorship. Many of the other mayordomias of lesser ritual value may not include a separate recibimiento of the type described below. All mayordomos, however, must formally acknowledge the transfer of the demandita, since the demandita is the symbol of the rights and obligations the mayordomo has toward the saint. Mayordomos must also provide a context for the weighing of the wax belonging to the image.

Recibimientos occur only when a cargo is first received since the demandita is already situated on his household altar if a man serves the saint a second year. The recibimiento involves a ceremonious removal of the demandita from the household of the outgoing mayordomo and its placement on the altar of the incoming mayordomo. Musicians may be hired and the dancers will be invited if they are active at this time. Recibimientos are major events, and more immediate kinsmen, compadres de fé, and others from the barrio contribute goods and labor when invited to participate. The fiscales must be formally invited as well to weigh the wax in order to ascertain the amount consumed by the previous mayordomo, which must be replaced by the incoming mayordomo. The quantity of wax belonging to each image varies from 20 kilos for mayordomias menores to 150 kilos for those associated with the most ritually valued images. The wax has been contributed bit by bit over the years through individual devotions. Mayordomos have the right to "borrow" and replace the wax consumed in sponsorship. The fiscales keep close count of these transactions and have the right to sell some quantity of wax to raise money for church projects. The wax sold must be replaced by the mayordomo.

On the day set for the recibimiento, the fiscales and their acompañamiento march in procession from the church to the house of the incoming mayordomo, who escorts them to the house of the outgoing mayordomo. The incoming mayordomo does not take part in this procession, since he has no right to involve himself with the demandita, a right activated by the recibimiento. Rockets are fired on arrival at the house of the outgoing mayordomo, after which a speech is made in Nahuat formally requesting the relinquishment of the demandita. The image, if a virgin, will be addressed as *nonana,* my mother, and if a saint, as *notata,* my father. Toasts and chanted prayers accompany the weighing of the wax, which is concluded by a burst of rockets. Respect is shown the saint by kissing and bowing to the demandita; candles and incense are burned. Flower petals thrown by the acompañamiento of the mayordoma cover those kneeling before the altar, who are crying over the loss of the saint. A procession is slowly formed outside to proceed to the house of the incoming mayordomo.

This procession, like all others, forms according to a specified order depending upon context. Position is determined by ritual rank. Dancers with their standards always lead processions when they are performing. The Santiagos are followed by the Tocotines, the Paxtes, the Guacamayas, the Negritos, and then the Correos, Toreodores, and Payasos. The fiscales follow the dancers and lead the cofradía. If the dancers are not involved, the fiscales lead, given their rank, authority, and obligation to carry the demandita, a position that symbolizes the collectivity. The fiscal primero carries the demandita, with the teniente to his right carrying an alms box and the alguacil to his left, each holding a large lit candle. Rockets (*cohetes*) are fired until halfway to the house of the entering mayordomo, when the man in charge of his rockets takes over. The diputados menores of the entering mayordomo gather up the large wheels of wax and the large, decorated storage bench in which the wax, clothes, and adornments for the image are kept and carry them to the house of their mayordomo behind the procession.

A formal encuentro follows the arrival at the house of the entering mayordomo. Encuentros formalize the distinction between the acompañamiento of the incoming mayordomo, that of the outgoing mayordomo, and the cofradía. Each acompañamiento represents a network of individuals who participate with and opposite each other as those who come and those who wait. Their transactions activate rights and obligations toward each other that make possible the tasks of the ritual occasion. In the recibimiento, the women in the acompañamiento of the entering mayordomo greet the procession with incense, candles, and flower petals or confetti just outside the portal of the mayordomo's house compound. Filing by to kiss the demandita, they join the fiscales in prayer, after which the mayordomo invites the cofradía to enter his house to place the demandita on his newly adorned altar. The floor of the room has been covered with pine needles and flower petals as is the custom to show respect and demonstrate welcome when something new and valuable is added to a dwelling. Following a prayer, the men of the cofradía are seated along a narrow bench against the wall in front of which a lower bench serves as a table.

Seating order is set. The fiscal primero is flanked by the teniente on the right and the alguacil on the left. Others sit on either side of these men in descending order of rank. Opposite the fiscal primero and teniente on smaller single benches are the mayordomo and his diputado mayor. Others are seated on benches around the remaining walls, and wives sit on mats in the center of the room facing the fiscales. The diputado mayor is busy offering cigarettes to everyone present and offers to each guest in turn a single shot glass of aguardiente while the mayordomo engages in an exchange of salutations with members of the cofradía. When aguardiente is offered, this act is accompanied by bowing (respect) and counter-bowing (respect returned). A refusal to drink implies disinterest in the shared purpose of the event. The glass is passed around several times before food is brought from the kitchen in bowls made from elaborately colored gourds. Others who attend are fed in the courtyard and many eat standing. Over three hundred people may be fed at a recibimiento of an important mayordomía. Each of the three fiscales and their wives receives a nacatzontet of one-half a cooked chicken, after which each will be served a normal portion of xole, followed by rice and mole with chicken or pork. Everyone is fed in turn, and at the conclusion of the banquet, the fiscales begin a long speech of agradecimiento to the mayordomo. Rockets announce the departure of the cofradía. If a recibimiento is held on the same day as the mayordomía mass, it is held after the mass and banquet sponsored by the outgoing mayordomo in order to diminish cost. The transfer of the demandita and belongings of the image occurs relatively unceremoniously, with only cigarettes and aguardiente offered to the cofradía by the incoming mayordomo once they arrive at his house.

4. The *labrado de la cera* or working of the wax refers to preparation of candles used during a mayordomía. In years past, all candles used for rituals were made locally, and the wax was stored in large wheels. Today, only the important mayordomias have what remains of this wax. The wax is melted and the candles are dipped two weeks before the mayordomía mass at a special ceremony in the house of the mayordomo. The mayordomo may be absent but his diputado will insure that this ceremony is carried out in the appropriate manner. If the services of a candlemaker are required, a wage is not paid. A pedimento of aguardiente and cigarettes will be made to the candlemaker, who is given a meal of mole with an especially large portion of meat. This is not a nacatzontet. Specialists are not ritually ranked and therefore require an agradecimiento that makes no other statement. Rockets are fired throughout the ceremony, and much aguardiente is consumed. If there is insufficient wax, contributions made by the diputados menores will increase the store. The diputados menores will be served a meal of mole when the candles are collected. If the mayordomo is willing, the labrado may resemble a recibimiento. The fiscales and the cofradía will be invited and nacatzontet will be served to them. Originally the contribution of the diputados menores was more symbolic than essential, a gesture of respect for the mayordomo who was in many instances a compadre. Today, commercial candles of white wax may be bought in Teziutlán and will be taken to the priest for his blessing before being offered to the mayordomo.

5. The *entrega de la cera* or delivery of the candles to the church occurs

before vespers on the night before a mayordomía mass. This allows the sacristanes and the diputados mensajeros time to arrange the candles on the main altar. Larger candles are placed in tall candlesticks along both sides of the main aisle. A pedimento of aguardiente and cigarettes has been made to the fiscales to invite them to the mayordomo's house and they arrive an hour or so before vespers. Those accompanying the fiscales to the mayordomo's house represent the initial congregation of members of the cofradía for that particular mayordomía. The mayordomo and mayordoma ceremoniously greet them and offer them aguardiente and cigarettes before the fiscales enter the house to pray briefly before the demandita. By 5:00 or 6:00 P.M. everyone has gathered and a procession forms to take the demandita to the church. Rockets accompany the procession, which stops along the route to allow people to emerge from their houses and express their devotion to the saint by kissing the demandita and offering a small amount of money to the saint. The procession can take more than an hour to arrive at the church, where the flowers and candles are handed to the sacristanes. The image has been removed from its niche and sits on a processional platform for use following the mass. The demandita is placed on the platform to the right of the image. Gladioli supplied by the mayordomo fill the twenty-four vases of the main altar, red for a saint, and white for a virgin.

6. The vesper service, held the night before a mayordomía mass, serves to announce a mayordomía, and vespers occur only on this occasion. If a band has been hired to play at the mayordomía, the band will begin playing just before vespers. The fiscales, the mayordomo, his diputado, and a few selected members of the mayordomo's acompañamiento recite several prayers before the image since the priest does not officiate. The church bells are rung and rockets are fired for fifteen minutes to announce the culminating event of the mayordomía the following day. Vespers conclude when the fiscales retire to the fiscalía for about an hour to talk and drink aguardiente supplied by the mayordomo before going home.

7. The mayordomía mass is a high mass, sung and concluded with the celebration of the Eucharist. The priest takes this opportunity to offer a sermon lasting roughly twenty minutes in which he invariably condemns the Indians for their commitment to the most overtly non-Catholic elements of the mayordomía, contributing to sentiments of many Indians that he is ignorant of the true desires of the saints. However, such admonitions are not without effect. For some time, there has been an insistent campaign by resident priests to undermine Indian customs by opposing indigenous elements in all rituals. Actions like these have recently been commented on by

DeWalt (1975); Ingham (1986), who presents fascinating accounts of abuse by priests in Tlayacapan; and Brandes (1988), who charts the desacralization and physical demise of the cargo system in Tzintzuntzan due to clerical action. In contrast to Ingham and myself, Brandes appears to attribute ingenuousness to the priests' actions. Brandes appears to believe that what the priests in Tzintzuntzan did had no damaging ramifications. This is a difficult position to sustain given the post–Vatican II dedication to homogenizing the rites of the church and thereby obliterating ethnic differences among native peoples.

Catholic rites of vespers and the mass, in Chignautla, have been embedded in the mayordomía complex since its inception. On the one hand, the Indians believe that the mass is an important rite, although they remain uneducated as to its full theological implications. On the other hand, the events of a mayordomía are fully imbued with indigenous sacred meanings and the mass itself is subsumed by them. The other events of a mayordomía are structurally arranged to enable the ritual actors to subliminally retain a distinction they make between the rites of the church, at which an outsider who is controlled by outside forces officiates, and elements that belong absolutely to them and are an integral part of Chignauteco identity. I refer here not to ethnic identity, but rather to a cultural morality as it must exist in folk religion, fully interwoven into the fabric of social life and the experience of the individual. For the Indians, the mass and vespers retain significance largely because of the concrete presence of the saints. The images are not confused with the supernatural power the saints embody. Their power is attributional, that is, it resides in the realm of expectations and assumptions made about the nature of the world. Other significata are the demandita and the fiscales, whose mediating presence symbolizes the Autoridad Eclesiástica and the collectivity, bridging these experientially discrepant contexts.

In the mass, the personal names of mayordomos are never used, but the sponsor of the mass always sits in the second pew behind the fiscales, who carry their staffs of office, all three being present at mayordomias of importance. For lesser mayordomias, only one fiscal need be present. By 7:30 A.M. musicians hired by the mayordomo have already begun to play for the 9:00 A.M. mass. The diputada and mayordoma rarely attend since they are busy preparing the ceremonial banquet to follow. Once the mass concludes, the procession for the image forms. The mayordomo distributes candles to carry in the procession, which circles slowly twice around the atrium, stopping at each corner for prayers. Bells and rockets accompany the procession. The priest follows the diputado mensajero, who carries an incense burner close behind the image. The three fiscales and the demandita follow behind the priest, leading those Indians who, for this mass, form the members of the parish congregation, and most of whom will be excluded from the following events. People throw confetti over the image as it moves slowly along.

Once it is returned to the church, people file by to kiss the image or demandita. The fiscales return their staffs to the sacristy, and, accompanied by the mayordomo and his diputado, retire to the fiscalía, where they are joined by the wives of the fiscales and other members of the cofradía. Any presently serving cargo holder or pasado of importance may attend these gatherings, and the diputado mayor is always present, since he must pass around aguardiente and cigarettes. A formal toast to the mayordomo is made by the fiscales, who offer their gratitude for his sacrifice, a gesture the mayordomo returns by saying: "Here you are, Señores Fiscales, with your mensajeros and the cofradía, and we would like you to accompany us to our house in the saint's honor and favor us by accompanying us for a *taquito* [snack]." The fiscales bow in acceptance. A relatively informal meeting then begins with a general discussion of ritual affairs in which recruitment is the central issue, a discussion the mayordomo joins since he now has a say in these affairs. People who are guests of the mayordomo but not of sufficient ritual rank to allow them to enter the fiscalía leave for their walk to the house of the mayordomo accompanied by the musicians, who will begin playing once they arrive at the mayordomo's house.

8. The collection of the candles and demandita by the sacristanes for removal to the house of the mayordomo signals the moment for members of the cofradía to form their procession. An agradecimiento will be sent to the sacristanes and diputado mensajero for their labor in church preparations and will consist of a serving of food and nacatzontet. The fiscal primero brings the postmass gathering to an end and announces his duty to accompany the mayordomo and the demandita. The entourage proceeds slowly to the mayordomo's house. Rockets are fired along the route, which, years ago, was covered with flower petals and pine needles, a custom that survives only for the mayordomias of Holy Week, San Mateo, and Guadalupe and is confined to the church atrium. All along the way, members of the community can observe and demonstrate their respect for the cofradía, at times emerging from their houses to bow to and kiss the demandita, reminding all that the mayordomo is making his sacrifice for the benefit of the entire community.

9. The encuentro at the house of the mayordomo follows the arrival of the procession after the mass. The various duties of individual cargo holders invariably include specifically defined obligations toward other cargo holders

in positions of either inferior or superior ritual rank. Ultimately, it is the right of senior-ranking cargo holders to insure appropriate comportment of all, and it is their obligation to insure the fulfillment of intercargo duties. Gestures of respect toward those of inferior ritual status override other principles operating in Chignauteco culture such as age and social position, which are determinant in secular affairs. The encuentro entails the same activities that occur in the recibimiento and serves the same purpose. When the women hear the rockets drawing near, they light incense and candles and go out to the street to meet the cofradía. Where they meet, more rockets are fired and each woman passes before the demandita to kiss it and welcome it to the house while others throw confetti or flower petals. The mayordomo invites the cofradía to enter the patio of his house compound. The mayordomo formally invites the cofradía to enter and the fiscal primero places the demandita on the household altar and kneels before it to lead a rosary. In prayer, the saint is addressed in the symbol of the demandita.

I have already discussed the significance of household altars, whose structure and function designates the house of the mayordomo as a sacralizing context. Household altars are portals between the realm of daily life and the realm of the sacred, sites marking a coalescence of venerative acts and sacred aims accomplished through the sacrifice undertaken by the mayordomo. As I have mentioned, the ancient Nahuas believed that all movement, whether in the development of an individual's life, societal changes, or naturally occurring phenomena such as the movement of the sun across the sky or the arrival of rain after the dry season, was linked to a spatial ordering of time (León-Portilla 1963). In cosmological time, balanced movement was essential to spatial and temporal harmony and required blood as a sacrificial offering. Soustelle (1940) has contributed to the articulation of Nahuatlan thought by what he calls "place-moment." Together, space-time and place-moment serve as a means for locating, combining, and relating to each other primary natural elements and cosmic forces, the direction of space and time, and human and natural events. Consequently, the household altar serves as the focus for the transcendence of the mundane into the sacred. Household altars invariably face north, betraying their association with the god Tezcatlipocha, who is also linked to sacrifice, death, and Mictlan (place of the dead). In Chignauteco experience, the force of custom dictates that supplications offered for the welfare of the soul during wakes occur before the household altar and prayers for the welfare of the community occur before the demandita placed on the household altar during a mayordomía. In this sense, the dead and the kinsmen and compadres of the deceased at a wake and the acompañamientos of the mayordomo and the fiscales are in a transformational state from one space-time and place-moment to another. Analogously, the demandita on the household altar and the images of saints in the church become interchangeable transcendental forces in movement between sacralizing contexts. During a mayordomía, the demandita, the mayordomo, and the cofradía are central foci. Each has a role in preserving the necessary order of the universe through participation in the sacrifice of the mayordomo.

The encuentro is the vehicle through which those who come and those who wait enter reciprocal interactions initiated by ceremonious salutations. The encuentro is a transitional interval, and in this case, a doorway to a context that is sacralizing. The tone is set for that which follows by the identification at the outset of who has the right and obligation to give and who has the right and obligation to receive throughout a series of agradecimientos, at ceremonial banquets, in provision of the nacatzontet, in prayer and in speeches—interactions clearly organized reciprocally around themes of harmony and balance.

10. The *rezo* or prayers following the encuentro center on the demandita and are led by the fiscales, who set the tone for the ceremonial banquet to follow.

11. The *comida* or ceremonial banquet of the mayordomía, whose preparation is laborious and costly, represents one of the most evocative events of the entire ritual-ceremonial complex. All ritual activities conclude with ceremonial banquets or celebratory meals that make tangible the effects of reciprocity, respect, and rank. Chignautecos believe that if a man gives only the mass and not the ceremonial banquet, as sometimes occurs among the Mestizos, it does not qualify as a sacrifice. This is captured in the words of an informant:

> To celebrate a saint, one must feed the people. A mayordomía is the sacrifice and the sacrifice is the fiesta. When I received my appointment, I at times began crying. At night I could not sleep and was troubled. A mayordomía is something that a man wears as part of his being. It is marked in his flesh and a mayordomo will always continue being one. And so it is with a sacrifice for a saint. Those who do not make their sacrifice do not benefit for not wanting to spend on a fiesta.

Ritual meals are invariably centrally positioned in the sacralizing contexts in which they occur. They provide a means for the transformation of the mundane stuff of life into that which is sacred. The sacred objects needed, the special foods offered and received, the respect and humility displayed mark the bonds established between themselves as Chignautecos and their chosen ritual representatives and the pantheon of folk Catholic supernaturals believed to intervene on their behalf. Goals of propitiation and thanksgiving are achieved in the ceremonial banquet and are embedded in the structure of favors given and received. Regulated strongly by core assumptions that implicitly guide these performances, ritual meals become consummate vehicles of sacralization around which expectations of the favor of the saints are generated.

Offering simple or elaborate meals within ceremonial contexts as thankmeals is a custom well grounded in both Nahuat and Christian traditions. For mayordomias, the manner in which a ritual meal is offered is rigidly proscribed, with little room for idiosyncratic expression. It is always called a *taquito,* a little snack. Such understatement stresses the humility of the mayordomo while focusing attention away from the banquet he must provide for the cofradía. The members of the cofradía are led to their seats of honor to the left of the household altar. For such events, the fiscales are invariably accompanied by at least one mayordomo mensajero and often a diputado mensajero and one or more past or present mayordomos of San Mateo. Directly opposite, on smaller individual benches, are the mayordomo, the diputado mayor to his right, and the mayordomo's father, brother, grandfather, or tío hermano to his left. On mats placed in the center of the room are the wives of these men. The wives of the fiscales sit opposite their husbands, and to their right sit the wives of other important members of the cofradía. Behind this line of women are wives of men of lesser ritual rank who have accompanied the fiscales that day. Aguardiente and cigarettes are offered to all. The food is then brought out in individual bowls from the kitchen hut across the courtyard by diputados menores, women of the household, and others who have been invited to help. The mayordoma and diputada remain in the kitchen.

The first food presented is the nacatzontet for the fiscales. If a fiscal is absent, he will be sent his nacatzontet the following day. The nacatzontet serves the same purpose as in compadrazgo. Once ceremoniously presented to a member of the cofradía, the nacatzontet is received with repetitive thanks only to be returned to the kitchen or handed directly to the fiscales' wives, to be carried home in jars hidden beneath their shawls. The nacatzontet becomes the object of silent admiration. The gesture of agradecimiento is completed by the offering and receiving of the nacatzontet, which is never eaten at the meal since this would, I believe, detract from the evocative power it symbolizes in so condensed a form. Food in exaggerated portions is offered to the members of the cofradía, who just sample the fare. The rest is handed to their wives to be taken home. This rite is followed by a general distribution of normal portions to all who attend.

The food served is defined by the class of mayordomía held. Mayordomias that involve the dancers or those of high ritual value begin the meal with xole served in elaborately decorated gourd bowls with two *cacalas* or special tortillas made into squares and flavored with salt and anise. A thin soup made from lamb and cabbage flavored with green chile follows. Stacks of tortillas covered in embroidered napkins are placed on the benches, which serve as tables. In mayordomias menores, xole is served, but it is followed by a thin mole with pork. Those invited to help in preparations, as opposed to those invited to participate as guests, are always served in the courtyard or kitchen because they become, for this occasion, members of the mayordomo's household.[3]

After the meal is concluded, the fiscales rise and the fiscal primero addresses himself to the mayordomo to ask if he desires to serve the saint another year. This is usually a formality, since the mayordomo's decision has already been communicated to the fiscales and they may already know who will be the next mayordomo should the cargo be released. Not without purpose, however, this act initiates the right of the fiscales to transfer the sponsorship in due time. The mayordomo may also make a formal endorsement of an individual or formalize a request to sponsor the cargo again after a rest of several years, since sponsorship entitles a man to retain rights to serve the saint just celebrated.

12. The despedida or farewell to the cofradía is a terminating event. All ritual events conclude with a formalized agradecimiento, whose overt purpose is to give thanks to those whose presence made the event ritually and materially possible. Despedidas are statements of agradecimiento in contexts in which ritual rank and respect are significant and are necessary to establish and realize the purpose of the event. Despedidas and speeches of agradecimiento designate complementary ritual positions activated through a pedimento that induces those needed to attend, thereby completing the roster of necessary personnel for the performance of whatever ritual task is on hand. These are structuralizations of reciprocity in which there is a transposition of those who give and those who receive extended to include the larger networks of those who come and those who wait. This transposition, then, concludes a ritual event without concluding the reciprocity intrinsic to it.

Despedidas also function as rites of transition, facilitating passage from a context absolutely determined by ideological constraints to moments of daily life in which the importance of form diminishes, as does the conscious concern with human-supernatural relations. In a despedida for a mayor-domía, the mayordomo and his diputado formally thank the fiscales for fulfilling their duties to the saints and to the community and especially for partaking in a meal offered in so humble a house. The fiscales in turn thank the mayordomo for the care given the saint's image and for the sacrifice offered in the saint's name and in the name of all Chignautecos before God. At the conclusion of this speech, the formal assembly quietly leaves and everyone relaxes. The musicians retire, for it is now evening.

In years past, mayordomias were typically followed by a secular dance, which was open to the residents of the barrio and often attracted young men from other barrios who came in search of potential wives. Excessive drinking and brawls were not uncommon and with the emergence of many other opportunities for young people to meet, this custom has almost completely faded.

13. The despedida of the diputado mayor is a terminating event. Obligations of the mayordomo toward his diputado mayor are fulfilled in a despedida dedicated to this purpose. Agradecimiento is achieved through the offer of a celebratory meal to the diputado, his wife, and their acompañamiento. Rockets are fired and nacatzontet is served, usually a whole cooked chicken, one-half for the diputado and the other the diputada. Or one live turkey may be offered so that the diputado may defray his expenses. After the meal, the mayordomo makes a formal speech of thanks and the diputado leaves to the sound of rockets.

14. The *entrega,* or transfer of the cargo to a new sponsor, terminates sponsorship and accompanies the recibimiento of the new sponsor. Recibimientos and entregas are structured so that all participants in a mayordomía alternately become givers and receivers. The outgoing mayordomo, once the receiver himself, becomes in the entrega the one who must give. This, in turn, activates the right of the incoming mayordomo to receive, only to be obliged to give at some unspecified time in the future, in a manner structurally replicating how Chignautecos relate to the saints. Recibimientos and entregas mirror each other in structure and function. The recibimiento enacts the obligation to receive respectfully, while the entrega enacts the obligation to respectfully give at the moment when the ritual relationship between these two men is becoming asymmetrical; that is, what the recibimiento gains for the incoming mayordomo is lost in the entrega of the outgoing mayordomo. The ritual rank of the mayordomo mirrors the asymmetrical reciprocity of

sacrifice (of sponsorship), which serves as a metaphor for human-supernatural relations and confirms, for Chignautecos, the instrumentality of the mayordomía. The teleological nature of this ritual system is further reflected in the composite events of the mayordomía, and it is in this sense that the recibimiento and entrega are reciprocal events initiating sponsorship and concluding the performance of associated ritual duties.

15. The velorio or wake for the saint, also called "vespers of the transfer of rights to celebrate the saint," is given by the outgoing mayordomo in his house on the eve of the entrega, to which the incoming mayordomo is invited with the core of his acompañamiento. Flanked by four candles and four vases of flowers, the demandita is once again the focus. An individual known for his ability to chant at wakes is invited to assist in the rosaries. Held at 9:00 P.M., when wakes are usually held for the dead in Chignautla, this velorio assumes much the same form discussed in chapter 4 except without game playing. The demandita rests as a body in state, not on the floor before the altar, but on the altar itself. Both the incoming and outgoing mayordomos contribute special breads, coffee, and aguardiente required for a wake.

The velorio lasts several hours. A meal of thin soup with tripe will be served by the outgoing mayordomo to other mourners, usually the diputado mayor, diputada mayor, close compadres who have served as diputados menores, and close kinsmen who contributed their labor and materials for the mayordomía.[4] As in all wakes, focus is on the spiritual, making this an introspective moment for all concerned. The mayordomo and his diputado have assumed the responsibility for caring for the saint during the year of sponsorship, and, as a child would do for a beloved parent, they bid farewell to the saint, to whom they feel a sense of profound attachment and for whom this event serves to affirm an enduring sense of commitment and responsibility. It is believed that a proper wake guarantees the blessings of the departed. At the concluding moment, all kiss the demandita and cry over the loss of the saint, for they fear that they may never serve the saint again. A formal agradecimiento given by the outgoing mayordomo to the incoming mayordomo concludes this event.

The Mayordomía in Its More Inclusive Contexts

There are other ceremonial events involving large numbers of ritual actors whose positions in the system are highly discrepant, although their obligations are vital to the realization of the aims of the cult. There are a number of cargos not formally associated with any image, such as the mayordomos of the Jubileos. These men borrow the demandita of the Santísimo Sacramento for a mass, recibimiento, and ceremonial meal. The sacristanes hold a celebration for the Niño Dios, whose image serves as their demandita. The sacristán mayor and segundo, in agreement with the fiscales, appoint a sacristán menor to serve as mayordomo for this mass, which is followed by a banquet with assistance from the other sacristanes as if they were the diputado mayor. Each year another sacristán serves so that each may make a venerative sacrifice.

The men of the Autoridad Eclesiástica are responsible for the coordination of all activities of the cult. The cargo of fiscal primero has the greatest burden of all. The man chosen to be fiscal is sent his letter of appointment in July. If he accepts, he must choose his teniente and alguacil by formal pedimento. This requires a *mecoyotzin*, a gift of respect in the form of a chiquihuite similar to that given by the mayordomo to his prospective diputado mayor but with contents in greater quantities. The teniente and alguacil serve as the primary ritual assistants to the fiscal. Once appointed, the entering fiscales hold their recibimiento before they assume office on January 1st. Their recibimiento is held on the day of the mayordomía mass for San Mateo 21, articulating the affinity between the patron saint and the fiscales. The incoming fiscales present themselves to the outgoing fiscales and offer an agradecimiento, after which the entering first fiscal sponsors a ritual meal of chicken mole for his teniente and alguacil and their wives. A mass dedicated to San Mateo is held at 6:30 that morning before the mayordomía mass at 11:00 A.M., with the larger share of expense falling to the fiscal primero. The mass is the occasion for the transfer of the staffs of office to the new fiscales and is followed by a ceremonial banquet in the house of the first fiscal. The sacred staffs are placed on the household altar before the ceremonial banquet. No one attends this event who does not hold an important ritual rank.

The fiscales are central actors in all celebrations held directly in honor of San Mateo and serve as intermediaries between the patron saint and the community. They are directly responsible for supervising the mayordomias of San Mateo and the appropriate performance of those who dance in his honor. The duties of the fiscales have previously been mentioned and are notably complex. The fiscales also sponsor a second Sunday mass each month, collect funds for Holy Week celebrations, sponsor a yearly project for the church, purchase church supplies, pay the debts of outgoing fiscales, and provide the supplies for the diputados mensajeros on their first day of service. The fiscales arrange the faenas of the mayordomos, and, with the mensajeros, contribute aguardiente and cigarettes. They make the general collection of funds from the municipio as a whole several times a year and supply the *mecoyotzitzin* (pl.) for the pedimentos of the sacristanes.

The Principios and Despedidas to San Mateo

The four-month period from the beginning of September through the end of December is dedicated to San Mateo and is when the cult of the saints finds its most elaborate, public expression in especially well-attended celebrations. The mayordomias of San Mateo on the 21st, 22nd, 23rd, and 28th of September are closely associated with the harvest. For their processions, the four images of San Mateo are heavily draped with dried ears of corn and numerous xochikoskat placed around their necks by individuals as expressions of personal devotion and respect. The evocation of the meaning of sacrifice is intensified in these activities since all actors are engaged in some form of ritual sponsorship. This intensification of the spirit of sacrifice is directly associated with renewal. The image of the patron saint with corn at his feet is reminiscent of pre-Hispanic sacrificial rites to Huitzilopochtli, in which commoners made offerings of ears of dried corn to the gods (Ingham 1986).

The mayordomias of San Mateo are enhanced by the performance of the dancers. Multiple activities forming a specific design commence on September 19th, which is designated *El Principio* or the Beginning. Although celebrations of the Principio occur at various locations within the municipio, in combination, their design takes the form of a recibimiento collectively performed for the community as a whole in honor of San Mateo. A ritual meal is given in turn by the dance captains and the Pilato mayor of each group to their respective dancers, and by their encargados on the 20th. The fiscales, as encargados of the Tocotines, are responsible for providing a ritual meal for them. The dance groups move between the village plaza, where they perform, and the households of the men who sponsor their agradecimientos in the form of celebratory meals. For example, the Negritos perform and then retire to the house of the Pilato mayor for xole and cacalas, aguardiente and cigarettes. Formal speeches are made to thank the dancers for their efforts, after which they return to the plaza to dance. Several hours later, they return for a meal of lamb and cabbage soup given at the house of the lead dancer of the Negritos, and so on for each group.

Within each dance group, the personnel are ranked. Each mayor reciprocates the dancers subordinate to him for their sacrifice in the fulfillment of their vows, demonstrating respect for performers of inferior rank. This is accomplished by supplying the dancers with meals, cigarettes, and aguardiente at appropriate intervals during the long period of their performances. If the mayordomo of the Virgen de la Natividad so wishes, he invites the dancers to perform for his mayordomía on September 8, two weeks prior to the formal Principio. The activity is intense: masses are held, dances are performed, toros are burned, and ritual meals are offered. The village plaza fills to capacity and many support personnel and kinsmen of the ritual performers remain all night under the porticos of the school and municipal palace. Processions of ritual personnel move between the church and the village plaza and the respective households of the mayordomos, the encargados, and the mayores. The component events of a mayordomía are replicated, accompanied by much drinking and rocketry, from 5:00 A.M. until midnight each day.

The mayordomias honoring the Virgen de Guadalupe in December are elaborated by the use of toros and ritual dancers. Celebrations honoring the Virgen are held in Tepepan and Coahuixco as well. A series of despedidas for the dancers represent the second most elaborate public celebration directly honoring San Mateo. In actuality, the dancers perform during two distinct periods: from September 7th at vespers for the mayordomía of the Virgen de la Natividad to October 16th, and from December 11th at vespers of the celebrations for the Virgen de Guadalupe to December 18th, when the final Despedida is held. In all, three public despedidas are involved. One is given by the Ayuntamiento on October 16th, in which the Presidente Municipal assumes the role of mayordomo in his sponsorship of the mass. He is assisted by the regidores, who help defray expenses for the ritual meal held afterward. If the Presidente identifies himself as Mestizo, this fiesta will contain Mestizo elements in the type of food given and in the value placed on vespers. If the Presidente identifies himself as Indian, this event will resemble an Indian mayordomía: the customary xole and cacalas and lamb and cabbage soup will be served to the cofradía, who will assume the usual position of honor at the table and in relation to the demandita borrowed for the occasion.

The second despedida is held the third Sunday of October. When combined with the first, it recreates the structural design of a mayordomía, and in fact, dancers have referred to the Ayuntamiento Despedida in this fashion. The same pattern obtains for the Principio: the encargados provide a culminating event to the initiating event sponsored by the Pilatos mayores and dance captains, therein duplicating the juxtaposition of those who come and those who wait. The mass to San Mateo of the second despedida is the obligation of the dancers themselves, each dancer contributing toward expenses. The Pilatos supply rockets of the type supplied for the despedidas in mayordomias. After the mass, the dancers retire to the houses of their respective encargados to receive a ceremonial banquet and perform the xochitis, exchanging xochikoskat and then dancing a xochipitzahuac. The xochikoskat used are made in the usual manner and placed by the encargados around the necks of the dancers. The fiscales hold a xochitis for the Tocotines and their Pilatos. The Tocotines are the largest dance group and the fiscales together make over four hundred xochikoskat for this occasion. The Pilatos have their own xochitis, followed by a ceremonial banquet with the required nacatzontet given to the captains and Pilatos mayores. The dancers do not become compadres through these ritual exchanges, but they do enact an exchange signifying obligatory respect, which embodies binding reciprocity among themselves and between themselves and San Mateo. At the close of this despedida, the entire complement of dancers go to the house of the fiscal primero, where they perform a xochitis and dance the xochipitzahuac, after which they are given a ceremonial meal and the mayores receive nacatzontet. For this occasion, the alguacil and teniente assume the role of diputados mayores to the fiscal primero. Following the banquet, a velorio is held all night in the church, in which all the dancers and fiscales participate.

The final despedida marks the end of the celebrations for San Mateo. On December 12th, the dancers perform for the mayordomía of the Virgen de Guadalupe whose image is in the parish church. On December 13th, they perform for the mayordomía of the image of the Virgen in Coahuixco's chapel. On December 16th, they perform for the mayordomía of the Virgen whose image is housed in the chapel in Tepepan, returning on the evening of the 18th of December to Coahuixco for the final despedida. After dancing several hours, each dancer lights a candle and kneels to pray before the image. Completing this short prayer, they embrace each other; a Tocotine embraces a Negrito, a Santiago embraces a Paxte, etc. Each group then returns to the house of its encargado. On this occasion, the dancers bring their wives and selected kinsmen and compadres for a ceremonial banquet and final xochitis, exchanging xochikoskat before dancing the xochipitzahuac.

As in compadrazgo, the xochitis here represents a cumplimiento through whose enactment sacred obligations are fulfilled. Ambiguously positioned in a system of ritual rank, the cargo of dancer within this complex as a whole derives its value from the relationship of the dancers to the patron saint, a relationship confirmed in the presentation of the nacatzontet and xochikoskat to them, ensuring them a position of respect among individuals holding clearly superior ritual rank. The xochitis serves a function analo-

gous to that of the nacatzontet when it is given to the sacristanes and diputados mensajeros for their assistance in adorning the church for mayordomía
masses and processions. I found quite interesting the comment of one Chignauteco when asked whether he would prefer to be Cortés of the Tocotines
or a mayordomo. He responded: "For a poor man like myself, I would want
the cargo of Cortés. A dancer like Cortés represents the whole community;
a small mayordomo represents only his barrio." When a person such as this
informant undertakes a vow to San Mateo, it is with the same intentions that
a mayordomo or fiscal has in sponsoring his cargo, and he expects to
achieve the same ends, even though his cargo involves a series of distinctly
different duties. His devotion provides an experience in which there is a
sense of contribution to upholding the social order and insuring that life
continues as it should for himself, his family, the community as a whole,
and the saints.

Semana Santa and Corpus Christi

There is not one day during Semana Santa (Easter Week) when the parish
church is not crowded to capacity to celebrate the mayordomía masses of
Domingo de Ramos (San Ramos), San Lázaro (Santo Entierro), and Señor
de la Resurrección and for the elaborate processions that occur amid many
more sacred activities that enact the Chignauteco version of the Passion,
Crucifixion, and Resurrection of Christ. The Last Supper, the imprisonment
of Christ, and the birth and renewal of the cult of the saints are enacted with
the participation of additional mayordomos whose images are "borrowed"
for this occasion. The duties carried out by the acompañamientos of these
mayordomos and the combined obligations of the Autoridad Eclesiástica and
the Ayuntamiento Municipal make Semana Santa an important celebration
but one lacking the emphasis on community identity typical of an altepeihuit.
The cooperation and respect between mayordomos from Arriba and Abajo,
the burden displayed in their sacrifice, the relatively evenly distributed duties
of the civil and administrative authorities, and the deference enacted in reciprocal exchanges between individuals of differing ritual rank evoke themes
of balance and harmony intrinsic to sacralizing contexts that sustain and
confirm major elements of the Chignauteco cosmovision.

By Thursday before Palm Sunday, the entrance to the church has been
draped in black and purple cloth as a sign of mourning and the atrium is
adorned with palm leaves, ribbons, and respaldos. On Saturday, the entire
Ayuntamiento arrives at the parish house to join members of the Autoridad

Eclesiástica for a series of exchanges followed by a celebratory banquet. The topiles have brought palms from Tlapacoyan for the fiscales to distribute to all present. The palms are given in exchange for flowers before partaking in a meal offered to those present by the regidores de gasto. The meal concludes when the church bells announce vespers for the mayordomía mass and procession for San Ramos the following day, dedicated to the blessing of the palms and the appearance of the twelve Apostles portrayed by Indians costumed in long purple robes. After the mass, a band sponsored by the mayordomo plays amid volleys of rockets and bells as the procession forms and marches twice around the atrium with a stop for prayers at each of the respaldos.

During the days leading up to Holy Thursday, the transformation of the interior of the church is completed. Purple cloth is draped over the main altar and images, with the exception of the Virgen de los Dolores, to set the scene for the enactment of the Passion and Crucifixion. The mayordomos of San Mateo 21 and San Lázaro recreate Calvary in front of the main altar by erecting three crosses that stand between two pine trees. The baptistry becomes the cell for the image of the Divino Preso and bottles of colored water with flags representing tenebrae adorn the floor of the rear of the church. Following a mass sponsored by collection, the priest ceremoniously washes the feet of the Apostles and divests the fiscales of their staffs of office, marking a loss to enable celebration of rebirth and renewal. In the procession with the images of San Pedro, San Juan, and Padre Jesús to follow, the fiscales carry the monstrance. The Apostles are then provided a meal of twelve courses, sponsored by the regidores de gasto and signifying the Last Supper, before joining the rosary that announces that the Divino Preso will be placed in his cell at midnight.

The ritual process that enacts the Passion of Christ on Good Friday becomes the sacrifice of the mayordomo of San Lázaro. Wooden noisemakers, trumpets, and clarinets substitute for the bells, which may not be rung again until Easter. By 11:00 A.M., many people have gathered around the processional platforms of the images of Padre Jesús, San Pedro, San Juan, San Lázaro, San Ramos, María Magdalena, the Virgen de los Dolores, and the Virgen de la Soledad. This procession enacts the Stations of the Cross, after which the church is closed to allow the mayordomos to place the image of Padre Jesús on the central cross. Many return to the church at 5:00 P.M. to witness the removal of the image of San Lázaro from the cross by four hooded "Jews" wearing sackcloth. Now representing Santo Entierro, this image is placed in a glass coffin guarded by "Roman soldiers," actually six topiles carrying rifles, for a series of processions. In the first procession,

María Magdalena and the Virgen de la Soledad are carried on the right while Padre Jesús and San Juan are carried on the left. During the second procession, the Virgen de los Dolores is carried by unmarried women. The white candles supplied to the crowd by the mayordomo will be collected after the processions conclude. The church remains open until midnight for a velorio, for which the Apostles remain in attendance. The mayordomos jointly sponsor a celebratory meal of agradecimiento for all ritual personnel involved. Sabado de Gloria begins with a rezo at dawn to bless the buckets of holy water in which flowers have been placed for general distribution, holy water that will be used to bless the newly weeded milpa. Candles now adorn the main altar and aisle. After the congregation is blessed with holy water, a mass is held. At midnight, to the sound of rockets and noisemakers, the drapes are removed from the images by the mayordomos while the priest unveils the altar. The priest then returns the staffs to the fiscales to signal the birth and renewal of the cult of the saints. Explicitly structured by themes central to Catholic theology, Semana Santa is also a cosmic drama of transition structured by more implicit notions of change, sacrifice, and inevitable destructions and rebirth of successive eras of the world, notions lying at the heart of the cosmological design of the universe, human beings, and gods among the Nahuat. Such dramas resemble themes embodied in the actions, costumes, and meanings attributed to the Paxtes and Guacamaya dance groups as previously discussed.

For Easter Sunday, the mass is announced by records played by the priest over a loudspeaker system. The atrium floor has been decorated by three scenes designed in flower petals for three encuentros during the procession. Encuentros occur between San Juan and La Inmaculada Concepción, whose image is borrowed from the Mestizos, between San Pedro and Señor de la Resurrección, and between the Virgen de los Dolores and the Virgen de la Soledad. Replete with symbols of both duality and reciprocity, the images respectfully bow and greet each other as onlookers shower them with flower petals in the same manner as would occur between ritual actors performing an encuentro during a mayordomía. After the mass concludes, a cofradía consisting of all members of the Autoridad, the officers of the Ayuntamiento, and the topiles retires for a ceremonial banquet held at the house of the mayordomo of Señor de la Resurrección.

The four mayordomias of Corpus Christi in June are sponsored by the mayordomos of the Santísimo Sacramento, who, along with their diputados mensajeros, sponsor the consecutive masses and ritual banquets of the Corpus Christi celebrations. This is the major ceremonial obligation of these cargos. The mayordomía of Domingo de Corpus concludes the sacred rituals of Corpus Christi. That weekend, preparations take place under the aegis of the Ayuntamiento Municipal for a major altepeihuit. Horse races, greased pole and pig competitions, and a large secular dance are some of the entertainment provided, sponsored by collection of funds from each section. Interbarrio rivalries and ethnic antagonisms play no part, for this is a secular municipal fiesta. Such events allow the Indians and Mestizos of Chignautla to share an identity as the people of Chignautla and affirm their participation in the wider cultural whole of the region and nation. The Corpus Christi celebrations are an amalgamation of different types of events that, upon closer inspection, reveal the subtle changes that are occurring in the ceremonial lives of people of the rural municipios of Mexico.[5]

The altepeihuit once was a religious event and did not include secular activities. With the emergence of governance in the hands of the Mestizos, the nature of such events changed and they could no longer retain most of their indigenous referents. This form of desacralization is leading ritual expression in traditional communities like Chignautla to a more isolated position, eroding a relatively enduring and integral worldview. New patterns in behavior will ultimately undermine the ideological basis of ritual action and leave it devoid of its original meaning. I believe failure to pay attention to this dimension of experience will make it difficult indeed to understand the position fiestas have in the lives of Mexican peoples. This appears to be a problem in Brandes's (1988) book *Power and Persuasion: Fiestas and Social Control in Rural Mexico,* which is devoted to how public celebratory events function as mechanisms of social control in the village of Tzintzuntzan in the state of Michoacán. Brandes writes that in order to study social control, one must "discover the precise content of those beliefs and practices and their meaning to the people themselves" (1988, 10). This would be difficult to accomplish without addressing the fact that the Tarascan underpinnings of fiesta organization in this community have been engulfed by national culture. That is, Tzintzuntzan is a Mestizo community located relatively close to the reaches of influence of Mexico City and has become a significant tourist attraction. On the one hand, the ceremonial complex in Tzintzuntzan appears to be largely desacralized and the fiestas described have long since been divested of the beliefs that once moored them to the cultural system he admits once existed. On the other hand, Brandes describes a totally new form of fiesta that has emerged in this community. He charts the decline of the religious cargo system and the religious authority vested in it. But new forms of fiestas have emerged along with new festivities, some of which are conscious revivals of traditional events brought about by individual inclination and "nostalgia" (1988, 51). What Brandes appears to be describing is culture loss. This is not to say that the people of Tzintzuntzan do not hold public fiestas that are important to them. Rather, there appears to be no normative basis for these events.

What emerges is a description of religion devoid of the very content that in my thinking is a powerful mechanism of social control. That fiestas in this community reflect the nature of Tzintzuntzan society today is axiomatic. However, Brandes fails to substantiate his claim that devotion to the saints is an important component in these fiestas, which would allow for their characterization as sacred. Group activity does not make an event either sacred or secular, and both types of events may function as mechanisms of social control albeit through different means. From my perspective, it is the meaning captured in beliefs articulated in an event that defines it as either sacred or secular, traditional or desacralized, Mestizo or Indian, which, in turn, determines the expectations individual participants have about what will result from their efforts. While all ritual acts serve to guide and constrain behavior and may even be experienced by the people as having this purpose, it is the degree to which this purpose is actually achieved that matters in a study of social control. If Brandes had ascertained what the people of Tzintzuntzan did believe, he would also have come to know what they did not believe, which might have been something they used to believe in past generations but now consider irrelevant. This would have allowed him to grasp the significance of changes in beliefs that might have led to a more meaningful analysis of the nature of the fiesta system in its combined sacred and secular attributes.

In Chignautla, the cult of the saints is an ethical system pervasive in its constraining influence on behavior. The premises structuring the cult of the saints and individual experience rest on notions of a cosmological order in which all beings are bound to each other in making the world safe for existence. Whether in the form of pre-Hispanic gods who demanded blood sacrifice to maintain that order, or the saints who are repaid for their favors through the sacrifice of sponsorship, a cosmovision emerges in which harmony rests on the balance achieved between that which is given and that which must be reciprocated.

Chapter 6

The Structural Design of Participation

The principles ordering the practice of the cult structure the choices individuals make regarding which cargo best suits their intentions and when a cargo should be requested or accepted. Membership in a given household and descent group and residence either Arriba or Abajo constrain an individual's choice of sponsorship, determining which cargos he will expect to hold and ultimately will be granted by members of the Autoridad Eclesiástica, who make recruitment decisions. Thus, selection of individuals for sponsorship follows a recognizable pattern reflecting the most salient attributes of Chignauteco social organization and religious belief.

In the past, consideration of the needs of the collectivity was a major concern of the Autoridad in selection of ritual personnel and took precedence over the precise manner of sponsorship undertaken by any individual. Population increase and access to new forms of wealth have heightened competition between prospective cargo holders. The past decades have been witness to a more energetic pursuit of certain forms of sponsorship than others and barrio members have become more actively involved in the selection process in order to secure and retain sponsorships among their membership. This trend coincides with a diminution of the authority of the fiscales and the influence of the hueytatoanime in recruitment decisions, men of high ritual rank whose position in the system formerly allowed them to enforce collective goals. The hueytatoanime always epitomized ideal conduct. When they acted as a group, they could wield sufficient influence to force individuals to accept cargos or resign from them if their comportment was viewed as detrimental to community interests. The sacred status of these men insured that interactions between cargo holders and between Chignautecos and the saints remained balanced and harmonious.

The Ideological Foundation of Participation

Individuals who request or accept cargos are guided by consciously held beliefs that stipulate the correct and incorrect manner in which ritual action

181

must be undertaken in order to successfully achieve consciously held aims. As we have seen, Chignautecos believe that the saints cannot be fooled by unwarranted refusals nor obligated through unwarranted sacrifices. Such actions are believed to contain coercive intentions that are experienced as incompatible with the goals of sacrifice and the respect that sacrifice implies. It is from this perspective that cargo sponsorship may be seen as organized reciprocally and understood as being both voluntary and obligatory in the experience of Chignautecos. Correspondingly, individuals can neither be coerced into accepting cargos nor refuse. Chignautecos experience pressure to make their request for cargos because they believe themselves to be indebted to the saints once they have become successful enough to assume the burdens of ritual sponsorship. Chignautecos believe that the pursuit of self-interested goals, especially those involving greed, a quest for prestige, or any other self-involved ambition, is dangerous. Motivations of this type, once associated with requests for cargos, become the basis for explanations to interpret the misfortunes befalling individuals who fail to pay their debts.

In recent years, men of high ritual rank have complained that many individuals no longer willingly volunteer to sponsor certain cargos when formally asked, but are eager to obtain the sponsorships they wish. This indicates that the individual and common good, once structurally and ideologically undifferentiated, now conflict, and the means for obtaining cargos are less guided by traditional dictates. Immediate group interests, often represented by the voice of the mayordomos, at times challenge the authority of the fiscales, forcing the fiscales to consider the wishes of the mayordomos in the selection of ritual personnel. The insistence of the mayordomos is especially forceful when there is a disagreement regarding who should or should not be granted a specific cargo. The ability of the mayordomos to achieve their aims indicates that Chignautecos, without their conscious awareness, are redefining what constitutes appropriate conduct in regard to the saints while leaving unaltered the core assumptions that give rise to and sustain the traditional purpose of ritual sponsorship.

The Traditional Means of Recruitment

There are three types of formal gatherings dedicated to recruitment. The fiscales meet periodically throughout the year to select the majority of the mayordomos. At assemblies in the fiscalía after a mayordomía mass, plans for sponsorship are discussed. These are informal gatherings, and the intentions an individual has to sponsor a cargo will be evaluated in reference to his reputation. Throughout such discussions, other members of the Autoridad serve in an advisory capacity and their opinions are important to the fiscales. As I have mentioned previously, a second type of gathering that occurs in the fall of each year is dedicated to the appointment of the three fiscales and formalizing decisions informally made at other times regarding other cargo holders. The three fiscales are appointed by the four mayordomos of San Mateo, the four mayordomos of the Santísimo Sacramento, their four diputados mensajeros, and a minimum of eleven sacristanes (that is, only one of the twelve sacristanes menores may be absent for this meeting). The third type of recruitment assembly is dedicated to appointment of the mayordomos of San Mateo, who, for obvious reasons, are in a class by themselves. This is a special meeting of the fiscales in conjunction with the mayordomos of the Santísimo Sacramento, their diputados, and all twelve sacristanes menores. The sacristán mayor and segundo are rarely present at these meetings, but their influence is expressed by the sacristanes menores, who must attend and will voice their wishes.

The process of selection during these meetings is relatively uniform. In the absence of a formal request made within a reasonable amount of time before the duties of sponsorship must begin, the members of the Autoridad solicit suggestions during these meetings of specific individuals waiting or able to receive a cargo. This information is often provided by the sacristanes. What is most useful to the fiscales is information concerning the observed comportment, known reputation, and productive base of these individuals. The individuals' previous ritual experience and the quality of their performance of duties will also be at issue. The sacristanes are generally well aware of an individual's intentions to serve if they have been mentioned casually in a cantina or during ritual events. The fiscales and other high-ranking cargo holders who form a particular cofradía have the same opportunity as the sacristanes for observation of other Chignautecos.

Members of the Autoridad have represented a permanent locus of legitimate authority in religious life for as long as informants can remember. The teleological attributes of this ritual system are crystalized in the formal position of these men: ideological givens are confirmed in the achievement of these individuals, whose dedication to the cultural ideal is demonstrated by the favor the saints have shown in reciprocation for compliance with the dictates of traditional belief. The fiscales always relied upon the advice of the hueytatoanime in issues of cargo recruitment. The informal authority of the hueytatoanime insured that a consensus was achieved without discord or disrespect between men of differing ritual rank who might have different points of view and facilitated good will and the continuity of spiritual leadership. The fiscales also relied upon the sacristanes to uphold the ideals embodied in the cargo of fiscal. The sacristanes assist the fiscales in their duties and hold their cargos for life, but they are granted neither formal leadership responsibilities nor authority to make decisions. Effectively recognizing those men most likely to carry out the sacred responsibilities of sponsorship, the sacristanes have always been in a position to provide adequate information to the fiscales so they could select men who publicly and privately conform to the prescribed character of humble success and respectful obedience.

Recruitment decisions have always been achieved through consensus. Individuals in authority are careful not to appear to use unjustly the power vested in them. However, the actual process of decision making occurs rather informally. Once a decision is made, written notification is taken to the house of the candidate and the fiscales must wait for a response. If the individual selected fails to make an appearance at the fiscalía within the proscribed time, a letter will be sent to someone else. Refusals carry implications. They are noted by the fiscales and are taken into consideration for the future. If an appointment is refused, another meeting must be called, but the time lost may force the fiscales to bypass normal considerations for selection.

The Distribution of Cargos

While the successful management of one's resources in large part establishes the possibility for bearing the burdens of sponsorship, wealth measured in productive capacity alone does not guarantee selection. Individuals affiliated with a given barrio display their level of success in life by requesting sponsorships of a certain type and ritual value. Barrios whose residents belong to families who have generally succeeded economically will seek to obtain sponsorships that are believed to further their accomplishments. They will depend upon their most influential kinsmen, who have achieved a significant ritual rank, to assist in their selection. Access to certain sponsorships, then, becomes an issue of collective interest, and a barrio's success in acting corporately in these matters is believed to affect the quality of life for barrio residents. That is, through individual and collective efforts, the residents of a barrio attempt to maintain a balance between the actual success of individual residents and access to cargos already sponsored by barrio members. This localization of interests inevitably generates opposition between individuals of different barrios who are placed in competition for the same cargo.

The alliances resulting from these processes within and among barrios reflect and incorporate the division of the barrios into Arriba and Abajo.

There is a direct relationship between observable well-being and cargos sponsored. In experiential terms, a balance is maintained between perceived supernatural favor and responsive venerative acts. Increased local services like schools and electrical power, general health and welfare, and material affluence are attributed to supernatural favor, which correlates with the type and number of cargos requested and obtained by those individuals who have attained success. This balance is also structurally realized in a relatively fixed distribution of cargos held by individuals living Arriba and those living in Abajo and is a product of the struggle of the component barrios of Arriba and Abajo to keep certain cargos circulating among their members. Once a sponsorship is obtained by an individual affiliated with a component barrio of either set, it becomes difficult to relocate it across this imaginary ritual boundary. If a relocation of the cargo across this boundary does occur, Chignautecos experience a loss of opportunity to use that cargo to pay their debt. In short, the cargo will remain beyond their reach because those individuals who control the cargo will not relinquish it. Therefore, a relatively equal distribution of sponsorships between Arriba and Abajo represents only one possible structural expression of these processes.

Informants agree that the division into Arriba and Abajo is as old as the community itself. Informants also agree that Tequimila is the oldest barrio Abajo, while Calicapan is the oldest barrio Arriba, and all other barrios differentiated themselves from these. Neither Calicapan nor Tequimila has a small population, and at least one-fourth of all individuals residing there are adult men able to sponsor some type of cargo. Calicapan has a population of over 850 people and Tequimila has a population of over 900 people, making these barrios powerful in recruitment decisions. The principles governing participation in this system of sponsorships express not only the importance of descent in Chignauteco culture and the socioterritorial bifurcations existing within this community, but the balanced nature of reciprocal engagements between individuals and groups who participate in events of ritual importance. In effect, these fissiparous tendencies reach a balance. If an individual living in Arriba seeks a cargo currently and therefore customarily held by an individual living in Abajo, he must respectfully wait to implement his intentions. Not unlike the ritual actors who form the opposing groups of those who come and those who wait in a xochitis or the acompañamientos for a mayordomía, Arriba and Abajo are groupings whose members have mutual obligations and rights toward each other. In the midst of competition to secure cargos concordant with the needs of individual barrio members, interdependence is a sufficient and necessary cause for the cooperation demanded by the members of the Autoridad to insure proper veneration of the saints and the filling of all cargos; that is, cargo holders must act respectfully toward each other, no matter what residential affiliations they have, in the fulfillment of ritual obligations toward the saints.

The distribution of mayordomía sponsorships reflects the partisan interests of the barrios. However, even in the presence of these competitive processes, certain patterns emerge, once the total distribution of cargo sponsorships is charted over a significant number of years. The mayordomos of San Mateo tend to be equally divided between Arriba and Abajo although the sponsors for San Mateo 21 traditionally come from Tequimila, and the cargos of the mayordomo for San Mateo 21, 22, and 23 are more ritually valued than is the cargo of mayordomo for San Mateo 28. For at least the past hundred years, the mayordomos of the Santísimo Sacramento and their diputados mensajeros have been distributed so that two sponsors are from Arriba and two are from Abajo. But once again the mayordomias sponsored by these cargo holders are ranked and the two most valued tend to be sponsored by individuals living Abajo. It is rare that all three fiscales will come from either Arriba or Abajo, although this has occurred. More commonly, the fiscal primero and the teniente come from one set, while the alguacil comes from the other. The sacristán mayor and segundo have never come from the same set, and the men serving as sacristanes menores are affiliated randomly throughout the barrios with a generally even distribution between Arriba and Abajo. This distribution of the cargos insures a balanced representation from Arriba and Abajo among cargo holders within the Autoridad and insures that the cargo holders empowered with the administration of the cult are relatively constrained in their actions so that the partisan interests that might develop never come to fruition in a way that would affect the operation of the system as a whole.

If asked, cargo holders of high ritual rank will always state that all cargos are open to all men in good standing if they can afford a sponsorship, but they will also readily acknowledge that it matters where an individual resides. In fact, residence Arriba or Abajo is an overt consideration for members of the Autoridad in recruitment decisions. Even though cargos that are replicated are ranked in order of ritual importance, they also are replicated by numbers easily divisible by two, as we have seen. The sponsors of the mayordomias of Las Animas and Los Angeles associated with Todos Santos have almost always been divided equally between Arriba and Abajo for as long as informants can remember. The exceptions are the eight Jubileos, whose distribution, as far as I can tell, is strictly a function of kinship, since these cargos have been held by only two family lines for many years. The dance personnel are distributed in a different manner. The cargo of encargado is never requested but is appointed by the Presidente Municipal from among men who can afford the expense or from among those who have avoided serving as regidor de gasto. Sons of dancers usually dance, and since the members of each dance group tend to be from a specific barrio, the encargados are usually chosen from the respective barrios. The encargados select the head dancers and their Pilatos who, in turn, select those below them. Informants cannot recall a time when the dance groups were unevenly distributed between Arriba and Abajo, nor would it really matter to them. The dancers perform in honor of San Mateo and therefore function as communal symbols.

Tables 6–8 reveal a relatively even distribution of ritual sponsorships for the year 1971, which is not unusual. It is interesting to note that Abajo has a virtual monopoly on cargos of the first group, whereas Arriba has a monopoly on cargos of the second group; these monopolies tend to balance out because there are more cargos in the second group than in the first group. The removal of important cargos from one set to the other is typically a very gradual process. The importance of balance in the distribution of cargos derives from the importance of balance as an organizing principle in Chignauteco thought and cosmology and is central in the cult's ideological foundation.

Balance as an Attribute of Cargo Distribution

The forces that impinge on life in the municipio either perpetuate a relatively consistent distribution of sponsorships among the barrios or result in processes that will gradually or even precipitously alter their distribution without either ideological or structural change in the system as a whole. Since 1908, five priests have served Chignautla's parish. All resident priests leave their individual mark, especially if they remain in residence for many years. Yesterday's gossip has become today's legends, and people remember how the actions of a given priest either deleted from or added to their religious practices. The priest who arrived in Chignautla in 1952 was to remain for thirty-four years. During this time, he significantly interfered with the customary mode of recruitment for ritual personnel, but without transforming the fundamental nature of the ritual complex, which he was able to utilize for his own benefit.[1] He enlarged the role of the sacristanes by granting them

TABLE 6. Distribution of Cargos for 1971

Arriba	Abajo
Fiscal Primero	Alguacil
Teniente	
Santísimo Sacramento 2	Santísimo Sacramento 2
San Mateo 22, 28	San Mateo 21, 23
Diputado Mensajero 2	Diputado Mensajero 2
Sacristán Mayor	Sacristán Segundo
Sacristán Menor 7	Sacristán Menor 5
Cristo Rey	Jubileo de Carnaval 4
San Antonio Abad	Jubileo de Las 40 Horas 4
Día de la Candelaria	San Matías
Divino Preso	Virgen de los Dolores
San José	San Ramos (Domingo de Ramos)
Santos Reyes	San Antonio de Padua
San Lázaro (Santo Entierro)	La Santa Cruz
Señor de la Resurreción	San Martín de Porres
Señor de la Columna	Sagrado Corazón de Jesús
San Marcos	Virgen de Ocotlán
Santísima Trinidad	Sagrado Cuerpo del Padre Jesús
San Juan Bautista	Virgen de la Natividad
San Pedro	San Martín Caballero
Preciosa Sangre de Cristo	Virgen de la Soledad
Virgen del Carmen	Santa Cecilia
María Magdalena	Los Angeles
Dulce Nombre de María	Las Animas
Santa Teodora	Virgen de la Asunción
Virgen del Rosario	San Isidro Labrador
Divino Pastor	Immaculado Corazón de María
Virgen de Guadalupe	
Los Angeles	Niño de la Cruzada
Las Animas	San Rafael
Dancers 32	Dancers 38
Dance Encargados 3	Dance Encargados 4
Dancers Mayores 12	Dancers Mayores 9
Pilatos Mayores 8	Pilatos Mayores 6
Pilatos Menores 14	Pilatos Menores 24

Total

Cargos of the Autoridad	16	14
Other mayordomos	23	28
Dancers	69	81
	108	123

more power in matters of recruitment in a manner inconsistent with their traditional ritual rank and the ritual value of the cargo of sacristán, thereby undermining the balance of power among the members of the Autoridad Eclesiástica and altering the correlates of respect and rank among these cargo holders forever. His actions also upset the balance of influence between the currently serving mayordomos, who represented their individual barrios, and the hueytatoanime, who were distributed throughout the municipio and represented the collective interests of the parish.

The duties of the sacristanes are centered in the church and include assisting the priest during mass and informing him of affairs in the community. The sacristanes owe the priest their allegiance, which ideally would never conflict with the loyalty they owe the fiscales and other members of the Autoridad. This priest's interference with the traditional means for recruitment of ritual personnel resulted in an extreme response that altered the administrative function of the Autoridad Eclesiástica, whose position within the system's operation allowed the cult to remain self-perpetuating and self-regulating for over 250 years.

After his arrival in 1952, the priest solicited information from the sacristanes about those individuals requesting cargos. He then refused to confirm the selections made by the fiscales and instead confirmed individuals of his own choosing. It rapidly became impossible for the sacristanes to carry out the wishes of the fiscales without disregarding the wishes of the priest, a conflict whose resolution produced a profound effect on the distribution of cargos throughout the barrios. The sacristanes were in a compromised position. As a group, they had both more to lose (access to cargos desired for the future—often superior cargos of the Autoridad) and less to lose in upholding the traditional sanctity of the cargo of sacristán with its proportionately low ritual value and less potent behavioral constraints. The sacristanes did not

TABLE 7. Distribution of Mayordomias by Relative Ritual Value

| | Number of Cargos | |
	Arriba	Abajo
Group 1	1	4
Group 2	5	1
Group 3	2	1
Group 4	4	5
Group 5	6	3
Group 6	7	6
Group 7	2	12
	27	32

wish to incur the anger of either the priest or the saints as represented by the fiscales. In their experience, their compromise betrayed no sacred premises. On the one hand, the priest was always seen as an agent of the church, God, and the superimposed laws of the state and orthodox Catholicism, a system of legality and morality that fit somewhat uncomfortably into Chignauteco ontology. On the other hand, the presence of these authorities in the community fostered and perpetuated an attitudinal and expectational distinction between formal and less relevant obligations toward a remote God and immediate and essential rights to the favor of the saints. In acting as agents of the priest, the sacristanes gained informal power and their actions as a body became a counterforce to the centralized influence of high-ranking members of the Autoridad and the interests of individual supplicants from within their own barrios.

The ritual value of all cargos and the duties they entail, although ritually ranked, had never represented a chain of command. The traditional right of the fiscales to refuse an individual a sponsorship by upholding the cultural ideal was replaced by the priest's ability to refuse individuals already chosen by the fiscales on the basis of his personal interests. The source of the priest's power was his ability to withhold necessary ritual services such as performing mayordomía masses, baptisms, weddings, or last rites. The authority of the fiscales was eroded and transformed in its influence to function analogously to that of the important mayordomos, since the fiscales could no longer act to uphold the integrity of the collectivity. The priest was able to use the sacristanes, the diputados mensajeros, and the fiscales politically without divesting these cargos of their sacred purpose, which remained unaltered. The continuing reluctance of people to talk about these events bears witness to the tension created within the men who were torn between their need to assure harmonious interpersonal and personal-supernatural relations and their inevitable participation in generating disharmony. The fiscales retained their right to administer the affairs of the cult, but they did not retain their binding influence in recruitment decisions, that is, the efficacy of their sacred author-

TABLE 8.   Set Affiliations of the Fiscales from 1953 to 1972

Fiscal	Arriba	Abajo
Fiscal primero	9	7
Teniente	8	8
Alguacil	5	11

Note: Balance is displayed in the overall distribution of the fiscales, who hold their cargos as a group from one to three years before occupants of these cargos change.

ity, a role assumed by the mayordomos, who were forced to act more asser-
tively in the interests of their barrios in a manner uncommon before the
arrival of the priest. Whether or not the intention of the priest was to reduce
the instrumentality of strongly held beliefs, he did increase the politicization
of recruitment so that competitive activity increased as well.

The priests before 1952 had left ritual procedures to custom. The fiscales
had final say in who would receive cargos and what church projects would
be carried out. The sacristán mayor and the fiscales worked closely with the
priest in an advisory capacity, and the priest would be informed of a man
chosen to hold a cargo and give his approval based on the fiscales' recommendation. This was all to change. Chignautecos had been unhappy with two
other priests and they were dismissed from the parish. Both had raised the
price of ritual services, unreasonably in the eyes of Chignautecos, and the
fiscales and hueytatoanime were able to organize a coalition of the mayordomos against these priests. Members of the Autoridad complained to the
Archbishop of Puebla, and the priests were removed. Looking back, informants interpret the choice of the succeeding priest as a *castigo de Dios,* a
punishment sent by God for having rebelled in the first place. In 1952, the
newly installed priest quickly made it known that he was raising the fee for
ritual services and was tripling the cost of a mayordomía mass, which immediately generated opposition from the fiscal primero, who had been instrumental in removing the previous priests. But his term was drawing to a close.
The fiscal again organized the cargo holders against the priest, but consensus
could not be achieved about what action to take. People had become afraid.
Residing Abajo, the fiscal hoped to be joined by the hueytatoanime, many
of whom were from Abajo. But the priest insisted upon making the appointment of a new fiscal himself and refused the recommendation of the fiscales.
He chose a man from Arriba who had requested the cargo of San Mateo 21
for a number of years without success. Before this time, fiscales primeros
rarely came from Arriba; by the selection of this man and a new group of
mayordomos mensajeros and their diputados, the priest destroyed the normal
process of selection and the traditional balance inherent in it.

Chignautecos felt compelled to respond. The retired fiscal organized the
mayordomos into a force demanding the suspension of all ritual activity in
hopes of dissuading the priest from remaining in the parish. The plan failed,
however, because a new group of mayordomos from Arriba chose to follow
the new fiscal, blaming the previous fiscal from Abajo for bringing the priest
to the parish in the first place. By this action, they hoped to secure a newly
won access to some of the more ritually valued cargos denied them in the

past by the strength of the cargo holders from Abajo. The former fiscal was aware that this opposition was an expression of antagonisms that had always existed between Arriba and Abajo rather than anger at his actions, but he was not aware that the priest was skillfully manipulating these antagonisms to secure his position, which certainly would have been endangered by a unity between Arriba and Abajo. This structural disjuncture facilitated an individualistic opportunism normally checked among men willing to serve the saints but now possible through the encouragement of the priest who neither valued nor participated in this cultural universe. The priest found an individual who would serve his purposes, an individual who had entered service in the church as diputado mensajero under the new fiscal.

When the former fiscal closed the church, it was reopened by this diputado mensajero, who presented his conduct as an act of respect for the saints. The sacristanes told the diputado mensajero to relinquish his cargo and return home because they fully intended to remove the priest bodily and, if necessary, the new fiscal. But fearing no physical harm in the church itself, the diputado mensajero remained to keep the church open. Frustrated and angry, the mayordomos withdrew, and those currently serving finished their terms without incident. The diputado mensajero assumed the cargo of sacristán segundo, which he continues to hold and could hold for life. This individual had not come to reject sacred dictates of his culture, as individuals converting to Protestant sects have. Rather, he chose to ensure for himself the benefits intrinsic to them. At the end of the year, all ritual personnel changed, and none of the opposition retained positions of authority, since only men approved by the priest were chosen by the new fiscales, mayordomos, and sacristanes. The fiscales no longer represented a point of coalescence for traditional practice and beliefs. These events also lowered the age of men able to sponsor ritually valued cargos and altered a number of practices that determined access to this mode of human-supernatural engagement.

The Nature of Appointment to Cargos

The two most common motives for requesting cargos are to fulfill a vow to give thanks to a saint for favors attributed to the saint's beneficence and to fulfill an inherited vow offered by a close kinsman in exchange for a gift of real property. Once an individual requests a cargo, many factors are considered by the Autoridad. If personal misconduct becomes generally known, an individual's chances of obtaining a cargo are gravely reduced. As we have seen, a man estimates his ability to assume a sponsorship on the basis of milpa production, his ability to buy, raise, or sell animals, and the income he anticipates from cash crops or wage labor. Further, although men of Calicapan may wish they could sponsor the mayordomía of San Mateo 21, they will generally not request this cargo, just as men of Yopi, Abajo, do not expect to sponsor Señor de la Resurrección, even if they can afford it. They know that they will not receive these cargos because they are customarily held by individuals residing in the barrios of the opposing set. Such expectations reflect principles of selection framed in beliefs that articulate the relationship between land, descent, and how human beings relate to the saints.

Chignautecos believe that vows made to the saints create a sacred and enduring bond of rights and obligations between the individual, specific groups of individuals, and specific saints. Venerative efforts become multidimensional collective acts embodied in the position of the household head, the associated acompañamiento, and the alliances within a barrio and across the boundary between Arriba and Abajo. Certain assumptions are latent in beliefs about the association between an individual's tie to his land, barrio affiliation based on residence, kin ties established by descent, and relationship to the saints significant to a physical and social corner of the Chignauteco universe. The nature of their association becomes manifest in a history of sponsorship, which Chignautecos come to conceive as customary for a given individual.

Residence as Determinant in Selection of Ritual Sponsors

De facto residence is the most compelling basis for assumption of rights to a sponsorship, and men born and raised in the barrio in which they continue to reside can activate the strongest claim to a given image that has been sponsored by others in their barrio. Claims made to cargos by virtue of de jure residence are inevitably weaker. Men who live in this manner would not be trusted to validate the barrio's influence over the sponsorship, nor could they easily compete against men holding de facto membership to obtain a cargo. A son born to a man who changed residence but remained within the same set has little difficulty in receiving a cargo of his father's natal barrio; but if he is born in a barrio of the other set, strong pressures can be brought to bear against his sponsorship by other men of his father's natal barrio. He could obtain the cargo, however, if a special request were made asking to borrow the image for one year. This would require "borrowing" a house from one of his close kinsmen for the entire year of service.

Occasionally, skillful genealogical manipulation is used. This is illustrated by the efforts of a man to become the mayordomo of San Mateo 21, a man born in Tequimila to a successful descent group with a history of sponsorship of this cargo. Unhappy that his younger brother was chosen to inherit his father's house, he purchased land in Calicapan, Arriba, and became independent of his father. He defended his right to sponsor San Mateo 21 on the basis of his birth in Tequimila and his father and father's father having held the cargo. His request was not refused, but the saint was to return to Tequimila in two years' time. This type of manipulation and contractual agreement is not common, but may occur when the individual in question has a strong position in a network of ritually influential men. A favorable relationship with the current mayordomo is essential, since it is he who has the right to refuse a selection made by others. A man also betters his position by winning the favor of a number of sacristanes, for they can influence the priest. One informant made this comment: "Before when a man not of the right barrio wanted a cargo, he would talk with the mayordomo and fiscales. Now they talk to the priest. Before a man would gather about him all the pasados to exert influence. Now we must ask a favor of a sacristán."

I must mention that compadrazgo ties are never used for personal leverage in this context. Such desperate efforts would be incompatible with the respect inherent in relationships between ritual kinsmen. It is for this reason that ties of kinship and barrio affiliation remain important in requesting a cargo. If an outgoing mayordomo from the same barrio fails to give a strong recommendation to the fiscales, there is little chance of securing the cargo. Not even the fiscales can overrule the veto of a mayordomo. If a man is able to obtain the backing of powerful pasados, it is more difficult for the fiscales to simply refuse a request by saying that the cargo had been promised to someone else. One informant summed up these actions in a rather candid statement about the nature of selection of ritual sponsors:

If a man from over there [Arriba] requests a cargo, the fiscales will tell him that they cannot give it to him. The people [Abajo] won't let it go. Even if I go to the fiscal, the mayordomo will tell me to take another cargo if I want to serve. It would do a man no good to speak to the mayordomo and make a promise to return the image. But there can be no payoffs. People are even foolish to think about passing a cargo over there if they want to avoid squabbles.

New precedents can be established. When there is an attempt either to remove a cargo from its usual barrio or to retrieve it, the component barrios of Arriba or Abajo act collectively. For example, the mayordomía of the

Virgen de los Dolores was originally sponsored by an individual from San Isidro, Arriba. This cargo never lacks a sponsor and individuals who live Abajo also desire it. It was precisely when an unexpected frost destroyed a profitable plum crop Arriba that the sponsorship became vacant for the following year. A man of good reputation from Coaxicalco, Abajo, was able to enlist the aid of men from Tequimila and successfully obtained the cargo, which he held for three years. A similar transaction occurred for San Lázaro, originally sponsored Abajo but now sponsored Arriba, after it was once loaned to a resident of Calicapan. San Lázaro is valued more than the Virgen de los Dolores. When it became apparent that the mayordomo would retain the cargo beyond expectations, the men of Tequimila acted, convincing another man from Coaxicalco to consider sponsoring the Virgen as an act of retribution. Today, the Virgen de los Dolores remains in Coaxicalco and San Lázaro remains in Calicapan.

Descent as Determinant in the Selection of Ritual Sponsors

Previous sponsorship in the patriline often determines cargo requests, as well as appointments likely to be made by the Autoridad. Significant kinsmen in such determinations are father, tío hermano, and older brother, in descending order of importance. Kin of no bearing are primos hermanos, affinal kin, and matrilateral kin. Relationships among core members of the descent group provide a basis for the evaluations Chignautecos make about character, and a father's and son's achieved reputations are reciprocally influential. Cargo requests may be refused by the fiscales on the grounds that a father or brother acted improperly by falling asleep in the street when inebriated. This type of behavior is neither abhorrent nor rare, but will become an issue when there is an intention to deny a request for a cargo.

As we have seen, there is much pressure to follow in a father's footsteps in serving the saints. A young man's first sponsorship may be of a mayordomía menor, provided that his father did not hold as his last cargo one of significant ritual value. Such requests would not be denied but they are unlikely, because sons rarely request cargos ritually incompatible with those sponsored by their fathers and grandfathers. Young men who have not yet achieved their full potential in production but who are sons of important pasados may request cargos that reflect more directly their current economic standing, but not without embarrassment and not without making known their future plans to sponsor cargos closer in value to those ultimately held by their fathers.

Achieving a high degree of success confirms both conscious beliefs and latently operative assumptions about the role of the saints in human affairs. The conscious experience of success is accompanied by a compelling but less articulated experience of indebtedness, which reaches consciousness in a sense of obligation to reciprocate the saints' favors appropriately. How a father utilizes favors he has received from the saints matters: a household head should provide for his sons so that they will have the means for continuing their father's success. This promotes and enables future generations to perpetuate a balance in reciprocity with specific saints attributed with safeguarding the lives of members of the descent group. In effect, anticipatory notions of reliably forthcoming protection from the saints embody the same ideological principles that are structurally incorporated into notions of descent and organize relations between significant kinsmen, whose patterns of interaction reveal the efficacy of these principles within multiple and overlapping contexts. Men with genealogies relatively devoid of sponsorships will be given a minor cargo initially, most commonly a mayordomía menor, since a pattern of service has not become intertwined with genealogical reckoning. I must point out that men interested in pursuing cargos of the Autoridad normally seek the cargo of diputado mensajero or sacristán initially, or mayordomo mensajero if the service of their fathers permits, since their intention would be to serve as fiscal at some point in the future. Serving as diputado mensajero allows these men to learn the skills necessary to be a successful administrator while they are still young.

From among the adult men of a barrio, individuals of important ritual rank are always aware of others who wish to serve. The mayordomos mensajeros who sponsor the mayordomias of the Santísimo Sacramento know of men who wish to serve as diputados mensajeros and will choose their diputados from among these individuals. A diputado mensajero need not be affiliated with his mayordomo's barrio, but he will not be from the other set. It is better if a man's intentions are known before a formal pedimento is made to the fiscales. Men invariably request the most ritually valued cargo they can afford, as they believe that this action is the most prudent, but a specific choice of a cargo will always incorporate plans for the future. In the words of an informant:

He may go to the fiscal and say that he wants to serve but no one remembers him for diputado mensajero. If he asks for the Santísimo, they won't give it to him even though young men still try. Instead, they will give him a small mayordomía and passing this well, they can give him diputado mensajero and so he enters the church.

Formal Appointments to Ritual Sponsorship

The value of sponsorship is experienced egocentrically and particular beliefs are either more strongly or less strongly held by individuals regarding their relationship to the saints. The value placed on particular sponsorships is also determined by the position an individual holds within the family. Appointments to ritual office are experienced by members of the Autoridad from a different perspective from that of the supplicant. This is a parallel experience to that of those who have a right to give and those who have an obligation to receive at any given moment in time, depending upon their position in this chain of reciprocal obligations. Letters of appointment from the fiscales typically arrive after it is known who would be willing and able to sponsor a given cargo. Instead of directly informing the fiscales, men who wish to serve have previously made their intentions known in other contexts so that when a cargo becomes vacant, the fiscales are already aware of who is awaiting appointment. Some men are afraid that the current fiscal will reject them, and they will wait until there is a fiscal more favorably predisposed. A man might make his intentions known three to six years in advance, whereas one year is sufficient if a formal agreement has been reached with the fiscales or the outgoing mayordomo, who then informs the fiscales himself. The process is further facilitated if a man approaches a pasado of that cargo and is able to secure his backing.

The more ritually valued a cargo is, the more competition will develop over who is appointed to sponsorship, and the longer it will take those desiring such cargos to succeed in obtaining them. If there has been an especially good harvest in corn, coffee, or fruit, more men will desire a sponsorship. In poor years, the Autoridad must struggle to fill vacancies until the economic trend reverses. A story related by a fiscal is revealing:

He approached me and told me listen, do you know what I was thinking. I want to serve San Juanito but they won't believe me because I never go to church. I don't have any money but I have my work. I was thinking since my family is well, with what shall I give thanks? We can't know what will happen tomorrow. I replied to him that you must ask them because I think they will appoint you. Then he told me that there was someone there who didn't want him to serve, and so he asked me to set them straight. I did and they asked me if he were drunk. No, I said, he really wants to serve. They said he could when a year comes when no one wants the cargo.

If a man asks for a cargo, his actions have the potential to affect everyone. Therefore, the content of such conversations tends to travel quickly. A common path taken toward obtaining an appointment to a cargo begins with innocent conversation between neighbors. A man will share his thoughts with his wife. Such plans are always discussed, and nothing more may be said about it between them. The following day or week, his wife will go to the fountain or stream to wash clothes and will mention the conversation to a neighbor. There is no overt reaction, but the neighbor will tell her husband, who, in turn, spends time in a cantina or goes to work and mentions the intentions of his neighbor, generally or specifically, to a sacristán, a cargo holder, or a pasado. The role of gossip in the operation of cargo systems has been well noted by many writers; see Bricker 1973, Haviland 1977, and Gossen 1974. But gossip alone does not determine who will or will not receive a cargo. Actually, only a very small percentage of the population could be appointed if there were total compliance with what is known to be the right and just way to serve the saints. Informants agreed that it is better to leave a cargo unoccupied than to give it to someone whose behavior, attitudes, and motivations are not appropriate, thereby angering the saints. However, no matter how closely an individual's conduct adheres to set standards, if he cannot afford a cargo, he will not be asked to go into debt. A cargo will, at times, be given to an individual in the hope that he will correct poor behavior since sponsorship is believed to change a person's nature. In the words of an informant:

At times they give a cargo as a punishment. Between the people over there [the Autoridad], the fiscales, the sacristanes, one from among them will say let's give it to so-and-so. He won't be any good because he has a questionable character. Well, then who? They look for another. Then they say, let's give it to him; he's pretty saucy. He has some reputation, this and that. We will give it to him so that he will feel the burden. He has to come. Here, in the fiscalía, we are going to beg him to take the cargo. When he arrives to respond, with a crowd of people, like the sly one that he is, he will say yes.

Mayordomos may retain their sponsorships for another year rather than relinquish the cargo to someone who will not serve their interests. The mayordomos of the constituent barrios of Arriba and Abajo have several informal meetings to discuss the distribution of cargos throughout their sets: who is seeking which sponsorship, whether or not a fiscal is favorably disposed toward them, and the possibility of losing a cargo for lack of a sponsor. When a man is appointed to a cargo, the mayordomos and pasados from his barrio or an adjacent barrio go to his house to offer their advice, their main concern being the cargo holder's choice of replacement. They will arrive with a bottle of aguardiente and cigarettes to discuss what action should be taken so that the cargo will not fall into the hands of an individual living in the other set, possibly suggesting replacements from among themselves. If no one is willing, they agree to lighten the burdens of the current sponsor by contributing goods and labor so that he may serve another year, leaving the mayordomo to pay for the mayordomía mass.

This strategy is not without problems. When emotions run high over the possibility of losing a cargo that has traditionally circulated among a specific group of individuals, and there is aguardiente to drink, people will more easily commit themselves to promises made to other men rather than the saints, promises that they will not want to keep a year later. As one man commented: "Yes, yes, they say they will help me and then give me another drink. When I am drunk, I agree to continue my sponsorship, but aguardiente will not help me pay for the mass and fiesta a year from now." This situation occurs only when a barrio is extremely attached to a particular image.

For the mayordomo, his mayordomía represents his personal contribution to the collectivity. For the cofradía, attendance at a mayordomía enacts the fulfillment of public duty in representing the community to the saints. The function of the cofradía is important. Its membership includes high-ranking individuals from both Arriba and Abajo and thereby represents the repository of cultural ideals epitomizing nonpartisan interests. When the cofradía forms as the acompañamiento of the fiscales, this group is experienced as the "keepers of the faith" because the presence of the cofradía evokes shared values. Misuse of the sacred trust given those cargo holders of high ritual rank is constrained in two ways: decisions must be arrived at by consensus rather than unilaterally by fiscal, in most respects the most influential position in the system. Certain cargos carry the right and obligation to suggest possible choices in their replacement, while others must actually nominate individual ritual sponsors. On the one hand, the sacristanes and diputados mensajeros have the right to propose possible candidates, even though the diputados mensajeros are morally bound to support their mayordomos. On the other hand, only the fiscales, the mayordomos mensajeros, and the mayordomos of San Mateo have the formal authority to appoint ritual personnel. The fiscales also have the obligation to veto candidates they feel will not successfully carry out the duties of sponsorship in an appropriate manner. The teniente and alguacil are bound in support of decisions made by the fiscal primero. Any mayordomo, of course, can also legitimately veto a nomination made by the Autoridad regarding his sponsorship. Through this right, the mayordomo achieves equal influence in recruitment decisions to that of the fiscales, the mayordomos mensajeros, and the mayordomos of San Mateo. The mayordomos mensajeros and the mayordomos of San Mateo have a right to speak against a candidate, but they are compromised by the interests of their respective barrios. High-ranking pasados and the hueytatoanime have the right to offer opinions bringing pressure to bear on those who can suggest and nominate as well as those who have the right to veto.

The sacristanes and diputados mensajeros are in a unique position to assist some individuals while creating obstacles for others. Far less constrained by their lower ritual rank, these men use slander as no other cargo holder may. It would be impossible for a fiscal, a mayordomo mensajero, or a mayordomo of San Mateo to denounce others since it is unbefitting to their ritual rank. Chignautecos state that sacristanes can do as they wish, while the fiscales are responsible to the people. These consciously held ideals are translated into the constraints that bind those individuals whose rank simultaneously provides power and prevents them from misusing it. Those individuals capable of pursuing their interests relatively unencumbered by such constraints have little means for realizing personal or partisan interests.

The place of the mayordomos in the operation of this system must be understood in the context of the balance maintained between themselves and the fiscales, between the interests of the community as a whole and the particular interests of individuals within segmental groupings of the population. The ritual obligations and sacred rights of the members of the Autoridad, the ritually high-ranking and low-ranking mayordomos, and the interdependence of all ritual actors in the system create a sacralizing vehicle through which behavior is molded to ideals embedded in the ideology and experience of these people. In effect, the mayordomía complex successfully sacralizes interpersonal relations.

Chapter 7

Conclusions

This book has been devoted to a study of the pragmatic attributes of Chignauteco religion. The systematic body of religious beliefs and cosmological premises that give meaning to the cult of the saints represents what Chignautecos hold to be true about themselves and their world. In large part, this ritual-ceremonial complex is an expression of the mediating role Chignautecos attribute to the saints in their experience of both good and bad fortune. Celebrations held in honor of individual saints in reciprocation for their favors and the complex of substantive and symbolic actions they entail are sponsored by specific networks of individuals and reflect, affirm, and maintain Chignauteco values. The personal and collective instrumentality of these celebrations highlights the relationship that is believed to obtain between human beings and the saints, defining that relationship in a context of interdependence that is comprehensible in the experience Chignautecos have of each other. This interpretive stance insists upon an analysis that goes beyond description of the outward trappings of Chignauteco religious practice, a catalogue of beliefs, or a functional analysis of the cargo system. The literature is already replete with ethnographic treatments of this sort. What distinguishes this work is my assumption from the outset that beliefs must be differentiated from the patterns of interaction that constitute the structural configuration of the system, and further differentiated from the experience of the participating actors. Throughout this work, these conceptual domains are analyzed in terms of their mutual influence and interplay. It is in this sense that I have described the mayordomía system as a central sacralizing vehicle in community life.

The Confluence of Experience and Ideology

There is a coherent logic ordering activities in the domains of ritual, kinship, ritual kinship, economics, and aspects of public life as I have described them. In the perspective I have assumed, analysis of behavior, when moored to beliefs, demonstrates the operation of core assumptions that frame experience so that meanings are structured according to a uniquely Chignauteco design. The system of causality implicit in Chignauteco thinking embodies patterned interpretations that give rise to generally held expectations and relatively standardized actions. Behavioral choices that follow from these expectations either confirm or undermine the validity of beliefs from which they arise. In my portrayal of interpersonal interactions, I have used a framework that presupposes a close functional relationship between the structuring of individual experience and the patterning of social conduct. I have taken the position that core assumptions and the ideological system of a people are inseparable epistemological entities insofar as they share a content and provide the basis for organizing activity. It is this organizing activity that gives the experience of individual Chignautecos and the institutionalized activities of social life their recognizable contours.

My study of the cult of the saints led to an analysis of a determinable ideology, which made it possible to understand the basis for the ritual performances I observed. The practice of the cult in Chignautla bears the mark of sixteenth-century Hispanic folk Catholicism, in which much has been retained from a cosmology indigenous to the Sierra Nahuat, whose beliefs reflect themes common to Nahua peoples as a whole.[1] What I sensed from my field experience and ultimately came to conceptualize were ontological themes important in the experience of Chignautecos. These themes also emerged in my structural analysis of interpersonal interactions. Within a wide range of contexts, organizing principles either directly or indirectly incorporated assumptions about the role of the saints in human affairs. Activities dedicated to propitiation of the saints are directly sacralizing because they are an explicit expression of pivotal ideological tenets. Cosmological premises also come into play unconsciously in interactions structured by principles evoking central organizing themes of a sacred nature. The ordering of both experience and interaction, accordingly, enhances the strength of significant sacralizing vehicles that result in or contribute to the sacralization of interpersonal relations.

The dominant components of Chignauteco ideology have served to establish a frame of reference through which the data are presented so that reliable conclusions about Chignauteco culture and society are possible. My interpretations of the nature of social life in this community are based on the repetitive occurrence of a unitary set of meanings that relate the domains of this society to each other to form a conceptual whole. In this manner, the structure of ritual performances, public life and economic practices, and the nature of interactions between individuals related to each other through ties of consanguinity and ritual kinship form a coherent pattern, linking these realms of experience to each other.

In Chignautla, the Catholic elements in this complex are relatively insignificant in comparison to the preoccupation Chignautecos have with the saints, who may best be understood as sacred personages with whom they share their existence. There is little concern with heaven or hell or formal doctrine regarding the relationship between the saints and the Virgin Mary or the Trinity. Each saint has a distinct personality and is available by characteristic inclination to participate in human affairs in an uplifting or threatening manner. As such, the saints are concretizations of underlying assumptions about human nature. Themes of interpersonal and personal-supernatural interdependence unveil injunctions about what is necessary to maintain a balanced and harmonious order in the universe. Giving and receiving only to give again predominates as an organizing premise. Reciprocally organized and therefore proscriptive modes of engagement are structurally realized in ritual sponsorship whether in the mayordomía complex or in compadrazgo—institutions that share a common ideological foundation.

Beyond contexts that are formally designated as sacred, the subjective potency of obligatory exchanges crystalizes in the Nahuat term *makwis makepis,* used in reference to a category of relationship or quality of interaction in which there is an expectation of assurance in exchanges of material and social support. The symbolic and substantive manifestations of the principle of reciprocity and the connotations of balance and harmony implied in them make reciprocity both pragmatic and sacred. Reciprocity is antecedent to rank and respect in the sacralization of interpersonal relations. Sacrifice embodies both harmony and balance. What is implied in sacrifice allows this dimension of ritual sponsorship to become antecedent to the sacralization of the activities that enact personal-supernatural relations. The sacrifice of sponsorship ties individual goals to collective aims while intensifying the experience of indebtedness to the saints and the importance of rules of conduct necessary to induce their favor. These ideological elements are the major sacralizing vehicles that sustain unconsciously held assumptions about the natural order of things and what may be expected to follow from venerative acts. They define notions of the possible, the probable, and the expectable in human social life. In Chignautla, all that is assumed to be essential is often what is held to be both traditional and sacred. Very often, "what ought to be" is what has persistently come closest to nuclear themes of traditional cosmology.

Assumptions regarding what the saints demand for their favors, whether they are housed in Chignautla's church or in the hotlands in La Garita's chapel, compel Chignautecos to sponsor mayordomias. While assumptions about the nature of the world indirectly organize expectations, these expectations do not generally become conscious unless there is a discordance between an expectation and actual experience. If expectations consistently prove false, they will become susceptible to challenge without necessarily altering the long-standing assumptions that generate them. In this way, the pull toward consistency in social life and the inevitability of change through transformation of experience becomes knowable. The development of new expectations through changing experience can only lead, over time, to new assumptions about the world, eventually producing a new ideology to confirm what has already been altered structurally.

Indians and Mestizos do not share the same cosmology. This ethnic division has implications for many aspects of life in which ethnicity is overdetermined. What affects Chignautla's Mestizos also affects the Indian population of the municipio, but interpretations and responses will differ. The Mestizos were never dependent upon subsistence agriculture. They have always eaten and dressed differently from the Indians and have always been dependent upon their ability to generate cash to purchase goods in the markets of Teziutlán and beyond. The Indians have, until recently, been far less dependent upon cash earnings and were able to produce most of what they needed. Cash outlays and cash earnings were consistent and balanced, engendering a sense of economic stability. This began to change during the 1950s with an increased monetization of the economy, which forced the Indians to augment their means for generating a relatively constant supply of cash. Yet, nothing pertaining to the intricate system of meanings and explanations changed because of these processes. Most changes are accepted largely as facts belonging to a modern existence, such as the use of corn mills, the use of confetti and candles purchased in Teziutlán to replace the flower petals or the sacred wax consumed in mayordomias, or the use of plastic sandals now worn by Indian women. These additions are not experienced as antagonistic largely because they do not challenge the major institutions of the society. An exchange of ideas and technology between sociocultural systems that occupy the same space and time is accepted as inevitable. The ritual system itself has accommodated many intrusions that do not yet generate conflict in individuals, who continue to reciprocate the saints for the successes they have achieved.

The Mestizos had the benefit of electric light in the first decade of the twentieth century because of the early construction of a hydro-electrical plant close by. The first Indian hamlet received electrical power in the mid-1960s, while the majority did not receive this service until the early 1980s. The use of manufactured items and the consumption of new foods that save time are changes that offer the Indians greater ease of living. Until very recently, it was generally believed that the saints would be responsive only if the sacrifice of sponsorship was undertaken humbly, the individual expending neither more nor less than what the saints provided from good harvests. Profits from capitalistic investments, however, have steadily increased since the 1970s, and other sources of a sustained cash income now interfere with the relationship between traditional production, consumption, and cargo sponsorship. Expectations are being recast to fit new experience and gradually altering underlying assumptions regarding the proper manner of living. That is to say, the absolute standard of behavior held necessary to invoke supernatural favor is being reinterpreted so that it is less absolute, but without calling into question the traditional interpretation of the reciprocal nature of human-supernatural engagement and the form ritual sponsorship should take to achieve its purpose. Similarly, the expectation of supernatural punishment for individuals who disregard the wishes of the fiscales has failed to be reliably confirmed. Indeed, those barrios most able to compete aggressively to secure valued cargos have become examples of the good results of ritual sponsorship achieved by different means.

When a system of explanation fails to be instrumental, underlying assumptions will be exposed as unworkable, especially when they fail to answer questions or solve problems to which they traditionally were addressed (Rokeach 1960). This is significant for the study of ritual systems in a context like Chignautla, in which certain material advantages are not uniformly distributed throughout the population and individual survival is increasingly dependent upon the success an individual has in navigating the world beyond Chignautla's ideological borders. It is then possible to understand why a number of Chignautecos have become successful construction workers in Puebla or Mexico City, using vacations to return for the central celebratory events of the sponsorships, to which they attribute their continuing success as wage earners. This contrasts with Cancian's (1990) report of increased proletarianization of Zinacantan's population, accompanied by loss of productive land and decentralization of religious authority in diminishing requests for cargos. He believes this to be an aspect of a larger process that will eventually destroy the religious cargo system of Zinacantan. Cancian remarked on Vogt's opposing view (offered in 1976) that community fission would lead to the development of additional cargo systems in different parts of the municipio, a process not unlike what is occurring in Chignautla. The political economy of the nation, especially today, has an effect on how life is lived in communities like Chignautla or Zinacantan, to which the cargo system adjusts, but only insofar as the ideology sustaining the operation of these systems remains sufficiently efficacious to promote individual participation. There is no need to challenge traditional beliefs if the success an individual achieves is already proof of the validity of what is to be gained from ritual sponsorship.

The Unifying Influence of Nahuat Cosmology

The most significant ideological-cosmological themes operative in the cult of the saints in Chignautla are realized in the organizing principles that I have designated as sacralizing vehicles. The following have emerged as most significant: the sacralizing effects of the ethic and action of reciprocity, whose evocative potency derives from and is entailed by the fundamental premises of balance and harmony; the explicit value and sacralizing effects of sacrifice in a context in which sacrifice is the ideational correlate of reciprocity; and the constraining effects of respect, enacted through distinctions of rank that assign rights and obligations to individuals in relationships of immediate and practical importance. These sacralizing vehicles intensify the effects of reciprocity in contexts not overtly dedicated to sacred aims. I have also used the term *ritual value* to designate the manner in which Chignautecos assign cargos particular significance, allowing the affinities and differences between them to emerge in the conceptual groupings I have charted. All of the above principles are implicit in the order in which ritual acts are performed, making understandable the nature of participation in the cargo system as a whole.

The Changing Nature of Chignauteco Existence

The remaining conclusions are devoted to a description and analysis of transformations of a way of life during the past twenty years, changing as well the nature of this folk Catholic complex. Like many rural communities in Mexico today, Chignautla is caught up in the throes of slowly accelerating but inexorable modernization of the material bases for existence, changing what is considered essential in order to live a good life. Indeed, the pragmatic basis of this ritual-ceremonial complex is exquisitely sensitive to shifts in the configuration of daily life brought about by the introduction of more efficient methods for dealing with life's concrete realities. Yet, compelling aspects of the sacred worldview of these Indians are so intricately interwoven into the experience of living that certain aspirations and perceptions of the world remain fascinatingly durable. Today, there is shameful discomfort in things traditional (and therefore Indian) and younger generations fail to insist, to the same degree that their parents and grandparents did, on proscribed modes of relating interpersonally and with the saints. Young adults no longer depend upon long-standing interpretations because they have learned alternate explanations for what occurs. But there is a quiet persistence of the "old truths," which emerge in times of stress, and Chignautecos have not yet replaced their ritualism with a more thoroughly secular existence, even though the meaning behind ritual acts may be concealed beneath a veneer of modern trappings.

The Modernization of Traditional Life

Today, in the last decade of the twentieth century, Chignautecos are far more oriented toward the nation than ever before. The majority realize their competitive disadvantage. The younger generation of Chignautecos have not retained the use of Nahuat but speak Spanish in a fashion that will allow them to be readily identified as Indians regardless of how they dress. People in Teziutlán used to comment that Chignautla was a strange place: there are wealthy men but they wear *huaraches,* the sandals traditionally worn by Indian men. With primary schools in all the barrios and a secondary school attended by Indians as well as Mestizos, a new locus of cultural change is available. Ideas and concepts are taught that concern making life better for the individual rather than making the world safe for existence. Formal education provides the means for opportunities antithetical to the functional interdependence of production and ritual sponsorship and the balance it maintains between household subsistence activities, reciprocal assistance, and wage work. These amendments to the Chignauteco lifestyle are consistent with the need to obtain skills for occupations in a national labor force, shifting importance away from the community well-being that was always entrusted to respected individuals who lived well and received the blessing of the saints.

An emphasis on the well-being of the individual and his or her nuclear family signals a loss of the Chignauteco preoccupation with the saints, who eventually will assume a position closer to the periphery of conscious concern. Modernization is affecting the pervasive influence of a sacred worldview and the customs through which it was always expressed. Most of the settled portion of the municipio now has street lights and potable water, and local bus lines between Chignautla and Teziutlán pick up and discharge passengers in Tequimila and Calicapan. There are many more televisions, cars, and trucks, and roads have been improved accordingly. Possibilities for modern health care have reduced infant mortality but with a consequence of increased population. Modern conveniences such as transportation, communication, processed foods, and manufactured clothes facilitate a preoccupation with the use of time in relation to money, since time is an essential ingredient in wage labor. Packaged foods are purchased to save effort even though they are not preferred to foods made in the home. Manufactured items are replacing those produced locally by household members or by specialists because they save time. Issues of convenience have penetrated the ritual domain as well. A wedding no longer takes three days, nor is the xochitis performed to initiate compadrazgo. There has been a gradual decline in the extent of reciprocal assistance asked for and received. Ayuda is gradually replacing makwis regardless of context, because it is disrespectful to ask individuals to give up their time without compensation now that time has an established value. Long journeys required to bring special materials, and the labor needed for house repairs before a fiesta, are now a form of labor for which a wage is paid.

Currently, although Chignautecos eagerly accept the material benefits of modernization, they remain reluctant to neglect their mayordomias. Mayordomos are far more likely to entrust ritual duties to their diputados or immediate kinsmen since the demands of wage work have forced a new evaluation of how time is best spent in the maximization of relatively traditional goals. Men are more eager to sponsor mayordomias than other cargos since most mayordomias involve important but discrete events of short duration. Other ritual events have become less elaborate because sponsors will gladly spend the money, but not necessarily excessive amounts of time in attention to detail. Extremely expensive cargos are held for more years consecutively, thereby enhancing the sacrifice of the sponsor while successfully reducing labor and cost. Important mayordomias are given less readily to individuals who live far from a Centro that is also expanding, and there has been an increase in the sale of land for new house sites, and a concomitant rise in rented houses. While more young men are able to hold more important cargos, the admonishments typically forthcoming for not conforming to usual custom, for example, serving mole instead of lamb and cabbage soup, are not as constraining, and there is greater room for individual choice than ever before in the manner in which the saints are celebrated. In effect, these are outward signs of change in response to a new distribution of critical resources that have not yet modified the value of the most evocative symbols centrally positioned in traditional venerative acts. Not only have the pragmatics of life been altered, but the more peripheral activities of the mayordomía complex are already changing and will more readily succumb to the pressures of scarce time. That is to say, a reorganization of sacralizing contexts is occurring so that elements that come into conflict with efficiency are more readily deleted from ritual performances, while the more evocative components will be condensed to symbolic portrayals rather than direct enactments. Events like the xochitis hold little value today, since compadrazgo will continue without it. Similarly, if only one fiscal and one sacristán form the cofradía for a mayordomía, the purpose of the mayordomía is still achieved.

It is not surprising, then, that what constitutes national Catholicism is beginning to hold greater appeal for Chignautla's Indians than ever before. Aside from the encouragement of the new priest to join religious associations of one type or another and to attend Sunday mass regularly, this form of religious practice requires less time, addresses the individual rather than the collectivity, and allows women to uphold the faith more openly and independently of their husbands. The regulatory effects of reciprocity, respect, and rank on interpersonal conduct are being replaced by a system of personal interest and morality. Thus, as a more orthodox Catholicism becomes heir to modernization, there is promise of a rewarding afterlife without concern for a harmonious passage through life. However, for the Indians, mayordomias still generate an intense sense of partnership, in contrast to the church, which at times is experienced as a lonely place. Presently, this sense of partnership remains fundamental to the cult of the saints. It continues to be more compelling than the newly emerging value on individual success visible in increased secular activities, which is antithetical to a sense of timelessness characteristic of life in Chignautla only twenty years ago. There is a similar sense of timelessness to the cult of the saints, maintained in the continuity of its rituals. Insofar as mayordomias remain instrumental, the newer goal of a higher standard of living will not undermine the system, because greater economic success and skillful capitalistic investment can simultaneously serve a personally gainful and communally sacred purpose.

A major impetus for change derives from the demands of the national political organization and national economy. In the past, these domains of experience were never primary or differentiated from public life, the cult of the saints, or the manner in which social life in the barrios was organized. There is a growing discrepancy between traditional ideals of conduct and an environment increasingly conducive to competition, individualism, and self-reliance, producing discontinuity with a meaningful past. In this context, the struggle of the Indians to obtain a political identity is assuming greater importance. Chignautla's Indians are now seeking positions within the municipal government and in national political parties, not as the pawns of the Mestizos as they once were, but as representatives of their own interests even though they are aware that the power they seek corrupts. The Indians also realize that sponsoring San Mateo circumscribes their influence to a domain of public life that does not translate beyond Chignautla's borders.

Of all the domains within this society, the economy displays the greatest autonomous functioning, reflecting its role as a locus of secularizing influence. The first signs of desacralization of core institutions are bound to follow, leading ultimately to a society with a concomitant bifurcation of the sacred and the secular. I agree with Nutini (1988) that modernization, often consisting in the random selection of substantive additions, is necessary but not sufficient to transform an ideological core. It is the desacralization of intrinsic elements of ideology that results in a worldview whose structural expression cannot resemble that which came before.

The Desacralization of Existence

Chignauteco cosmology, in which both human and supernatural beings share a temporal and spatial existence, is showing signs of erosion. New elements are emerging that are characteristic of a society whose worldview positions human beings and saints differently vis-à-vis each other. As the saints move further from the center, their quality of relationship with human beings will change, as will the perceived nature of responsiveness between them.

Subtle shifts in the choices made by individuals are now apparent. Individuals seek to combine traditional and nontraditional goals through means that will eventually erode the primacy of ritual in regulating interpersonal relations. As desacralization proceeds, the saints will be granted a less and less pivotal role in human fate. Some individuals already experience themselves as the primary agent in what befalls them or willingly blame others and even the state for inequities resulting from a national system of stratification in which Indians remain despised and disadvantaged. Newly politicized awareness is closely associated with greater emphasis on wealth and power and is reinforced by national political parties, which, like the Spanish friars, are busy competing for souls to fill their ranks with new converts. Thus, the different spheres of activity that Chignautecos are eagerly entering today place greater and greater demands on their time, and the hustle and bustle of modern living is already obvious. It is not a long journey from timelessness to being time bound, and it is an even shorter journey between a framework of time and one in which the saints play a role less significant in making the world safe for existence than money. When this transition is completed, the saints venerated for so long might still reside in the church and shrines that dot the landscape, but they will hold a position in religion rather than social life, and the ideological premises that form the basis for life in Chignautla will have become fully desacralized.

Desacralization of Economic Endeavors

Chignautla's economy today displays an amalgamation of sacred and market principles. No longer are engagements between specific categories of individuals inherently reciprocal. That is to say, important relationships like those based on descent offered the possibility of reliable assistance whenever needed, intensifying the bond between these individuals. Hence, mutual assistance was not defined by task. Today, makwis has largely been replaced by ayuda, indicating a loss of a sense of timelessness in reciprocal obligations. This trend indicates a preference for utilitarian engagements that concern little more than the money that will be spent and earned and it is likely that ayuda will be reliably forthcoming only from individuals with whom one already has some type of relationship. Today, the search for wealth has taken on new meanings. The amassing of wealth is undermining the influence of those whose authority was based on the perceived favor of the saints and there are a significant number of Indians who have become wealthy. In the past, wealth alone could not assure influence; those who failed to live up to stated ideals found themselves denied the ritual sponsorships they requested. Today, the respect one merits and one's social standing is no longer confirmed by ritual rank and a stratification whose basis is solely economic is developing.

Chignautecos say that they no longer have time to maintain fields a great distance from their place of residence. Such fields are now readily sold as house lots. This is a response to their increased value in a context of land scarcity and the greater importance given to cash income not associated with the productive use of land. Previously, milpa cultivation and ritual sponsorship were not only functionally interdependent, but were symbolically and experientially merged in the minds of Chignautecos. To labor in the milpa and serve the saints was the ideal life lived well. Today, land is an important commodity and wage earnings are used to purchase both corn and land, producing a premium on cash income.

The Reorganization of Public Life

There is today a notable distinction between public and private life, between ties to the barrio and ties of kinship, and between the civil and religious authorities. Just as the ethical premises of life have become more circumscribed in their efficacy, civil and religious governance have grown further and further apart, the former associated with the future, the latter with the past. There has been an evolution from the sacred authority of the men of the Autoridad to an increased emphasis on the moral authority of the priest and the legal right of municipal officials. This coincides with recognition of the importance of the legal system, now experienced by the Indians through its impact on their lives.

In the past, each of these institutions of public life operated successfully as a means of social control, but they remained distinct experientially and had different implications for the conduct of social life. Respect had been an expression of the formal authority granted to those individuals holding religious offices. In recent years, increased possibility for personal aggrandizement independent of concerns for the collectivity has undermined the importance of men of high ritual rank as guiding symbols. Indeed, ritual participation has become more truly voluntary, but for reasons reflecting allowance for individual choice where previously there was little choice if an individual hoped to please the saints.

What was originally a man's personal and social duty has become a rewarding undertaking for the individual, rather than an absolutely essential task necessary for the well-being of everyone else, even though Chignautecos are not yet at the point where the risk of noncompliance allows them to ignore the saints. Belief in supernatural reprisals has also become a less potent constraint since they are now interwoven with other explanations for personal calamities. The saints are less likely to be seen as causative agents when sickness or natural disaster occurs, even less likely than witches, or mal de ojo, indicating an increase in interpersonal rivalry formerly mitigated more successfully. This is clear in the interpretation offered by Chignautecos for two events some thirteen years apart in their occurrence. In 1972, church robbers seeking the valuable sacramental objects of silver and the image of

Dulce Nombre de María with her large gold heart surreptitiously removed these items from the parish church. The damaging storm the following day was interpreted as San Mateo's castigation for the carelessness shown by the diputados mensajeros and sacristanes in residence in the church. In 1985, the alms were stolen from the collection box just after the mayordomía mass for the Virgen de Guadalupe. People gossiped for days about who could have stolen the money, but in the end, nothing came of it.

In this altered social climate, there is greater personal isolation. What is being lost is not yet replaced by something else of value. The sense of emptiness individuals experience, especially those unable to achieve even the smallest measure of success given their new expectations, has increased their resentment at signs of success aimed at impressing others, a display that can only lead to a greater struggle for wealth and power. In growing desperation, respect has become all too easily replaced by abuse and higher levels of interpersonal violence than ever existed before.

In general, traditional beliefs are less consistently expressed in action and there is less compliance with what was upheld and publicly realized through the lives of the hueytatoanime. Not only have the hueytatoanime fallen into a comparatively ambiguous position within this society, but their formerly generalized influence is much curtailed, as is the overt display of respect accorded cargo holders outside of ritual contexts. The hueytatoanime are usually older and typically cling to the past. Their belief in the traditional way of life makes them appear antagonistic to things modern and they cannot hold the attention of the younger men, who are now held in high esteem for the cargos they hold early in their lives or because of the good wages they earn. But admiration does not have the same sociological implications as respect.

The injunction to serve the saints without pride is now challenged by a growing concern with communal identity that can serve as a meaningful bridge between Chignautla and the world beyond. The altepeihuit has taken on new importance but as a fiesta fully divorced from the sacred mayordomias that were centrally positioned within it. The altepeihuit is now an event aimed at generating pride in being Chignauteco and fiestas are arranged so that visitors will attend, strangers formerly resented as intruders. Consequently, there is a new sense of doubt associated with the belief that the saints will be responsive to people who engage in all the activities that are supposed to assure a positive outcome because, in effect, that outcome has ceased to be fully certain.

The Desacralization of Kinship

In comparison to 1972, there is a marked restructuring of interpersonal relations at the level of the household, the nonresidential kin group, the barrio, and the set as the functional integrity of these primary social units erodes. Individuals cannot maintain the level of face-to-face contact typical of the past: economic pressures force sons to earn a living independent of their fathers and establish house sites for their own families where they can. It is not uncommon today for young men to leave early in the morning and return late in the evening from jobs they hold in Teziutlán. This coincides with a weakening of respect and reciprocal expectations that gave the relationships between fathers and sons and between brothers their instrumentality. In fact, the growing scarcity of land, addressed initially by building two-story dwellings to continue the residential proximity of these kinsmen, now forces individuals to move further from the households of previous generations and members of the nonresidential kin group are rarely localized within the same or neighboring barrios or even within the same set. These individuals turn to ties of friendship for the assistance they need.

The stigma attached to residing uxorilocally is also disappearing, and civil marriage is now occurring along with marriage in the church. The reliability inherent in the reciprocity expected between husbands and wives, parents and children, and among siblings is being replaced by a new certainty emanating from laws that regulate the disposition of property. Barrio endogamy intensified ties between residents of a barrio that were further solidified through ritual kinship. Today, marriage partners are chosen from anywhere within the municipio or from other communities where young men have the opportunity to find work. With the changing nature of these interactions, ritual kinsmen are becoming a significant social resource for the individual or young couple. Compadres are sought among individuals who share a similar experience rather than a similar ritual rank, and people today are beginning to turn to ritual kinsmen in much the same manner as they once turned to members of the descent group.

More important, perhaps, are the structural transformations affecting the convergence of rights in land, in people, and therefore in saints, dismantled under new economic and demographic pressures. The strength of the barrio in securing rights to saints and in solidifying patrimonial land was a function of patrilineal descent and patrineolocal residence operating to establish entitlement to cargos. Reciprocal ties between fathers and sons were generationally extended through the custom of dejar dicho, which intensified the func-

tional significance of patrilineality in recruitment to cargos. With a break-
down in reliable assistance between members of the descent group and normative patterns of postmarital residence, the barrio no longer functions to
uphold the alignment of kinsmen and cargos. Recruitment will continue to
become more dependent upon the individual, independent of descent, barrio,
or set affiliation.

The Demise of Balance and Harmony

On my last visit to Chignautla, I noted that the clouds that impale themselves
on the peaks of Mt. Chignautla still gave the community nestled at its foot a
magical quality. The sense of timelessness captured in the ideology that
evolved in this community is being severely challenged by what I experienced, at that moment, as an abrupt intrusion upon my senses. My eyes were
drawn to the bulge of population emanating from Teziutlán, houses extending to the very borders of the municipio to join new houses built by Chignautecos in creating a formless mass of the stuff of progressive modernization that will eventually engulf what is left of Chignautla's original essence.
Indeed, the harmony and balance at the heart of the indigenous cosmology
of these Sierra Nahuat Indians and expressed throughout the institutions of
their society is gone, and there remains far less of either harmony or balance
in the Chignauteco experience. The disturbance, which lies just below the
level of conscious awareness, is an absence of something there before, the
compelling presence of immediately involved supernatural beings who were
attuned providers of all that made life worth living. Forced to replace their
pre-Hispanic gods with Catholic saints, the ancestors of today's Chignautecos embraced the saints without altering too greatly the characteristics as-
cribed to their supernatural benefactors or what was expected from their
favor or disfavor. A ritual-ceremonial complex evolved, anchored firmly to
the institutions that created a style of life that remained self-confirming and
self-regulating until the last decade. Today, the transformation of this complex is central to the observable changes taking place in Chignautla, which
are not yet equally at the center of Chignauteco awareness, because this type
of experience would be far too devastating were all of its implications understood. But the mind maintains a protective shield for only so long, and as the
substantive basis of beliefs and practices of the cult of the saints continues
to erode, Chignautla's Indians will come to know that what was can no
longer be.

All the changes that I have described in these conclusions have not been fully noted consciously by Chignautecos themselves as of serious consequence, or even as changes. They are accepted as evolving aspects of life. Mayordomias continue to be sponsored as they have always been, even though their instrumentality contains new purposes. Certain rules of conduct remain significant and even recognized, but they are no longer determinant. Injunctions formerly captured in consciously held beliefs are not backed by social sanctions because they are no longer backed by belief in supernatural sanctions as they once were. These injunctions now function as consciously held ideals for those who wish to live up to them. Most individuals still hold to traditional beliefs about paying one's debts to the saints even though conduct expressing this belief is losing ground to the demands of the priest to abandon practices that do not conform to the orthodoxy of the church. Turning to a nationally promoted religious system allows Chignautla's Indians to fit more comfortably into the world of the Mestizo, and many mayordomias are growing closer in form to those held by Mestizos. Furthermore, the successful entrenchment of Protestant sects in the community encourages a disbelief in the sacred truths of the past, since many of these converts have become quite successful without the favor of the saints. Regardless, the Indians who have turned to Protestantism, and the vast majority who have remained Catholic, are equally left with the distance and remoteness of a God less immediately involved in the facts of daily life than the saints, who, like Chignautla's Indians, are being forced into a secondary position in the ultimate scheme of things. For the time being, the conceptual system encouraged and taught by the priest can only offer explanations that poorly fit what Chignautecos have always assumed and experienced to be true, and such explanations will be less likely to interpret specific local happenings convincingly than many beliefs so readily did.

The actions of the current priest, unlike the priest before him, are an important impetus to change, and his presence in the community will discourage the perpetuation of the mayordomía complex in its traditional form. The previous priest understood well the intricacies of the mayordomía system, and, in his quest for personal gain, was able to utilize its structural properties successfully without interfering with its ideological basis. In 1952, the intensity of feelings surrounding participation was still largely intact and beliefs appeared to be confirmed by experience. Chignautecos were able to react to the priest's intrusions with a strike of the mayordomos, again affirming the depth of their beliefs and their attachment to their mayordomias. The current priest, in contrast, arrived in Chignautla in 1986 in the midst of a morass of uncertainty between two systems of belief tied to two substantively contradictory ways of life that had already come into severe conflict. Intention, occasion, and capacity combined in such a manner that this priest took the opportunity to make changes that will gradually have a profound effect on the nature of Chignautla's folk religion.

Unacknowledged as problematic by Chignautla's Indians, a series of changes the new priest has instituted since his arrival are very telling and will result in the obliteration of the boundaries between the sacred world of the Indian and the secular world of the Mestizo. Aside from the religious associations the priest has established, he has created a church choir for young adults, and he offers communion, confession, baptisms, weddings on a regular basis and usually on Sundays, and daily masses and rosaries. These are not unusual events in and of themselves even though they represent a more rigorous adherence to orthodox practice than was ever offered by the last priest. But in the context of other events that he has instituted, a pattern emerges. When a major mayordomía such as San Mateo 21 is celebrated, the priest not only insists upon a procession with this image, but he includes in the procession several of the most nationally important saints, such as the Virgen de Guadalupe and the Virgen de Ocotlán, and several regionally important saints, such as the Virgen del Carmen. All of these saints are closely associated with national and therefore Mestizo society. This dilutes the evocative potency of what is symbolized by the patron saint, especially during the celebrations held in his honor, by undermining the importance of distinctions in ritual value (and the associated sacrifice) attributed to the different saints. Such distinctions emphasized the ideological position of San Mateo, who epitomized Indian identity and the role attributed to the mayordomía complex as a whole in insuring general well-being. Several other images introduced in the procession for San Mateo, such as San Matías, are images of saints of little ritual value, while others, such as San Miguel, are not celebrated in the Indian system at all. Hence, the ideological boundary between these two systems of belief is made structurally irrelevant.

The use of the parish church for both Mestizo and Indian mayordomias affirmed and articulated the ethnic division that was sustained through the spatial and temporal means I have described. Each system retained its integrity but sanctified the discrepancy in social position between these ethnic groups. Mestizos and Indians were always "separate but equal" in Chignautla's church and in social life. During the mayordomias of the Indians, the church and its atrium became an Indian sanctuary; during the religious fiestas of the Mestizos the church belonged to them. The processions instituted by the new priest disturb the precarious balance between these two systems of belief. An ideologically random conglomerate of saints now marches in procession from the church through the streets of the Centro. Such elaborate processions encourage and validate prideful and public displays of devotion rather than the humble acceptance of responsibility that expressed confidence in the individual who served as a chosen representative to fulfill collective aims toward the saints by means not visible to the public.

Such changes clearly facilitate the mestizoization of Indian ritualism, by integrating Indian ritual forms into a general desacralized design that obliterates the reciprocal roles of the church and the household of the ritual sponsor. The priest has succeeded in convincing the sacristanes that cleavages in the community between the Indians and the Mestizos, between the barrios and the Centro, and between Arriba and Abajo are detrimental to spiritual well-being. Consequently, neither residence nor ethnic identity overtly remains an issue in the sponsorship of mayordomias, even though competition has now arisen between the Indians and the Mestizos over mayordomía sponsorship for images that are highly valued in much the same manner as competition existed between Arriba and Abajo. In 1989, a Mestizo sponsored the mayordomía of San Mateo 21 after the cargo was relinquished by a resident of Calicapan. In response, the highly prized Mestizo image of the Virgen del Carmen was requested by a man from Coaxicalco who has sponsored the image for two years and has successfully insured that another man from his barrio will sponsor the image in 1992. Although informants state that the mayordomo of San Mateo fulfilled his duties to the saint, they noted that certain elements of a traditional mayordomía were eliminated by the Mestizo sponsor. Similarly, the mayordomo of the Virgen del Carmen was forced to combine a number of elements of both Mestizo and Indian practice, whereas the mayordomo who will take his place intends to sponsor his mayordomía in a fashion that fully conforms to traditional Indian practice.

However, the most compelling change forced by the priest has been the replacement of these distinctions with one based on religious difference; that is, a denominational difference aimed at bringing Chignautla's Indians into the modern world. In this way, the priest is disallowing the ideological isolation that protected Chignauteco culture and the organization of individual experience for all these years. A recent event that heightens the ideological crisis that is progressively destroying whatever internal sense of harmony and balance remains for these Indians occurred over what was to be a publicly celebrated funeral held for a man greatly respected in the community. A hueytatoani, he had served as the mayordomo of San Mateo, fiscal, and Presidente Municipal years ago and represented the essence of the sacred core of Chignauteco existence. Because of what he symbolized and his influence in public life, the church was crowded to capacity for a public mass, an honor given only to those men who have achieved this level of importance. But the mass was never held. The priest appeared and simply announced that he would not officiate at a mass for an individual of a different religion. Stunned, the people left the church. Conversations with them revealed that many people suddenly became frightened, experiencing consciously, and perhaps for the first time, a sense of culture loss.

Whether or not this hueytatoani had actually turned to some Protestant sect (as many have in his barrio) is not as important as the fact that he had participated in and belonged to the Indian world, and during his life had embodied its values. His participation in the many sacralizing contexts that cross-cut the institutions of this society enabled the people to place him within their cultural universe, through which they could know and respect him. That this man might have privately come to question or even relinquish certain beliefs about the role of the saints in human affairs made him no different from many others in the community today. The people came to pay their respects not only to him, but to what they were being forced to surrender in themselves. The conflict unfolding in this incident is not between two religions, as the priest implied, but rather between the integrative nature of Chignauteco ideology and belief and the more secular and segmental worldview of the priest. The priest's organization of experience reveals his perception of religion as an autonomous domain, as it exists on the national level in Mexico today, distinct from the economy and politics of national life. The priest had, by his action, not only removed this man from the community of the saints, but from the community of his people. Events like this capture the disharmony occurring now in Chignautla, and it is precisely this type of event that, as it is repeated, will bring into full consciousness the changes that have already occurred and that I have attempted to portray as the final contribution of this book. The history of Chignautla's sacred cosmology will be obliterated by time when there is no more memory of it, since history, like experience, must become memory to be preserved. But when events and their meanings are lost to the experience of Chignautla's Indians, their memory of their history will no longer exist.

Appendixes

1971 Calendar of Ritual Events of the Indians in the Public Arena

Event	Date	Type
Month of January		
Change of fiscales, mass to San Mateo	Jan. 1	O
Niño de La Cruzada de los Sacristanes	Jan. 3	O
Church faena—milpa	Jan. 6	—
Los Santos Reyes	Jan. 6	M
Niño de La Cruzada	Jan. 10	M
Mass of fiscales, second Sunday each month		O
San Antonio Abad	Jan. 17	M
Month of February		
Día de La Candelaria	Feb. 2	M
Church faena—milpa	Feb. 15	—
Jubileo de Carnaval del Primer Día	Feb. 20	M
Jubileo de Carnaval del Segundo Día	Feb. 21	M
Jubileo de Carnaval del Tercer Día	Feb. 22	M
Jubileo de Carnaval del Quarta Día	Feb. 23	M
Divino Preso (Ash Wednesday)	Feb. 24	M
San Matías	Feb. 27	M
San Mateo 23, Recibimiento	Feb. 28	M
Month of March		
San José	Mar. 19	M
Preciosa Sangre de Cristo	Mar. 26	M
Change of mensaje	Mar. 31	O
Month of April		
Virgen de los Dolores	Apr. 2	M
Semana Santa (Easter Celebrations)		
Vespers, San Ramos	Apr. 3	M, RC
Domingo de Ramos (Palm Sunday)	Apr. 4	M
Lunes Santo, Adoracíon Nocturna	Apr. 5	S
Martes Santo—preparations for Passion of Christ	Apr. 6,7	RC
Jueves Santo (Holy Thursday): Last Supper of the Apostles	Apr. 8	CO, RC
San Lázaro (Good Friday): Enactment of Passion of Christ, Velorio	Apr. 9	M, CO, RC

Event	Date	Type
Sábado de Gloria (Holy Saturday)	Apr. 10	RC, M, CO
Señor de La Resurreccíon (Domingo de Gloria or Easter),		
Los Tres Encuentros	Apr. 11	M, RC
Divino Pastor	Apr. 24	M
Señor de la Columna	Apr. 25	M
Month of May (Mes de María)		
Daily rosaries at 5:00 P.M., barrio fiestas celebrating		
La Santa Cruz		
San Marcos	May 2	M
La Santa Cruz	May 3	M
First communion of Niñas	May 5	CO
Mass for Inmaculada Concepcíon	May 8	S, CO
Mass for Mother's Day	May 10	CO
San Isidro	May 15	M
San Martín de Porres	May 17	M
Annual Mass, La Vela Perpetua	May 20	S
Santa Cruz in San Isidro and Tequimila	May 25	O
Church faena	May 30	—
Mass for deceased mothers	May 31	CO
Church faena—milpa	May 31	—
Month of June (Mes de Jesús)		
Daily rosaries at 5:00 P.M.		
First communion of Niños	June 5	CO
La Santísima Trinidad	June 6	M
Church faena	June 6	—
Mass for living fathers		
Corpus Christi	June 8	CO
Primera de Corpus	June 9	M
Jueves de Corpus	June 10	M
Domingo de Corpus	June 13	M
San Antonio de Padua,		
Corpus Christi—Coahuixco	June 14	M
Corpus Christi—Coahuixco	June 15	M
Octava de Corpus	June 17	M, A
Sagrado Corazón de Jesús	June 18	M
San Juan Bautista	June 24	M
Mass for deceased fathers	June 28	CO
San Pedro	June 29	M
Annual mass, Sagrado Corazon de Jesús	June 30	S, CO
Change of mensaje	June 30	O
Month of July		
Presidente names encargados, encargados name Pilatos,		
fiscales appoint Tocotines		
Appointment of first fiscal	July 5	—
Virgen de Ocotlán	July 10	M

Event	Date	Type
Virgen del Carmen	July 15	M
Annual mass, Virgen del Carmen	July 16	S, CO
Fiscal primero chooses teniente, alguacil	July 20	—
María Magdelena	July 22	M
Nombramiento received by teniente	July 22	—
Nombramiento received by alguacil	July 23	—
New fiscales meet with priest	July 28	—
Month of August		
Sunday practice for dancers		
New fiscales meet with sacristanes	Aug. 2	—
Sagrado Cuerpo del Padre Jesús	Aug. 6	M
Virgen de la Asuncíon	Aug. 15	M
Virgen del Inmaculado Corazón de María	Aug. 22	M
Month of September (Tiempo de San Mateo)		
Jubileo de Las 40 Horas	Sept. 2	M
Jubileo de Las 40 Horas	Sept. 3	M
Jubileo de Las 40 Horas	Sept. 4	M
Jubileo de Las 40 Horas	Sept. 5	M
Vespers, Virgen de la Natividad	Sept. 7	M, DO
Virgen de la Natividad	Sept. 8	M, DO
Dulce Nombre de María	Sept. 12	M, DO
Santa Teodora	Sept. 17	M, DO
Principio de San Mateo	Sept. 20	O, A, RC, D
Vespers for San Mateo 21	Sept. 20	M, A, D
San Mateo 21	Sept. 21	M, A, D
Recibimiento of fiscales	Sept. 21	O, D
Vespers for San Mateo 22	Sept. 21	M, A, D
San Mateo 22	Sept. 22	M, A, RC, D
Vespers for San Mateo 23	Sept. 22	M, A, D
San Mateo 23	Sept. 23	M, A, RC, D
Formal meeting of Autoridad Eclesiástica	Sept. 25	—
Vespers for San Mateo 28	Sept. 27	M, A, D
San Mateo 28	Sept. 28	M, A, RC, D
Change of mensaje	Sept. 30	O
Month of October (Tiempo de San Mateo)		
Dancers perform in Atempan	Oct. 4–6	—
Vespers, Virgen del Rosario	Oct. 6	M, DO
Virgen del Rosario	Oct. 7	M, DO
Church faena—milpa	Oct. 10	—
San Mateo of Ayuntamiento Municipal	Oct. 16	RC, O, DO
Despedida of Centro (3d Sunday)	Oct. 17	O, D
San Rafael	Oct. 24	M
Las Animas (Todos Santos)	Oct. 31	M
Section masses for Todos Santos (7)	begin Oct. 31	CO

Event	Date	Type
Month of November		
Los Angeles (Todos Santos)	Nov. 1	M
Las Animas	Nov. 2	M
Los Angeles	Nov. 2	M
San Martín Caballero	Nov. 11	M
Virgen de la Soledad	Nov. 15	M
Las Animas, public masses	Nov. 14–20	—
Cristo Rey	Nov. 21	M
Santa Cecilia	Nov. 22	M
Despedidas de Todos Santos, Los Angeles	Nov. 29	M
Las Animas	Nov. 30	M
Month of December		
Annual mass, La Purísima	Dec. 9	S, CO
Recibimiento, San Mateo 21	Dec. 10	M
Vespers, Virgen de Guadalupe, Chignautla	Dec. 11	M, D
Virgen de Guadalupe in Chignautla	Dec. 12	M, D
Virgen de Guadalupe in Coahuixco	Dec. 13	M, D
Despedida, Virgen de Guadalupe, Coahuixco	Dec. 14	M, D, O
Annual mass, Virgen de Guadalupe	Dec. 15	S, CO
Despedida, Virgen de Guadalupe, Tepepan	Dec. 16	M, O, D
Posadas with daily rosaries	Dec. 16–24	CO
Final despedida of dancers	Dec. 18	M, O, D
Niño Dios for the parish	Dec. 24	M, RC
Barrio fiestas for Niño Dios	Dec. 20–25	O
"Promisias" (special collections)	Dec. 17–31	—

Note: CO = mass sponsored by collection
M = composite event of a mayordomía
RC = events involving civil and religious office holders
A = viewed as an altepeihuit
O = sponsored ritual event analogous to mayordomía
S = event sponsored by a sodality (association)
D = dancers perform
DO = dancers optional.

Appendix 2

Range of Yearly Income for 1971–72, in Pesos

Occupation	Daily Wage	Minimum	Maximum	Average
Campesino/agricultural labor	10–12	2,500	3,500	3,200
Factory work, Teziutlán	25–45	7,800	14,000	10,900
Truck/bus driver	25–45	7,800	19,300	18,000
Blue collar, Teziutlán	25–45	7,800	19,000	18,000
Mechanic, Teziutlán	20	4,600	6,200	5,000
Cal factory (limeworks)	20–25	6,500	8,400	7,800
Mason/construction worker				
Chignautla	18.50	4,800	5,700	5,700
Teziutlán	25	6,500	7,800	7,800
Puebla/Mex. DF.	30–45	8,000	10,000	9,300
Security guard	25–28	6,000	9,000	8,500
Textile worker/Teziutlán	25–30	7,800	9,300	8,500
Baker	20–30	6,200	9,300	7,800
Baker's assistant	20	3,100	6,200	5,800
Machetero (cargo loader)	12	3,200	3,700	3,600
Animal regatón	—	4,000	15,000	10,000
Vegetable regatón	—	4,000	7,000	6,500
Fruit regatón	—	5,000	9,000	7,000
Stone cutter/gravel beds	8–10	2,000	4,000	2,800
Corn mill owner	—	10,000	40,000	25,000
Barrio grocery/dry goods store	—	4,000	6,000	5,000
Cantina owner	—	5,200	15,000	8,000
Seamstress	—	1,400	3,000	2,000
Domestic help				
Chignautla	—	1,200	3,400	2,400
Teziutlán	—	3,000	6,500	4,300
Carpenter	—	1,500	8,000	6,000
Tailor	—	2,000	5,000	3,000
Charcoal maker	—	1,000	4,000	3,000
Butcher/store owner	—	4,000	13,000	9,600
Leñero/kindling (12 pesos per load)	—	2,000	5,000	3,000
Tortilla maker	10–15	3,000	3,700	3,400
Washerwoman	—	800	2,000	1,200
Midwife (50 per birth)	—	300	1,000	600
Gelder	—	250	1,000	500

227

Occupation	Daily Wage	Minimum	Maximum	Average
Musician	30–50	500	2,000	1,200
Curandero	—	700	3,000	2,000
Brujo	—	200	1,500	1,000
Cohetero (rocket maker)	—	2,000	7,000	5,000
Ritual paraphernalia artisan	—	200	1,000	500
Animal slaughter	—	200	800	400

Age, Landholdings, and Occupation of Ritual Sponsors, 1971

Cargo Title	Age	Landholdings	Occupation
Mayordomo Mensajero	53	2¹/₄ hec.	Agriculture
V. de la Natividad	32	1¹/₄ hec.	Factory work
Diputado Mensajero	33	1¹/₄ hec.	Agriculture
Fiscal (teniente)	57	4¹/₂ hec.	Agriculture
San Matias	26	³/₄ hec.	Limeworks
San Mateo 28	43	3 hec.	Federal roads
Jubileos de Las 40 Horas	23	4 tareas	Agriculture
Pilato Mayor, Negritos	29	1³/₄ hec.	Regatón
Encargado, Guacamayas	53	³/₄ hec.	Cantina owner
Diputado Mayor, San Mateo	47	2 hec.	Mason
V. de Guadalupe	32	1 hec.	Machetero
Fiscal Primero	42	5 hec.	Agriculture
Las Animas	34	1³/₄ hec.	Agriculture
Sacristán Mayor	60	4 hec.	Agriculture
Diputado Mayor,			
V. de Guadalupe	58	2 hec.	Sheep herder
San Mateo 22	49	5 hec.	Agriculture
V. del Rosario	31	2¹/₂ hec.	Agriculture
Pilato Viejo, Santiagos	62	1¹/₂ hec.	Agriculture
Santa Teodora	37	1 hec.	Cohetero

Comparative Cash Value of Sponsorships

Sponsorship Title	Average Cash Value (in pesos)
Cargos of the Autoridad Eclesiástica	
Fiscal	10,000–15,000
Mayordomo San Mateo	7,000–15,000
Mayordomo Mensajero	7,000–15,000
Diputado Mensajero	2,000–4,000
Sacristán	200–400
Sacristán responsible for Niño Dios	1,200
Mayordomias by Conceptual Groupings	
Grouping 1	7,000–15,000
Grouping 2	4,000–9,000
Grouping 3	4,000–8,000
Grouping 4	2,000–5,000
Grouping 5	1,000–3,000
Grouping 6	500–2,500
Grouping 7	500–1,000
Dancers	
Encargados	500–2,500
Dance Capitain	400–1,500
Pilato Mayor	400–1,500
Dancer	50–300
Pilato	50–350
Barrio Sponsorships	
Coahuixco	
Virgen de Guadalupe	7,000–10,000
Corpus Christi	3,000–5,000
All others	800–4,000
Tepepan	
Virgen de Guadalupe	1,500–3,000
All others	500–2,000
Mayordomos de Pila	300–800
Santa Cruz in May	400–1,000

Note: These are average and not inclusive figures. Certain sponsorships may have increased cost depending upon preferential elaborations, purchases made for the image such as new clothes, contributions made to the church, whether or not a separate recibimiento was held, and the amount of contributions made from the sponsors acompañamiento.

Approximate Cash Value of Ritual Expenses for Compadrazgo, in Pesos

Event	With Xochitis	Without Xochitis
Baptism		
Those who come	600–1,000	300–400
Those who wait	500–600	250–300
Wedding		
Bride's family	800–1,500	400–800
Groom's family	2,000–4,000	1,000
Padrinos	500–2,000	400–800
Confirmation	Same as baptism	Same as baptism
First Communion	Usually no xochitis	250–500
Funerals with Wakes	—	2,000–3,000
Dia del Santo	—	100–600
Ritual Object	—	100–200

Note: For a hueyxochit these figures may be tripled. These costs reflect averages for 1971, when 12.50 pesos equalled US $1.00. The costs have steadily increased given the inflation of prices and the devaluation of the peso.

Expenditures in Cash Value for Ritual Sponsorship in 1971 of San Mateo 21 Held without Diputado Mayor

Goods	Cash Value (in pesos)	Food Items	Cash Value (in pesos)
Mass	350	Aguardiente	240
Cohetes	576	Coffee	40
Castillo	180	Sheep, 6	600
Toros, 2	900	Pigs, 4	1,782
Cigarettes	48	Cabbage	36
Decorations	100	Chickens	108
Light bill	20	Turkey	180
Incense	4	Xole	150
Confetti	6	Bread	28
Flowers	150	Beans	30
Dishes, etc.	13	Rice	23
Kindling	180	Mole	440
Gourds	10	Corn	
Music	400	Tortillas	500
Tax for toros	30	Cacalas	80
Paint	100	Xole	36
Arco lujo	50		4,273
Charcoal	80		
Matches	2		
Lime	15		
Rope	18		
Roofing material	131		
New processional platform	210		
Plastic covers	10		
New household altar table	35		
	3,618		
Combined Totals, 7,891			

Goods	Cash Values (in pesos)	Food Items	Cash Values (in pesos)
Church faenas			
Cigarettes	18	Aguardiente	80
Paint	50	Corn	50
	68	Pig	372
			502
Combined Totals, 570			
Recibimiento			
Music	250	Corn	100
Cigarettes	12	Pigs, 3	1,140
Cohetes	180	Aguardiente	200
Candles	30	Mole	380
Confetti	3	Coffee	7
	475	Beans	30
		Bread	15
		Xole	80
			1,952
Combined Totals, 2,427			
Pedimentos			
Cigarettes	2	Aguardiente	16
Rituals for wax			
Cohetes	72	Foods	122
Cigarettes	6		138
	80		
Combined Totals, 218			
Total cost of sponsorship, 11,106			

Appendix 7

Cash Value of Cargo of the Santísimo Sacramento, 1971, in Pesos

Mayordomo*		Diputado	
Items	Cost	Items	Cost
Mass	350	Castillo	180
Cohetes	420	Music	70
Music	380	Cigarettes	12
Flowers	150	Decorations	82
Cigarettes	18	Light bill	10
Decorations	125	Kindling	18
Light bill	20	Charcoal	15
Kindling	89	Lime	10
Charcoal	30	Candles	45
Dishes	85	Pig, 1	680
House repair	175	Chickens, 3	54
Lime	40	Turkey, 1	78
Candles	75	Corn	100
Pigs, 4	1,125	Beans	13
Chickens, 15	282	Bread	25
Turkeys, 3	275	Mole	25
Xole	183	Coffee	40
Corn	500	Aguardiente	120
Beans	40		1,577
Bread	45		
Mole	680		
Coffee	65		
Aguardiente	312		
	5,464		
Recibimientos, for Rotations			
Meat	1,116	Meat	420
Aguardiente	420	Aguardiente	40
Music	280	Music	70
Cohetes	208	Cohetes	72
Mole	380	Food items	100
Cigarettes	6	Cigarettes	6

Mayordomo		Diputado	
Items	Cost	Items	Cost
Corn	150	Corn	50
	2,380		758
Food for diputado while in church for 3 months	450		
Thursday masses	480		240
Cleaning equipment for mensaje of diputado	100		
Church faenas	800		200
Total expenses for year	9,224		2,775

*These costs reflect the cost of items in 1971.

Appendix 8

Expenditures for Ritual Sponsorships in 1971

Cargo Title	Items	Total Monetary Value (in pesos)
	Virgen de Guadalupe	
	Mass	300
	Cohetes	360
	Toros	900
	Music	400
	Flowers	250
	Aguardiente	380
	Corn	550
	Meat	2,500
	Other	1,485
		7,125
	San Antonio Abad	
	Mass	250
	Cohetes	252
	Flowers	150
	Mole	560
	Aguardiente	156
	Cigarettes	12
	Meat	715
	Light bill	20
	Bread	6
	Coffee	10
	Other food items	150
	Fixing house	190
	Chickens, 4	72
	Candles	30
	Corn	150
		2,723

Cargo Title	Items	Total Monetary Value (in pesos)
	Jubileo de Las 40 Horas	
	Mass	250
	Cohetes	108
	Candles	24
	Light bill	20
	Music	67
	Corn	80
	Flowers	75
	Foods	380
		1,004
	Santos Reyes	
Mayordomo		
	Mass	250
	Cohetes	108
	Flowers	150
	Candles	20
	Light bill	20
	Corn	100
	Foods	300
	Other	287
	Music	175
	Aguardiente	64
	Cigarettes	6
		1,480
Diputado		
	Aguardiente	40
	Cohetes	72
	Candles	12
	Corn	10
	Foods	175
	Other	58
	Music	50
		417

Combined Total, 1,897

	Encargado of Negritos	
Pedimentos	Aguardiente	185
	Cigarettes	12
Dance Practice	Aguardiente	96
	Sheep, 1	100
	Pig, 1	490
	Other foods	189
	Corn	57

Cargo Title	Items	Total Monetary Value (in pesos)
Principio	Sheep, 2	200
	Corn	75
	Cabbage	12
	Other foods	189
	Cohetes	72
Despedidas, 2	Corn	100
	Cohetes	108
	Music	75
	Xochikoskat	114
	Plates	48
	Other foods	380
	Miscellaneous	235
		2,737

Itemized Cargo Expenditures, 1971

Event	Item	Cost (in pesos)
Dance captain (Cortés)	Costume	380
	Aguardiente	160
	Cigarettes	36
	Food	740
	Miscellaneous	287
	Corn	42
		1,645
Pilato menor	Quota	10
	Collections	15
	Costume	350
	Cigarettes	12
		387
Pilato mayor	Costume	234
	Quota	10
	Corn	50
	Mole	380
	Aguardiente	180
	Other foods	250
	Cigarettes	18
		1,122
Dancer	Costume	275
	Cigarettes	6
	Quota	10
	Aguardiente	40
	Candles	5
		336
Diputado menor of mayordomía of Divino Preso	Wax	8
	Cigarettes	6
	Aguardiente	24
		38

Appendix 10

Sample Household Composition

Actual Composition	Number of Households
Mo, Da with spouse and children	27
Mo, 2 Das, So with spouse and children	4
Fa, Mo, Da with spouse and children	11
Fa, Mo, So, 3 Das, So with spouse and children	58
Fa, So with spouse and children	31
Fa, Mo, 3 Sos with spouses and children	17
Mo, 2 Sos with spouses and children	23
Independent nuclear family	181
Nuclear family—uxorilocal	31
Single person dwelling	12
Total	395

Appendix 11

Entries from the Book of the Fiscales

Mayordomía de Jubileo de Carnaval del tercer día, Sr. José Aparísio
Wax 28¹/₂ kilos, an escaño
14 of February, 1956

The mayordomía of Divino Pastor received by Sr. Tomas Antonio
Items belonging to the mayordomía:
Worked wax 49 kilos, An *escaño* without a key, A demandita of the Divino Pastor, a picture frame, two altar cloths, one drum, two wooden candlesticks, one metal chain, a brown dress, a robe of velvet, a small bed cloth, an escaño which is in the church
15 of February, 1956

Inventory of items of the mayordomía of San Antonio Abad:
The wax weighed 48 kilos, an escaño with its key, a demandita of San Antonio, a new pole for the procession platform
Señor Lorenzo Castro of Section 1 received these items on the
20th of May, 1956

Mayordomía of Octava de Corpus received by Teodoro Andrés
Wax in the quantity of 148¹/₂ kilos, 6 glass vases, an escaño with a key, an alms plate, a pallium in the color white
July 1, 1956

Mayordomía of Virgen de Guadalupe: mayordomo Sr. Juan Rodrigo
Wax 152 kilos, one curtain, a demandita, two palliums, one tablecloth, an escaño
15 of July, 1956

Mayordomía of the Virgen de Guadalupe del barrio de Coahuixco
El mayordomo Sr. Leobardo Romero
Wax 84 kilos, one demandita, one bell, one cloth for altar, two candlesticks, one cámara (explosive chamber)
16 of July, 1956

Mayordomos del Santísimo Sacramento and other images:

Cayetano Climaco gave	50 kilos of wax
Alberto Ibañez	50 kilos of wax
Crisanto Lucas	125 kilos of wax
Trinidad Hipolito	50 kilos of wax

Filipe Benito	50 kilos of wax
Miguel Rodrigo	75 kilos of wax
Silvino Peña	40 kilos of wax
Marcelino Moralez	50 kilos of wax
Viginio Ortiz	25 kilos of wax

Transaction in sale of wax by fiscales:

Eulalio Martínez	bought	14 kilos of wax @ 5.00	70.00	May 2
Trinidad Hipólito	bought	50 kilos	250.00	Jan 3
Odélon Rodriguez	sold	29 kilos	147.00	Jan 3
Refugio Santos	sold	16^1/2 kgs.	82.00	Jan 3
Anselmo Castro	sold	32 kilos	160.00	——
Anatolio Magdaleno	sold	11 kilos	55.00	Sept 1
Viviano Santos	sold	63 kilos	315.00	Nov 5
Amando Cesario	bought	7 kilos	35.00	Dec 1

The above concerns the mayordomía of San Mateo 28:
Wax 121 kilos, a demandita, an escaño, two altar cloths, two andas
Dec. 30, 1956.

Quota for the renovation of the balance weight of the bells was collected from the following citizens:

Rosendo Benito	Vincente Aparicio	Cayetano Climaco	Emiliano Benito
Viviano Ramón	Rafael Jiménez	Odelon Rodriguez	Isidro Esteban
Bernardino Lucas	Encarnación León	Jacinto Lara	Vacilio Reyes
Nicolas Andrés	Francisco Camacho	Modesto Ramón	

Notation of case brought before fiscales:
Felipe Benito received 121^1/2 kilos of wax while Simon Gonzáles was fiscal. He returned 156 kilos of wax before the fiscales Benito Esteban, etc., and stated before these men that he had not received from Simon González a receipt when the transaction was made.

The Parish Church of
San Mateo Chignautla

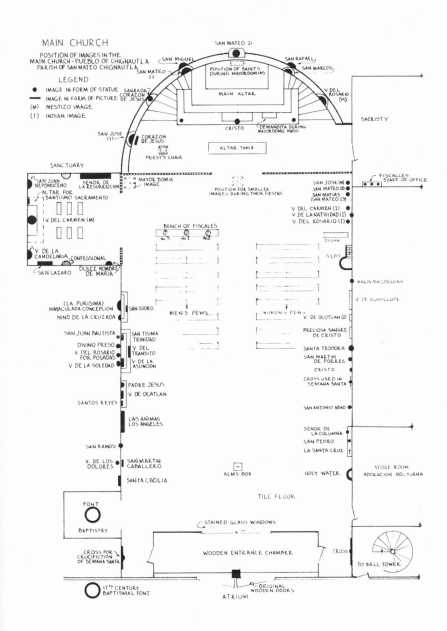

Notes

Introduction

1. I have adopted David Carrasco's term *cosmovision* because it captures the importance of the interplay of supernatural forces, natural forces, the gods, and human life in the worldview of the indigenous peoples of Mesoamerica. He defines *cosmovision* as "the ways in which Mesoamericans combined their cosmological notions relating to time and space into a structured and systematic world view" (1990, xix). He also stresses the significance of the parallel realities of the time and space of the gods and the time and space of forms of life on earth, elements emerging over and over again in the cosmology of the Nahuat Indians of Chignautla.

2. For a more detailed discussion of the role of Chignauteco women in community life see Slade 1975. Stephen (1990), Mathews (1985), Taggart (1983), and Chiñas (1987) have also made this point.

3. My thrust in this book has been to arrive at a meaningful conceptual bridge between individual experience and shared meanings based on a premise that the intrinsic structure of experience develops very early in life. Primary experiences are replete with contents and colorations that determine our experience of ourselves and the world and the actions we will take (Slade and Moskowitz 1988). My approach derives in part from my knowledge of the nature of social life as anthropologically conceived, and in part from my knowledge of the subjective life of the individual from the perspective of clinical psychoanalysis specifically informed by a view from Self Psychology. Understanding and communication between individuals is a central issue in all psychoanalytic schools of thought, each of which deems its mode of investigation superior, even though each is, in fact, theory bound (as all methods of data collection must be). Be that as it may, an analyst must grasp the complex psychological configurations that are the raw data of human experience before attempting to explain them. That is, the analyst must come to know another person and must be able to communicate that knowledge purposely. This is not unlike the goal of anthropological research, although the knowledge gained is certainly put to a different use. From the perspective of Self Psychology, insight into a patient's subjective life and past experience is possible because the structure of experience organized in the past continues to be functionally effective and remains available for mobilization in the clinical setting. Themes of the patient's life are either overt or provide a background organization for the patient's interpretation of his or her own experience. The analyst's perception and understanding of the patient is filtered through the analyst's apperception of the patient's organization of experience, an inevitability incorporated into both theory and method in the practice of psychoanalysis. Thus, psychoanalysis, like field research,

is a play within a play. Unknowingly, we organize our observations along unconscious, but familiar paths while we observe our subjects organizing their preconceptions of the world. Since we cannot observe organizing principles, nor can they be directly descriptive, it is imperative that we remain aware of the principles organizing our own experience in order to avoid imposing them on the experiential universe of those we are attempting to understand comprehensively.

4. In the studies of belief systems offered by Rokeach (1960), he corroborates the view that ideology, belief systems, and individual experience share organizational properties and contents. He writes: "We have come more and more to view a given personality as an organization of beliefs or expectancies having a definable and measurable structure. We have also come to conceive of man's cognitive activities—thinking, remembering, and perceiving—as processes and changes that take place within a person who has already formed a system of beliefs we can describe and measure" (1960, 7).

Chapter 1

1. Franciscans were notably skillful in their conversion efforts. As mendicant friars, they were granted parochial and sacramental powers that enabled them to realize their missionary goals. I agree with Gibson (1964) that the Indians could easily adopt the overt attributes of Spanish Catholicism of the period, constructing churches, holding celebratory processions with images of saints, etc., without altering the systematic assumptions of indigenous cosmology. A more detailed history of Chignautla may be found in Slade 1973.

2. The immediate region of the Sierra Norte in which Chignautla is located is also strongly united by a series of regional markets with staggered market days so that goods flow from the periphery of the region toward the city of Teziutlán. Similarly, a staggered system of ritual interchanges occurs among nearby municipios in celebration of their patron saints, those most important to Chignautla being the municipios of Atempan, Cuetzalan, Hueyapan, La Garita, Jalacingo, San Juan Acateno, Xuitetelco, Xochitlán, Yaonáhuac, and Tenextatiloyan.

3. Teziutlán was founded in 1552 and became the head town of a religious and administrative district in which Chignautla was a subordinate community. The territorial domain of Teziutlán was created from lands of four relatively small indigenous ceremonial centers of the region: Chignautla, Acateno, Mexcalcuatla, and Xuitetelco. A small pyramid remains in the center of the head town of Xuitetelco.

4. The *calpulli* was a pre-Hispanic form of social and territorial organization. Often used interchangeably with the Spanish term *barrio*, the term *calpulli* indicated an organizational unit whose function related to land tenure and use, kinship, and political leadership. Under calpulli leadership, calpulli lands were the common property of a certain number of families with usufruct rights. Barrio organization superimposed on calpulli organization became a colonial institution utilized for tribute collection, population control, and administrative functions that were originally assumed by one or more calpultin (pl.) in Indian communities (Olivera 1976).

5. Many structural characteristics and ideological elements in this society display the influence of a system of pre-Hispanic numerology in which the number four

has particular significance, as in the division of the cosmos into four quadrants marking four sacred directions, each associated with specific natural and supernatural forces.

6. It is interesting to note that an Indian ruler or leader was referred to in Nahuatl as *tlatoani,* he who speaks, a term deriving from the root *tlatoa,* to speak, which forms the terms *tlatolli,* language, and *tlatocayotl,* state, combining to form *tlatocan,* a supreme council, the speaking place and the place from which power emanates (Soustelle 1961). Soustelle also comments that the basis for the power of the tlatoani (in Nahuat, *tatoani*) was the dignity and ease with which these individuals spoke in public, a capacity highly valued by the Aztecs. These terms and their meanings clearly indicate a value placed on persuasion and wisdom that remains operative in Chignauteco society today.

7. Ejidos are tracts of land appropriated by the Mexican government after the Revolution from haciendas or municipal communal properties, held in usufruct by individual household heads or groups of families. These tracts are passed to heirs so long as they remain cultivated. There are 10,464 hectares of municipal land: 3,332 hectares privately owned, 2,132 communally owned, and 5,000 devoted to ejido. Originally the ejido had 4,070 hectares. Another 1000 hectares were taken from the communal lands during a struggle over the disposition and use of the ejido that continues today. Only 5 percent of the ejido is arable, and is inhabited by some 150 families.

8. The term *barrio* has many indigenous meanings confounded by designations applied to these socioterritorial units in the literature. I refer the reader to Hunt and Nash (1967) and Nutini, Carrasco, and Taggart, eds. (1976) for excellent summaries of these problematic issues. In Chignautla, what appears initially as a multiple barrio system in which the barrios surround a village that serves as a central nucleus with its church, plaza, government offices, and stores in fact adheres more closely to a dual barrio system once the function of the barrios becomes clear.

Chapter 2

1. Kertzer (1988) echoes the thoughts of Geertz (1973) and Turner (1969) when he defines ritual as behavior that is symbolic, repetitive, and socially standardized with a capacity to legitimate the status of the actors, their actions, and their intentions. Unlike other social activities, ritual combines strong affect with symbols reflecting social reality and thus has an evocative capacity to create a sense of sharing in the absence of conformity in either meanings or beliefs.

2. Todos Santos is celebrated by an elaborate sequence of rituals involving the church and household. Most of these rituals are clearly of indigenous origin. Todos Santos lasts for three days and the household altar serves as the focal point. On the 31st of October, the altar is decorated to receive the souls of unbaptized children. Water from the church is placed on the altar and represents the desire of their mothers to offer them baptism. November 1st, the Day of the Angels, celebrates the souls of baptized children and adolescents. Their presence is honored and enticed with offerings of foods like sweetened milk, gruels, rice, chocolate, sweet breads, and sweet tamales placed on the household altar. An exchange of these special foods occurs

between godchildren and their godparents, between ritual kinsmen and kinsmen who visit and exchange gifts. November 2 is the Day of Adult Souls. The household altar is again decorated with paper figures and foods for the souls of members of the immediate family. Candles, mole, chocolate gruel, fruits, and tamales are placed on the household altar. Special rosaries of bread and flowers (xochikoskat) made for the dead adorn the entranceway to the house. The graves are cleaned and ultimately decorated with these foods, rosaries, and holy water. Women conduct general collections in each section to sponsor a series of masses dedicated to departed souls. The four mayordomias of Todos Santos are celebrated in the usual manner in the mayordomo's house. In the past, they were also celebrated in the church by the sacristanes, who collected special foods from each section and placed them on the main altar. In 1963, the priest refused to allow these rituals to continue and this custom died.

3. The demandita is a significant ritual object recognizing the relationship between the mayordomo, the saint, and the community. The demandita is a replica, in miniature, of the saint's image. Encased in a glass box, the demandita may be carried by hand to facilitate its use in all rituals of the mayordomía, but otherwise remains on the household altar of the mayordomo during his tenure.

4. There are seven religious associations in Chignautla. In 1972, they had just under 350 members, of whom 117 were Indians. This form of veneration has increased in popularity under the guidance of the current priest.

5. I am not implying that the Mestizos in Chignautla are irreligious. They are devoted to their saints even though the type of devotion characteristic of their religious practice is more private and emphasizes formal doctrine; that is, religion among the Mestizos is a form of folk Catholicism devoid of indigenous meanings that give emphasis to the collectivity. Some saints are more popular than others, and I list them here in descending order: Niño Dios, Virgen de Ocotlán, Coronación de la Virgen, Virgen del Carmen, Inmaculada Concepción, Virgen del Rosario, San Miguel, San Rafael, Niño de la Cruzada, Virgen del Tránsito, and San Juan Nepomuceno.

Chapter 3

1. In 1972, the exchange rate of U.S. dollars to pesos was $1.00 to 12.50 pesos. The average wage for agricultural labor was 10 pesos a day; for skilled labor, 15 to 20. Certain jobs in Teziutlán offered a wage of 25 pesos, but these were difficult to obtain. It cost 50 centavos (100 centavos to 1 peso) to take the bus from Chignautla to Teziutlán, and a kilo of corn cost from 90 centavos to 1.40 pesos. The costs in this book are based on this rate of exchange, which remained stable until 1984, when the stability of the Mexican peso crumbled, producing an upward spiraling inflation that continues today. A mass that cost 350 pesos ($ 28 US) in 1972 cost 100,000 pesos ($ 32 US) in 1991; a man who earned 10 pesos in 1972 earns today 10,000 pesos and can rent a house for 70,000 pesos a month.

2. One hectare equals 2.471 acres.

3. If capital is viewed as any productive input aimed toward further production, any good may be defined as capital by its use, whether material or intangible. Chignautecos believe that ritual sponsorships have a role in the production of wealth because they serve as major production stimuli. Sponsorships involve a trade-off in consump-

tion of time, labor, corn, and money. Chignautecos believe that ritual expenditures improve their level of living because the individual must work harder after sponsorship lest the investment be lost; this idea is reinforced by the custom of never holding a cargo of lesser value. Cargos function as capital assets because they foster wealth accumulation and have a definite monetary exchange value compared to other forms of consumption. For far greater detail regarding Chignauteco economics and the economic basis for ritual sponsorship see Slade 1973.

4. The saints are quite distinct from other supernatural entities embedded within the subjective experience of Chignautla's Indians. The anthropomorphic spirits who also inhabit this cultural universe have a role in the lives of the people and merit distinctive propitiatory responses that insure a sense of balance and harmony once contact with them has occurred. Spiritual beings of significance include El Charro, a mounted figure resembling a Spanish rancher in full dress, La Llorona, the Wailing Woman, and El Diablo, literally the devil but actually an ambiguous, syncretic figure not quite Catholic nor indigenous but powerful and dangerous. Altered states that indicate a loss of balance within the mind or body, including panic, anxiety, rage, depression, and illness, are explained by the existence of other supernatural beings with whom contact is dangerous. A person can suffer from the ill effects of an *ataque de espíritus* or spirit attack, *espanto* or fright, *mal aire* (evil wind), or *mal de ojo* (the evil eye). Wandering souls are also dangerous and may cause illness or even death through fright. There are beings who bridge the world of humans and spirits and are endowed with supernatural powers: *brujos* (witches), *curanderos* (curers), and especially *nahuales*. Brujos and curanderos live in society in a relatively normal fashion. Their services may be purchased and their power is available for good or evil aimed at another individual. Curanderos are believed to be able to undo the harm done by brujos. Nahuales are somewhat distinct. Individuals who are nahuales are born with a capacity to transform themselves into turkeys, dogs, and other small animals, and they inflict harm either passively by fright or actively by causing illness and possibly death, usually out of spite, greed, or envy. Nahuales typically transform themselves at night and escape capture because they are able to fly. Sacred or enchanted places and objects, such as dolls, crosses, rocks, caves, mountains, and springs, are also potentially helpful or harmful depending on how they are used. Protective and purifying rites typically involving herbs, incense, and crosses are used to counteract these forces, especially in vulnerable states such as illness, menstruation, the weeks following childbirth, infancy, or when witchcraft is suspected as the cause of misfortune or illness. The saints may also be petitioned for their help at these times.

Chapter 4

1. The Mestizos recognize a bilateral network of kin supported by patterns of postmarital residence. Kinsmen who share a paternal surname have an importance that is not consistently reflected in recruitment of individuals for favors or assistance. Because of the dominant position of males in household management and the favoring of sons in inheritance, households of patrilaterally related kin tend to cluster together. Mestizos generally marry legally, and women often receive an inheritance in real property or a share in a commercial enterprise, making matrilocal postmarital resi-

dence attractive. Assistance is sought from either maternal or paternal kin depending upon intimacy and residential proximity rather than on a sense of mutual obligation. Intermarriage and ties of ritual kinship make the Mestizo enclave tightly knit in that all families are related to each other in one manner or another. Compadres are important members of the individual's social network locally and outside of the community, but such ties are comparatively devoid of the interactional constraints typical of compadrazgo among the Indians.

2. The role women have in ritual sponsorship mirrors the role women have in daily life. Women have their own networks of individuals with whom reciprocal exchanges occur, providing much of the labor necessary for ritual sponsorship. In Chignautla, the structural position of women in the cult of the saints is tied to an ideology that emphasizes mutuality and complementarity rather than gender-based inequalities. I believe enough has been critically written to correct biases that resulted in a model of "male:female::public:private" for gender-based relations (see especially Warman 1980, Mathews 1985, Chiñas 1987, Sault 1988, and Stephen 1990). The interdependence of men and women deserves further investigation in terms of the complementary or parallel positions they hold in ritual activities.

3. Marriage and baptism were the sacraments originally celebrated by Chignautecos. During the 1950s, the priest insisted upon celebrating each sacrament. He refused to perform a wedding without the confirmation of the bride and groom, forcing many people to seek the ritual services of priests from other communities. The least important sacrament of first communion was rarely celebrated by dressing the child or by a xochitis. Compadrazgo was initiated by an exchange of embraces or what Chignautecos call *compadres de abrazo*. This custom persisted until the 1960s, when first communion became fully institutionalized. Unlike baptism and confirmation, first communion may be used as an occasion to enhance social networks (Nutini and White 1977).

4. Compadres offer help to each other on ritual occasions when their labor is needed. Money is rarely borrowed between compadres in case resentments develop that cannot be expressed overtly. Money is offered, however, in times of emergency such as illness.

Chapter 5

1. It was particularly difficult to learn how the various images housed in the parish church arrived in Chignautla. Chignautecos experience each saint in a unique way. San Mateo is believed to be the most responsive supernatural in the pantheon and is vested with the highest ritual value requiring the greatest sacrifice on the part of the sponsor. His role and authority is analogous to that of the fiscal primero. San Mateo keeps the book of the saints—he is portrayed with an open book and plumed pen—as the fiscal primero keeps the book of the fiscales. Chignautecos relate a legend regarding how St. Matthew (San Mateo) became their patron saint. San Mateo miraculously appeared in the barrio of Tequimila, the original indigenous settlement, and was so taken by the beauty of Mt. Chignautla and the nine springs at its foot that he remained. A capilla abierta that was built on the site still exists. The Franciscans assigned saints

to Indian communities on the basis of some attribute that would facilitate their conversion efforts and perhaps chose St. Matthew for Chignautla because of its location at the foot of a mountain. In 1962, an image of San Martín de Porres was contributed by the priest and has remained a cargo of the sixth grouping. Atypically, this cargo is often sponsored by collection.

2. This has only recently become a concern, since uniformity marked traditional dress: white trousers, shirts, square over-shirts, and sandals for men; woolen skirts, embroidered blouses, and shawls for women, who went barefoot.

3. It is interesting to note that the closer the house of the mayordomo is to the Centro, the more the meal offered will resemble the meal of a Mestizo mayordomía. Xole and cacalas are served, but in porcelain bowls as among the Mestizos, followed by colored rice and mole with chicken, also served by the Mestizos. However, compliance with the dictates of tradition continues for the mayordomias of San Mateo regardless of the mayordomo's residence.

4. Meals in which tripe is served are consistently associated with transitions. Rituals involving transitions, what Turner (1972) has called "contingent rituals," belong to the class of ritual events dedicated to life crisis events. In Chignautla, both marriage and death are transitions from one position in the social system to another that are marked by ritual activity within a ritual context. Such events underscore changes that affect not only the object celebrated, but a wider network of relationships in which the individual in transition is structurally embedded. Transitions alter relationships by initiating either future reciprocal ties or the transfer of ties from one set of actors to another. Such moments are marked to reaffirm continuity during transition, underscoring the thematic nature of reciprocal bonds in this cultural system.

5. The celebration at Christmas of the Niño Dios occurs in a form that is structurally transitional between a typical Indian mayordomía, a Mestizo mayordomía, and an altepeihuit. Sometimes as many as one thousand people participate in the refreshments offered by the mayordomo at his house, the breaking of the piñatas, and the procession to Midnight Mass. Hence, this mayordomía is costly. However, for the last several decades, the Niño Dios has been sponsored by an Indian in transition between his natal culture and the world of the Mestizos. The Indian images of the Virgen del Rosario and San José are requested from their mayordomos for the nativity enactment, to which the mayordomo invites those he wishes to participate in *posadas*. Eight piñatas are bought and coffee and special cakes are served to all who come. When the mayordomo of the Niño Dios is an Indian living close to the Centro and disengaged from his Indian heritage, the division between these ethnic groups is diminished; if he is Mestizo, the division will be accentuated even further.

Chapter 6

1. The parish priest to whom I refer arrived in 1952 and left in 1986. His coercive methods ultimately earned him the Indians' hatred and mistrust. To obtain a cargo, all debts to the priest had to be paid in full; that is, if the fee for a baptism could not be met, and his services were sought elsewhere, the fee would be owed for the baptism before the priest would consider rendering any further services.

Conclusions

1. It is interesting to note that Ingham (1986), in his study of Tlayacapan, Morelos, presents a number of ritual forms and describes religious practices and paraphernalia not unlike what I have described for Chignautla, although their meaning and placement in ritual activities differs, as does the significance Ingham attributes to them. From Ingham's perspective, this is an essentially Catholic complex in which indigenous traits are vestigial and, in fact, subordinate to Catholic symbolism and meanings.

Glossary

This glossary includes a selection of both Nahuat and Spanish terms used in the text. Note that certain terms have a usage peculiar to Chignautla and should not be confused with common usage elsewhere in Mexico.

Acompañamiento: a specific group of individuals who are central actors during a ritual event and form part of the entourage present.

Agradecimiento: a formal speech, gesture, or action acknowledging the fulfillment of obligations in a ritual or ceremonial context.

Aguardiente: an alcoholic beverage made from sugar cane.

Alcalde mayor: head of the municipal council.

Alguacil: the third fiscal.

Altepeihuit: a community-wide fiesta that includes sacred and secular elements.

Apellido: surname taken from the father.

Autoridad Eclesiástica: the formal body of cargo holders responsible for the practice of the cult and the administration of church affairs.

Ayuntamiento Municipal: municipal government.

Ayuda: contractual favors given materially or socially but devoid of reciprocal implications.

Barrio: the territorial domain and the people residing within this domain who act corporately for ritual purposes.

Cabecera: municipal head town; also called *El Centro.*

Capilla: chapel in which the images of saints are housed.

Cargo: religious office; also refers to a ritual sponsorship, a mayordomía, or the obligations associated with these offices.

Chiquihuite: a basket with designated contents used to acknowledge a favor requested in the context of some form of ritual sponsorship.

Chiquihuite de pedimento: see *Pedimento.*

Cofradía: term used to designate members of the acompañamiento of the fiscales for a mayordomía.

Compadrazgo: ritual kinship.

Compadres: ritual kinsmen (coparents).

Compadres de fé: compadres who have held a xochitis.

Cumplimiento: an event that finalizes ritual obligations.

Dejar dicho: a verbal covenant between two kinsmen in which a vow to a saint is fulfilled in exchange for an inheritance.

Demandita: small replica image of a saint representing the mayordomo's vow and cargo, used in the events of a mayordomía.

Despedida: formal farewell or concluding ritual event.

Diputado mayor: first deputy or ritual assistant to the mayordomo.

Diputado menor: one of many minor assistants to the mayordomo who contributes to a mayordomía.

Diputado mensajero: first deputy or assistant to the mayordomo mensajero (the mayordomo of the Santísimo Sacramento) and a member of the Autoridad Eclesiástica.

Encargado: dance group foreman.

Encuentro: ceremonial greeting in a ritual context.

Entrega: the transfer of an office, an image, or an object from one ritual actor or context to another.

Faena: mandatory donation in labor for a communal purpose.

Fiscal: fiscal officer, one of the three high-ranking cargos of the Autoridad Eclesiástica (pl. fiscales).

Hueytatoani: leader or old and wise person who has served the community well (pl. hueytatoanime).

Hueyxochit: literally great xochit, term used for the final cumplimiento in compadrazgo.

Iglesia de visita: subordinate church without resident priest.

Invitados: persons invited to contribute in labor or goods to a ritual event.

Labrado de la cera: one of the composite events of a mayordomía dedicated to candlemaking.

Llevada de la cera: one of the composite events of a mayordomía, in which the candles and demandita are taken from the church to the house of the mayordomo.

Los que esperan: "those who wait." Half of a reciprocal pair.

Los que vienen: "those who come." Half of a reciprocal pair.

Lugar: a named place or a component settlement of a barrio.

Makwis makepis: Nahuat term signifying reciprocal obligations.

Manda: vow or promise made to a saint in return for favors received from a saint.

Mayordomía: a composite of events venerating a saint.

Mayordomo: ritual sponsor of a mayordomía.

Mayordomo mensajero: ritual sponsor of the Santísimo Sacramento who is also a member of the Autoridad Eclesiástica.

Mestizo: Mexican national who is not an Indian.

Mexicano: dialect of Nahuatl language in which the "tl" phoneme has been replaced by "t."

Milpa: plot of land used to cultivate corn and beans.

Mole: a rich chile sauce served with chicken, pork, or turkey.

Nacatzontet: Nahuat term for special portion of meat given to central ritual actors as a sign of respect and agradecimiento.
Nombramiento: appointment to a ritual sponsorship.

Parientes: kinsmen.
Parientes carnales: blood kinsmen related in the patriline.
Parientes políticos: affinal kin.
Pasado: individual who previously held a cargo.
Pedimento: formal solicitation of a favor with social or ritual implications.
Pedir favor: to initiate an exchange of favors.
Pilato: a masked dancer who accompanies a dance group.
Promesa: vow to a saint.

Recibimiento: a composite event of a mayordomía. Formal transfer of duties from one cargo holder to another.
Regidores de gasto: a minor civil official with specific religious duties.
Rezo: a prayer or prayers usually chanted by a specialist.
Respaldo: altar-like object used during Easter as a spatial marker.
Respeto: literally respect; an attitude or quality of merit and positive regard demanding constraint.

Sacrificio: sacrifice offered to a saint. Used interchangeably with promesa, cargo, burden, *compromiso* (obligation).
Sacristán: sexton, low-ranking cargo of the Autoridad Eclesiástica.

Tarea: literally a task; one-twentieth of a hectare.
Tata'tzin: Nahuat term for a male saint to signify "our father."
Tatiotzitzin: Nahuat term for pantheon of saints.
Teniente: second fiscal and deputy to first fiscal.
Topil: policeman or minor civil official.
Toros: special rocketry used in important mayordomias.

Velorio: a wake held for a person or a saint.

Xochitis: a ceremonial event dedicated to establishing a bond of obligatory respect between two or more ritual actors.
Xochikoskat: ceremonial leis ("rosaries") made of orange leaves, flowers, and breads that are exchanged in a xochitis or as a sign of respect between two beings.
Xochipitzahuac: a ritual in the form of a ceremonial dance accompanying the exchange of xochikoskat.
Xole: a special corn gruel offered on celebratory occasions.

Bibliography

Acosta, J. de. 1590. *Historia Natural y Moral de las Indias*. Seville.

Assad, T. 1983. Anthropological Conceptions of Religion: Reflections of Geertz. *Man* 18(2):237–59.

Atwood, G., and R. Stolorow. 1984. *Structures of Subjectivity: Explorations in Psychoanalytic Phenomenology*. Hillsdale, N.J.: Analytic Press.

Beals, R. 1945. *Ethnology of the Western Mixe*. University of California Publications in American Archaeology and Ethnology, 42:1–76.

———. 1946. *Cherán: A Sierra Tarascan Village*. Washington, D.C.: Smithsonian Institute: Social Anthropology, Publication 2.

———. 1969. The Tarascans. In *Handbook of Middle American Indians*, vol. 8, ed. E. Vogt. Austin: University of Texas Press.

Beidelman, T. 1982. *Colonial Evangelism: A Socio-Historical Study of an East African Mission at the Grass Roots*. Bloomington: University of Indiana Press.

Beltrán, G. A. 1973. *Regiones de Rufugio: El Desarrollo de la Comunidad y El Proceso Domincal En Mestizo America*. México, D. F.: Instituto Nacional Indigenista.

Brandes, S. 1981. Cargos Versus Cost Sharing in Mesoamerican Fiestas with Special Reference to Tzintzuntzan. *Journal of Anthropological Research* 37:209–25.

———. 1988. *Power and Persuasion: Fiestas and Social Control in Rural Mexico*. Philadelphia: University of Pennsylvania Press.

Bricker, V. 1973. *Ritual Humor in Highland Chiapas*. Austin: University of Texas Press.

Bunzel, R. 1952. *Chichicastenango: A Guatemalan Village*. Seattle: University of Washington Press.

Cámara, F. 1952. Religious and Political Organization. In *Heritage of Conquest*, ed. S. Tax. Viking Fund Seminar in Middle American Ethnology. Glencoe, Ill.: Glencoe Press.

Cancian, F. 1965. *Economics and Prestige in a Mayan Community: The Religious Cargo System in Zinacantan*. Stanford: Stanford University Press.

———. 1967. Political and Religious Organization. In *Handbook of Middle American Indians*, vol. 6., ed. M. Nash. Austin: University of Texas Press.

———. 1972. *Change and Uncertainty in a Peasant Economy: The Maya Corn Farmers of Zinacantan*. Stanford: Stanford University Press.

———. 1990. Zinacantan Cargo Waiting Lists as a Reflection of Social, Political, and Economic Changes, 1952 to 1987. In *Class, Politics, and Popular Religion in Mexico and Central America*, vol. 10., ed. L. Stephen and J. Dow. Society for Latin American Anthropology Publication Series. Washington, D.C.: American Anthropological Association.

Carrasco, D. 1990. *Religions of Mesoamerica*. San Francisco: Harper and Row.

Carrasco, P. 1952. *Tarascan Folk Religion: An Analysis of Economic, Social, and Religious Interactions*. Middle American Research Institute Publication 17. New Orleans: Tulane University Press.

————. 1961. The Civil-Religious Hierarchy in Mesoamerican Communities: Pre-Spanish Background and Colonial Development. *American Anthropologist* 63:483–97.

————. 1969. Central Mexican Highlands: Introduction. In *Handbook of Middle American Indians*, vol. 8, ed. E. Vogt. Austin: University of Texas Press.

————. 1976. La sociedad mexicana antes de la conquista. In *Historía general de México*, vol. 1. México, D.F.: Colegio de México.

————. 1979. Las fiestas de los meses mexicanos. *Homenaje al Doctor Paul Kirchhoff*. México, D.F.: Instituto Nacional de Antropología e Historia.

Caso, A. 1958. *The Aztecs: People of the Sun*. Norman: University of Oklahoma Press.

Chance, J. K. 1990. Changes in Twentieth-Century Mesoamerican Cargo Systems. In *Class, Politics, and Popular Religion in Mexico and Central America*, vol. 10, ed. L. Stephen and J. Dow. Society for Latin American Anthropology Publication Series. Washington, D.C.: American Anthropological Association.

Chance, J. K., and W. Taylor. 1985. Cofradias and Cargos: An Historical Perspective on the Mesoamerican Civil-Religious Hierarchy. *American Ethnologist* 12:1–26.

Chick, G. 1981. Concept and Behavior in a Tlaxcalan Cargo Hierarchy. *Ethnology* 20:217–28.

————. 1984. Personality Attribute Inference and Religious Officeholding in a Tlaxcalan Village. *Ethos* 12:245–64.

Chiñas, B. 1987. Women: The Heart of Isthmus Zapotec Ceremonial Exchange. Paper presented at the eighty-sixth annual meeting of the American Anthropological Association, November 18–22, Chicago, Ill.

Cordry, D. 1973. *Mexican Masks: An Essay*. Fort Worth: Amon Carter Museum.

————. 1980. *Mexican Masks*. Austin: University of Texas Press.

DeWalt, B. 1975. Changes in the Cargo Systems of Mesoamerica. *Anthropological Quarterly* 48(2):87–105.

Douglas, M. 1966. *Purity and Danger*. London: Routledge and Kegan Paul.

Durán, Fray Diego de. 1967. *Historia de las Indias de la Nueva España e Islas de Tierra Firme*. 2 vols. Reprint. Mexico City: Porrúa.

Earle, D. 1990. Appropriating the Enemy: Highland Maya Religious Organization and Community Survival. In *Class, Politics, and Popular Religion in Mexico and Central America*, vol. 10, ed. L. Stephen and J. Dow. Society for Latin American Anthropology Publication Series. Washington, D.C.: American Anthropological Association.

El Guindi, F. 1986. *The Myth of Ritual: A Native's Ethnography of Zapotec Life-Crises Rituals*. With the collaboration of A. Hernandez-Jimenez. Tucson: University of Arizona Press.

Firth, R. 1951. *Elements of Social Organization*. London: Watts and Co.

————. 1957. *Man and Culture: An Evaluation of the Work of Bronislaw Malinowski*. London: Routledge.

————. 1963. Offering and Sacrifice: Problems of Organization. *Journal of the Royal Anthropological Institute* 93:12–24.

————. 1973. *Symbols Public and Private*. Ithaca, N.Y.: Cornell University Press.

Foster, G. 1953. Cofradía and Compadrazgo in Spain and Spanish America. *Southwestern Journal of Anthropology* 9:1–28.

————. 1960. *Culture and Conquest: America's Spanish Heritage*. Viking Fund Publications in Anthropology, no. 27. Chicago: Quadrangle.

————. 1961a. Interpersonal Relations in Peasant Society. *Human Organization* 19(4):174–84.

————. 1961b. The Dyadic Contract I: A Model for the Social Structure of a Mexican Peasant Village. *American Anthropologist* 63:1173–92.

————. 1963. The Dyadic Contract in Tzintzuntzan, II: Patron-Client Relationship. *American Anthropologist* 65:1280–94.

Friedlander, J. 1981. The Secularization of the Cargo System: An Example from Post-Revolutionary Central Mexico. *Latin American Research Review* 16:132–43.

Geertz, C. 1973. *The Interpretation of Cultures*. New York: Basic Books.

Gibson, C. 1952. *Tlaxcala in the Sixteenth Century*. Stanford: Stanford University Press.

————. 1964. *The Aztecs under Spanish Rule*. Stanford: Stanford University Press.

Good, C. 1988. *Haciendo La Lucha: Arte y Comercio Nahuas de Guerro*. México, D.F.: Fondo de Cultura Económica.

Gossen, G. 1974. *Chamulas in the World of the Sun*. Cambridge, Mass.: Harvard University Press.

————. 1986. Mesoamerican Ideas as a Foundation for Regional Synthesis. In *Symbol and Meaning Beyond the Closed Community: Essays in Mesoamerican Ideas*, ed. G. Gossen. Studies on Culture and Society, vol. 1. Institute for Mesoamerican Studies. Albany: State University of New York.

Gouldner, A. 1960. The Norm of Reciprocity: A Preliminary Statement. *American Sociological Review* 25:161–78.

Greenberg, J. 1981. *Santiago's Sword*. Berkeley: University of California Press.

Guiteras-Holmes, C. 1961. *Perils of the Soul: The World View of a Tzotzil Indian*. Chicago: University of Chicago Press.

Hallowell, A. I. 1955. *Culture and Experience*. Philadelphia: University of Pennsylvania Press.

Haviland, J. 1977. *Gossip, Reputation, and Knowledge in Zinacantan*. Chicago: University of Chicago Press.

Hawkins, J. 1983. Robert Redfield's Culture Concept and Mesoamerican Anthropology. In *Heritage of Conquest Thirty Years Later*, ed. C. Kendall, J. Hawkings, and L. Bossen. Albuquerque: University of New Mexico Press.

Hubert, H., and M. Mauss. 1964. *Sacrifice: Its Nature and Function*. Trans. W. Halls. Chicago: University of Chicago Press.

Hunt, E. 1977. Ceremonies of Confrontation and Submission: The Symbolic Dimension of Indian-Mexican Political Interaction. In *Secular Ritual*, ed. S. Moore and B. Myerhoff. Assen: Royal VanGorcum Ltd.

Hunt, E., and J. Nash. 1967. Local and Territorial Units. In *Handbook of Middle*

American Indians, vol. 6, ed. M. Nash. Austin: University of Texas Press.

Ingham, J. 1986. *Mary, Michael and Lucifer: Folk Catholicism in Central Mexico.* Austin: University of Texas Press.

Jiménez, G. 1978. *Cultura Popular y Religión en el Anahuac.* México, D.F.: Centro de Estudios Ecunménicos, Chalma.

Kertzer, D. 1988. *Ritual, Politics and Power.* New Haven, Conn.: Yale University Press.

Kirchoff, P. 1952. Mesoamerica: Its Geographic Limits, Ethnic Composition and Cultural Characteristics. In *Heritage of Conquest,* ed. S. Tax. Viking Fund Seminar in Middle American Ethnology. Glencoe, Ill.: Glencoe Press.

Kluckhohn, C. 1952. Values and Value Orientation in the Theory of Action. In *Toward a General Theory of Action,* ed. T. Parsons and E. Shils. Cambridge, Mass.: Harvard University Press.

———. 1960. Patterning as Exemplified in Navaho Culture. In *Language, Culture and Personality,* ed. L. Spier, A. I. Hallowell, and S. Newman. Salt Lake City: University of Utah Press.

Knab, T. 1986. Metaphors, Concepts, and Coherence in Aztec. In *Symbol and Meaning Beyond the Closed Community: Essays in Mesoamerican Ideas,* ed. G. Gossen. Studies on Culture and Society, vol. 1. Institute for Mesoamerican Studies. Albany: State University of New York.

Kohut, H. 1977. *The Restoration of the Self.* New York: International Universities Press.

Kurath, G. 1967. Drama, Dance and Music. In *Handbook of Middle American Indians,* vol. 6, ed. M. Nash. Austin: University of Texas Press.

Lebra, T. 1972. Reciprocity-Based Moral Sanctions and Messianic Salvation. *American Anthropologist* 74:391–407.

León-Portilla, M. 1959. *La Filosofía Náhuatl.* México, D.F.: Universidad Nacional Autónoma de México.

———. 1963. *Aztec Thought and Culture: A Study of the Ancient Nahuatl Mind.* Trans. J. Davis. Norman: University of Oklahoma Press.

Lévi-Strauss, C. 1953. Social Structure. In *Anthropology Today,* ed. A. L. Kroeber. Chicago: University of Chicago Press.

———. 1960. On Manipulated Sociological Models. *Bijdragen tot de Taal-,Land-, en Volkenkunde.* 116:45–54.

———. 1963. *Structural Anthropology.* New York: Basic Books.

———. 1967. *Mythologiques: Du Miel Aux Cendres.* Paris: Plon.

López de Castillo, H. 1862. *Crónica de los Seis Curas de La Villa de Tlatlauqui.* Church Archives, Tlatlauqui, Puebla.

Madsen, W. 1967. Religious Syncretism. In *Handbook of Middle American Indians,* vol. 6, ed. M. Nash. Austin: University of Texas Press.

———. 1969. The Nahua. In *Handbook of Middle American Indians,* vol. 8, ed. E. Vogt. Austin: University of Texas Press.

Mathews, H. 1985. We Are Mayordomo: A Reinterpretation of Women's Roles in the Mexican Cargo System. *American Ethnologist* 12(2):285–301.

Mendelson, E. M. 1962. Religion and World View in Santiago Atitlan. *Micro. Coll. in Middle American Cultural Anthropology,* no. 52, University of Chicago.

Nagel, E. 1961. *The Structure of Science*. New York: Harcourt, Brace.

Nash, M. 1958. *Machine Age Maya: The Industrialization of a Guatemalan Community*. New York: Free Press.

Nutini, H. 1967. A Synoptic Comparison of Mesoamerican Marriage and Family Structure. *Southwestern Journal of Anthropology* 23:383–404.

———. 1968. *San Bernadino Contla: Marriage and Family Structure in a Tlaxcalan Municipio*. Pittsburgh: University of Pittsburgh Press.

———. 1976. Syncretism and Acculturation: The Historical Development of the Cult of the Patron Saint in Tlaxcala, Mexico (1519–1670). *Ethnology* 15:301–21.

———. 1984. *Ritual Kinship*. Vol. 2, *Ideological and Structural Integration of the Compadrazgo System in Rural Tlaxcala*. Princeton: Princeton University Press.

———. 1988. *Todos Santos in Rural Tlaxcala*. Princeton: Princeton University Press.

Nutini, H., and D. White. 1977. Community Variations and Network Structure in the Social Functions of Compadrazgo in Rural Tlaxcala, Mexico. *Ethnology* 16:353–84.

Nutini, H., P. Carrasco, and J. Taggart, eds. 1976. *Essays on Mexican Kinship*. Pittsburgh: University of Pittsburgh Press.

Olivera, M. 1976. The Barrios of San Andrés Cholula. In *Essays on Mexican Kinship*, ed. H. Nutini, P. Carrasco, and J. Taggart. Pittsburgh: University of Pittsburgh Press.

Opler, M. 1946. Themes as Dynamic Forces in Culture. *American Journal of Sociology* 51:196–206.

Parsons, E. C. 1936. *Mitla: Town of Souls*. Chicago: University of Chicago Press.

Reck, G. 1977. *Religión y Sociedad*. México, D.F.: Departamento de Etnología y Antropología Social, Instituto Nacional de Antropología e Historia.

Redfield, R. 1930. *Tepoztlán: A Mexican Village*. Chicago: University of Chicago Press.

———. 1941. *The Folk Culture of Yucatan*. Chicago: University of Chicago Press.

———. 1953. *The Primitive World and Its Transformations*. Ithaca, N.Y.: Cornell University Press.

Reina, R. 1966. *The Law of the Saints*. New York: Bobbs-Merrill Co.

———. 1967. Annual Cycle and Fiesta Cycle. In *Handbook of Middle American Indians*, vol. 6, ed. M. Nash. Austin: University of Texas Press.

Reina, R., and N. Schwartz. 1974. The Structural Context of Religious Conversion in Péten, Guatemala: Status, Community, and Multicommunity. *American Ethnologist* 1:157.

Robinson, D. 1966. *Sierra Nahuat Word Structure*. Santa Ana: Dow, Robinson.

Rokeach, M. 1960. *The Open and Closed Mind: Investigations into the Nature of Belief Systems and Personality Systems*. New York: Basic Books.

Romanucci-Ross, L. 1973. *Conflict, Violence and Morality in a Mexican Village*. Palo Alto, Calif.: National Press Books.

Rus, J., and R. Wasserstrom. 1980. Civil-Religious Hierarchies in Central Chiapas: A Critical Perspective. *American Ethnologist* 7:466–78.

Ruvalcaba, C. 1972. Teziutlán de Mejía. Pts. 1, 2. *Presencia*, nos. 20, 21.

Sahagún, Fray Bernadino de. 1956. *Historia general de las cosas de la Nueva España*. 4 vols. Reprint. México, D.F.: Porrúa.

Sault, N. 1988. Patrons and Sponsors: The Network of Zapotec Women in the Oaxaca Valley. Paper presented at the eighty-seventh annual meeting of the American Anthropological Association, November 16–20, Phoenix, Arizona.

Sexton, J. 1978. Protestantism and Modernization in Two Guatemalan Towns. *American Ethnologist* 5(2):280–302.

Skinner, G. 1964. Marketing and Social Structure in Rural China: Pt. 1. *Journal of Asian Studies* 24:59–95.

Slade, D. 1973. The Mayordomos of San Mateo: Political Economy of a Religious System. Ph.D. diss., University of Pittsburgh.

———. 1975. Marital Status and Sexual Identity: The Position of Women in a Mexican Society. In *Women Cross-Culturally: Change and Challenge*. The Hague: Mouton.

———. 1976. Kinship in the Social Organization of a Nahuat-Speaking Community in the Central Highlands. In *Essays on Mexican Kinship*, ed. H. Nutini, P. Carrasco, and J. Taggart. Pittsburgh: University of Pittsburgh Press.

Slade, D., and L. Moskowitz. 1988. Pathognomic Mirroring and the Organization of Experience: A Developmental Factor in Self Pathology. In *Frontiers in Self Psychology, Progress in Self Psychology*, vol. 3, ed. A. Goldberg. Hillsdale, N.J.: Analytic Press.

Smith, W. R. 1977. *The Fiesta System and Economic Change*. New York: Columbia University Press.

Soustelle, J. 1940. *La Pensée Cosmologique de Anciens Mexicains*. Paris: Hermann et cie.

———. 1956. Apuntes sobre la psicología colectiva y el sistema de valores en México antes de la Conquista. In *Estudios Antropológicos Publicados en Homenaje al Doctor Manuel Gamio*. México, D.F.: Universidad Nacional Autónoma de México.

———. 1961. *Daily Life of the Aztecs on the Eve of the Spanish Conquest*. Stanford, Calif.: Stanford University Press.

Stephen, L. 1990. The Politics of Ritual: The Mexican State and Zapotec Autonomy, 1926–1989. In *Class, Politics, and Popular Religion in Mexico and Central America*, vol. 10, ed. L. Stephen and J. Dow. Society for Latin American Anthropology Publication Series. Washington, D.C.: American Anthropological Association.

Stephen, L., and J. Dow. 1990. Introduction: Popular Religion in Mexico and Central America. In *Class, Politics, and Popular Religion in Mexico and Central America*, vol. 10, ed. L. Stephen and J. Dow. Society for Latin American Anthropology Publication Series. Washington, D.C.: American Anthropological Association.

Taggart, J. 1983. *Nahuat Myth and Social Structure*. Austin: University of Texas Press.

Taussig, M. 1980. *The Devil and Commodity Fetishism in South America*. Chapel Hill: University of North Carolina Press.

———. 1987. *Shamanism,Colonialism and the Wild Man: A Study in Terror and Healing*. Chicago: University of Chicago Press.

Tax, S. 1937. The Municipios of the Midwestern Highlands of Guatemala. *American Anthropologist* 39:423–44.

———, ed. 1952. *Heritage of Conquest: The Ethnology of Middle America.* Glencoe, Ill.: Glencoe Press.

Turner, V. 1969. *The Ritual Process: Structure and Anti-Structure.* Chicago: Aldine.

———. 1972. Symbols in African Ritual. *Science* 179:1100–1105.

———. 1974. *Dramas, Fields, and Metaphors; Symbolic Action in Human Societies.* Ithaca, N.Y.: Cornell University Press.

Vaillant, G. 1962. *Aztecs of Mexico.* Garden City, N.Y.: Doubleday.

Vera y Zuría, P. 1925. *Cartas a Mis Seminaristas en la Primera Visita Pastoral de la Arquidiócesis.* Puebla, México: Escuela Linotipográfica Salesiana.

Vogt, E. 1969. *Zinacantan: A Maya Community in the Highlands of Chiapas.* Cambridge, Mass.: Harvard University Press.

———. 1973. Gods and Politics in Zinacantan and Chamula. *Ethnology* 12:99–113.

———. 1976. *Tortillas for the Gods: A Symbolic Analysis of Zinacanteco Ritual.* Cambridge, Mass.: Harvard University Press.

Warman, A. 1980. *We Came to Object.* Baltimore: Johns Hopkins University Press.

Wasserstrom, R. 1978. The Exchange of Saints in Zinacantan: The Socioeconomic Bases of Religious Change in Southern Mexico. *Ethnology* 17(2):197–210.

———. 1983. *Class and Society in Central Chiapas.* Berkeley: University of California Press.

Waterman, T. 1917. Bandelier's Contribution to the Study of Ancient Mexican Social Organization. *University of California Publications in American Archaeology and Ethnology* 7:249–82.

Wolf, E. 1955. Types of Latin American Peasantry: A Preliminary Discussion. *American Anthropologist* 57:452–71.

———. 1957. Closed Corporate Peasant Communities in Mesoamerica and Central Java. *Southwestern Journal of Anthropology* 13:1–18.

———. 1959. *Sons of the Shaking Earth.* Chicago: University of Chicago Press.

Zantwijk, R. Van. 1967. *Servants of the Saints.* Assen: Royal VanGorcum Ltd.

Index